BLACKBURN/BAE
BUCCANEER

All marks (1958–94)

First published in August 2018

A catalogue record for this book is available from the British Library.

ISBN 978 1 78521 116 4

Library of Congress control no. 2018935484

Published by Haynes Publishing,
Sparkford, Yeovil,
Somerset BA22 7JJ, UK.
Tel: 01963 440635
Int. tel: +44 1963 440635
Website: www.haynes.com

Haynes North America Inc.,
859 Lawrence Drive, Newbury Park,
California 91320, USA.

Printed in Malaysia.

Senior Commissioning Editor: Jonathan Falconer
Copy editor: Michelle Tilling
Proof reader: Penny Housden
Indexer: Peter Nicholson
Page design: James Robertson

BLACKBURN/BAE BUCCANEER

All marks (1958–94)

Owners' Workshop Manual

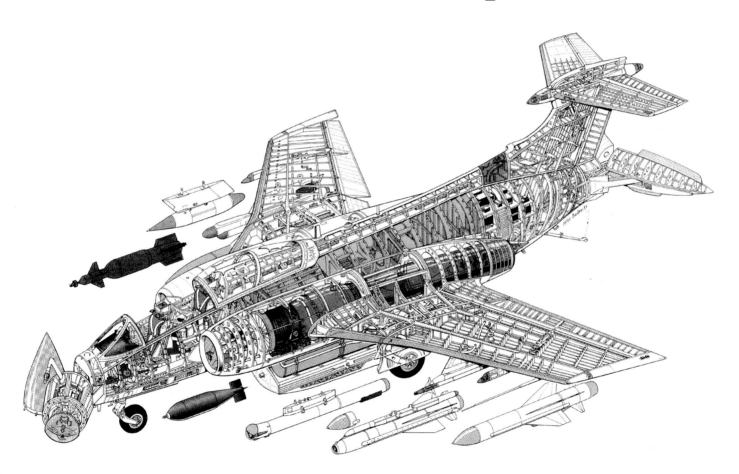

Insights into the design, operation and preservation of the
iconic Cold War carrier-borne and overland strike jet

Keith Wilson

An everlasting memory! Flying at low level through the Scottish Highlands, in very tight formation with another 12 Squadron Buccaneer, back in November 1992. *(Keith Wilson)*

Contents

Acknowledgements

A project of this nature requires the help and support of many people, who have contributed in different ways to make the book possible. The author would like to offer his sincere thanks to the following:

Dave and Andrew Webber of The Buccaneer Aviation Group (TBAG), Bruntingthorpe, for providing unlimited access to their amazing collection of Buccaneer jets. David and Andrew lead a team of committed volunteers who keep the Buccaneers 'live' at Bruntingthorpe. Both gave of their time and support freely while nothing seemed too much of a problem – despite my testing their patience on occasions. My personal thanks must also go to all of the members of The Buccaneer Aviation Group at Bruntingthorpe: a tremendous team of enthusiastic and knowledgeable individuals; and for allowing me to share in your passion of all things Buccaneer.

My individual thanks must go to:

Barbara Gilbert and Catherine Cooper of the Fleet Air Arm Museum, Yeovilton: for allowing me access to their archive as well as the tour of the Cobham hangar.

Howard Mason and Barry Guess at the BAe Heritage Centre at Farnborough: for allowing me access to their outstanding archive; and their help with images and information.

To Paul Lawson, Peter Hotham, Eric Barker, Dave Gresswell and John Cowper at the BAe Heritage Collection at Brough for allowing me to access their excellent archive; and for providing images and information.

To the various photographers who have kindly provided images to this book including: Lee Barton, Squadron Leader Rick Phillips, Group Captain Christopher Finn, Peter Wright-Gardner, Peter 'Ossie' Osborn, Francis Wallace, Mike Overs, Matt Wellington, Geoffrey Lee, Peter R. March and Ollie Wilson.

Sebastian Cox at the Air Historical Branch, RAF Northolt, for providing the Branch's support with access to the collection of images; along with his encouragement and sense of humour.

My thanks must also go to Lee Barton at the Air Historical Branch for his unwavering enthusiasm, vision and attention to detail during the image selection process. Also thanks must go to his research skills; unearthing new information and responding to the never-ending stream of questions.

My special thanks must also go to those individuals who have contributed the Buccaneer memories to the volume: Group Captain Christopher Finn, Squadron Leader Rick Phillips, Peter Wright-Gardner, Peter 'Ossie' Osborn and Ollie Suckling.

The history and operations of the Buccaneer in South African Air Force service have always appeared to be a little 'dark'. Thankfully, I had the considerable assistance of both Steve McLean and SAAF Buccaneer aficionado Johan Conradie in guiding me through the chapter on SAAF activities; while Johan also contributed a number of rare images of SAAF aircraft. I am most grateful to you both.

Throughout my research and writing of this volume I have been fortunate enough to have had Group Captain Christopher Finn looking over my shoulder and providing significant information and guidance, especially relating to the operations of the Buccaneer and its weapons systems. He also took the time to check the complete manuscript. A lifelong career navigator and Buccaneer aficionado, his contributions have been invaluable. Thank you Chris!

At Haynes Publishing, I would like to thank Jonathan Falconer, Michelle Tilling and James Robertson for their considerable input at key stages during the book's production; and for keeping me on track whenever I wavered.

Sincere thanks are due to my sons Sam and Oliver. Thank you for your patience and support throughout the project; I couldn't have done it without you. Finally, my special thanks must go to Carol – for just being there.

Introduction

'At 550 knots (633mph), 100ft above the waves, the ice-cold sea below looks just like a blur. At this level, the Buccaneer reveals why it earned the nickname "Easy Rider". Despite gusting winds indicated by the choppy seas below, the ride is surprisingly stable – as though it were on rails! The aircraft can be flown as low as 50ft above sea level, hands off. The ability to fly at high speed and at ultra low-level is the real strength of the Buccaneer. After more than 23 years in service with the Royal Air Force there are few other aircraft that can fly as fast; as low; or as far. There are none that can do all three. All this in an aeroplane that the RAF didn't even want!'

These words provide just one of many amazing memories I have of flying in the back seat of a 12 Squadron Buccaneer S.2, XX885, in December 1992. The aircraft was painted in low-vis grey but still carried its Gulf War artwork of *Famous Grouse*, the bomb mission marks along with an aircraft 'kill'. The words were published in a 1993 edition of *Air Pictorial* magazine as part of a farewell tribute to the amazing Buccaneer.

But we are getting a little ahead of ourselves.

Let's go right back to 1952 and the beginning of the Buccaneer story.

Countering *Sverdlov*-class ships

In the early 1950s, the Soviet Union embarked upon what was to become the largest build-up of naval power the world had ever witnessed. Every year during the 1960s, the Soviet Navy introduced a new class of cruiser, destroyer or submarine. This process continued well into the 1970s.

Included in this programme were plans to construct around 24 new heavy cruisers ideally suited to the merchant shipping raiding role. The *Sverdlov* class ships of around 17,000 tons, were offensively armed with 12 × 5.9in guns in four triple turrets, 12 × dual-purpose 3.9in guns in six twin turrets, and two quintuple 21in torpedo launchers. Defensive armament included twin guided-missile launchers along with no fewer than 32 × 37mm anti-aircraft guns. The *Sverdlov*-class cruisers would provide a formidable opposition to the large British merchant navy fleet. In the event, only 17 hulls

BELOW The prototype NA.39, XK486, at the Blackburn Aircraft Company factory at Brough on 9 April 1958. This was the very first publicity photograph of the type released. (BAE SYSTEMS Image BAL11515)

were launched from 1951 onwards and of these only 14 ships were completed and operational by the end of 1960.

The Soviet Navy was learning what Britain knew 150 years ago – that those who control the seas, control events. If the Soviet Navy ever needed confirmation of this fact, it came in 1962 during the Cuban Missile Crisis. When faced with the overwhelming power of the US Navy, the USSR backed down and recalled her merchant ships loaded with offensive, nuclear-armed missiles, en route to Cuba.

For Britain, the traditional method of countering the threat posed by the *Sverdlov*-class cruisers would have been to build bigger and bigger warships, carrying even larger weapons. However, the UK economic climate of the 1950s prevented such a race from being initiated. Britain needed an alternative strategy to counter the threat.

And so it was, that in June 1952, the Royal Navy issued NSR (Naval Staff Requirement) NA.39 for a high subsonic speed, twin-seat, twin-jet, carrier-borne strike aircraft intended to be able to penetrate beneath an enemy's radar cover in order to deliver nuclear or conventional weapons in all weathers. The head of the Naval Air Warfare Division of the Naval Staff, Admiral A.S. Bolt, concluded that an extremely cost-effective solution to the *Sverdlov*-class threat would be a specialised naval air strike aircraft capable of delivering a variety of conventional or nuclear weapons from a high-speed, low-level attack profile to avoid long-range radar detection. The achievement of tactical surprise by low altitude approach had been repeatedly demonstrated in fleet exercises and much of the training of aircrews at the School of Naval Air Warfare was directed towards achieving weapons accuracy in such attacks. The Korean War had demonstrated the success of this training.

NSR NA.39 specified a two-seat bomber able to fly at Mach 0.85 at a height of 200ft. It was to carry a nuclear weapon internally and other stores, and to have a radius of operation exceeding 400 nautical miles. Folding wings were specified to enable the aircraft to fit within the confines of Royal Navy aircraft carriers. Its range could be extended by fitting two 250-gallon drop tanks.

The bomb bay could, as standard, accommodate 2,000lb nuclear bombs or a battery of photographic flares and cameras. When drop tanks were not attached, a further four 1,000lb bombs could be carried beneath the wings, providing the aircraft with a maximum ordnance of eight 1,000lb bombs.

Blackburn B.103

A large number of British manufacturers were pursuing the contract, including Armstrong Whitworth, Fairey, Shorts, Westland and Hawker; a requirement they all felt able to meet, and almost fell over themselves in their eagerness to prepare submissions which began to arrive at the Ministry of Supply in February 1953.

Most of the projects were powered by either a pair of Avon or Sapphire engines and had large wing areas to provide the lift necessary for carrier operations. Several of the companies tackled the problem of reduced field or deck length by utilising the benefit of the jet deflection principle, which was about to be tested on a modified Nene-powered Gloster Meteor. The Hawker project – the P.1109 – was powered by four engines, while another project by no fewer than six!

Under the leadership of Barry Leight, the project team at Blackburn Aircraft initially favoured the jet deflection solution applied to a pair of Armstrong-Siddeley Sapphire engines but also pursued the benefit of boundary-layer control achieved by blowing hot, high-pressure air bled from the engines out of thin slits along the wings and in front of the flaps. This lift-increasing development had been pioneered in the USA by Dr John D. Attinello of NACA (National Advisory Committee for Aeronautics – now NASA) in association with the US Navy. Interestingly, the 'blown flap' was adopted on several US aircraft including the Lockheed F-104 Starfighter, which could barely fly without it.

Despite the abundance of interest in the project, Blackburn's B.103 – with the initial design being drawn up by Roy Boot – was soon the front runner. Blackburn also manufactured a wind tunnel model, although at the time, missions, profiles, weapons and equipment to be carried were a matter of guesswork.

By 1955, the B.103 was approaching its definitive shape, with a small wing of around 500ft², small plain flaps and large ailerons. In front of the flaps and ailerons were the vital full-span blowing slits. In place of the slats there was a second row of slits, facing rearwards in the upper surface of the outer wing close to the leading edge.

These tiny slits discharged air bled from the downstream end of the engine compressors. The bleed air was so hot that the ducting and the slit structure had to be made from heat-resisting alloy. The boundary-layer control system – sometimes referred to as 'supercirculation' – was designed to come on automatically when the flaps were lowered.

Another piece of advanced technology adopted on B.103 was that of 'area rule'. Once again, this feature was based upon pioneering NACA research in the USA, where the work of Richard Whitcomb showed the advantage of the total cross-sectional area of high-speed aircraft forming a smooth streamlined curve from nose to tail, with no bulge due to the wing. With a conventional aircraft, the wing adds a significant peak to the curve. With area rule, this peak is smoothed out by reducing the area of the fuselage in line with the wing and increasing aft of the wing.

Although the US research was aimed at supersonic aircraft, the idea could usefully reduce the drag of one designed to cruise at Mach 0.85. When applied to B.103, the result was rather crude with the wasp-waisting and bulged tail being very evident. The application of the rule significantly reduced the amount of thrust required for the maximum cruise. More importantly, it also provided a welcome bonus as a large amount of useful extra space in the rear of the fuselage was now available for equipment.

Underpowered

The application of the area ruling made a crucial contribution to the selection of powerplant. The choice of engine is always a major decision in the designing of a new aircraft, but it was of special significance to the B.103, on which valuable thrust would be used for the boundary-layer control.

To achieve the maximum range specified by the Navy requirement, it was essential to use the smallest possible engines. At this stage, the B.103 had two Sapphires, but assuming that every take-off would be assisted by a catapult, calculations indicated that with the area rule, a thrust of little over 14,000lb would provide the desired speed of Mach 0.85 at sea level.

With de Havilland studying a scaled-down version of its 20,000lb thrust Gyron turbo jet, the two-fifths scale Gyron Junior came into being with a modest thrust of 7,000lb and it was this engine that was selected by Blackburn for the B.103.

It was appreciated at the time that this amount of thrust was marginal and, sadly, this proved to be the case. The Buccaneer S Mk.1 never possessed sparkling performance, especially on take-off, and it wasn't until the Spey-powered S Mk.2 came into being that the design would eventually fulfil its maximum potential.

Royal Navy nuclear deterrent role

Following the termination of the Fairey guided nuclear programme – 'Green Cheese' – the free-fall tactical nuclear weapon 'Red Beard' was the Buccaneer's primary armament. Developed to meet Operational Requirement (OR) 1127, 'Red Beard' was a tactical weapon initially developed for service with the Canberra fleet and as a partial replacement for the 'Blue Danube' weapon carried by the first V-bombers.

BELOW XN526, the first Buccaneer S.2 taking off at Holme-on-Spalding-Moor on 17 May 1963. *(BAE SYSTEMS Image BAL19397)*

'Red Beard' weapons were carried by Royal Navy Scimitar aircraft from 1963 as an emergency measure pending the introduction of the Buccaneer. By modern standards 'Red Beard' was a primitive weapon with no in-flight arming facility. Once it was on board the Buccaneer, it was live, while fusing and delivery options were somewhat limited. However, it became the Royal Navy's weapon of choice for its nuclear deterrent and QRA standby role – a role emphasised by the all-over anti-nuclear flash white colour scheme.

Limited export success

Export success for the Buccaneer was limited, despite the NA.39 design being very carefully studied by the American authorities in 1957 under the terms of the Mutual Weapons Development Program (MWDP) treaty. After representatives of Blackburn were put through the technical 'hoop' by the MWDP authorities, they later declared that they were 'satisfied' that the NA.39 project was 'soundly based'. They also indicated that a similar operational requirement was in preparation for the US Navy, providing some hope to the Blackburn representatives. The US authorities, however, eventually opted for the Grumman YA2F (later A-6) Intruder aircraft for their Navy. Like the Buccaneer, the YA2F had virtually full-span flaps, but without boundary-layer control.

Negotiations had also been conducted by British Government officials with the West German Government with the S Mk.1 being seen as a potential replacement for the Sea Hawk Mk.100 and Mk.101 aircraft then in service with their Bundesmarine. However, it appears the negotiations were not conducted in a suitably professional manner by British Government officials and the Sea Hawks were subsequently replaced in service by the Lockheed F-104G Starfighter.

Nevertheless, negotiations between the British and South African Governments fared a little better as an order was received for 16 modified S Mk.2 aircraft (as the S Mk.50) for the South African Air Force. However, this order was jeopardised when the British Government almost reneged on the agreement under which the aircraft were to be supplied, with the result that options on a further 20 aircraft were summarily cancelled.

Politics rears its ugly head

The Buccaneer S Mk.1 had enjoyed a relatively smooth entry into Royal Navy service with the Intensive Flying Training Unit in May 1961. The Rolls-Royce-powered S Mk.2 joined 700B Squadron in April 1965. Eventually, the Buccaneer would serve with Nos 700Z, 801, 800, 803, 700B, 809 and finally 736 Squadrons. Buccaneers saw valuable service on four aircraft carriers – HMS *Victorious*, *Hermes*, *Eagle* and *Ark Royal*. However, in 1968, the issue of politics was about to rear its ugly head.

On 16 January 1968, Harold Wilson announced to parliament the cancellation of the RAF's purchase of 50 F-111K aircraft. These, in turn, had been ordered to replace the cancelled TSR-2 project. Eventually, in July 1968 an RAF order for a batch of 26 new-build Buccaneer S Mk.2B aircraft was announced to replace them.

The run-down of the Fleet Air Arm's carrier force was also proclaimed with an agreement reached for the RAF to take over the complete inventory of FAA Buccaneer S Mk.2 airframes as the Navy squadrons ran down and disbanded. That said, significant modifications had to be completed to de-navalise the design with the first RAF aircraft delivered to a squadron arriving at RAF Honington on

BELOW South African Air Force S.50 example '413' photographed at Holme-on-Spalding-Moor. Sales to the South African Air Force were to be the Buccaneer's only export success. *(BAE SYSTEMS Image BAL20885)*

1 October 1969. All were ex-Navy machines refurbished to an interim Air Force standard.

RAF nuclear deterrent role

On 1 October 1970, No XV Squadron was formed at RAF Honington to provide the RAF with its second Buccaneer unit. As with No 12 Squadron before it, No XV Squadron had previously flown V-bombers. Unlike No 12 Squadron though, the second squadron received new-build aircraft in the form of S Mk.2Bs directly from the production line at Brough. Destined for RAF Germany to replace the ageing Canberra B(I).8 aircraft which had provided the strike alert, XV Squadron moved to RAF Laarbruch in January 1971.

The First Gulf War

Despite having been informed that Buccaneer aircraft 'were not required' to participate in the First Gulf War, aircraft were transferred into theatre on 23 January 1990. Apparently, the Tornado GR.1 aircraft were delivering their ordnance with the accuracy of a Second World War bomber. What was required was the ability to designate for laser-guided bombs (LGBs), so Buccaneer aircraft and crews from Nos 12 and 208 Squadrons were called upon to form a single operating unit. Initially, the aircraft were employed purely in the designator role, with Tornados carrying the LGBs. However, towards the end of the conflict they carried a

ABOVE Buccaneer S.2B XV350 was the first airframe to emerge from Mod 1499 as well as being the first airframe officially handed over to the RAF. XV350 never saw squadron service; instead, it remained as a test airframe primarily with the A&AEE at Boscombe Down. *(Crown Copyright/Air Historical Branch Image TN-1-6262-106)*

single LGB each as a back-up and destroyed two Iraqi aircraft on the ground with them.

Buccaneer production

Production of the Buccaneer totalled 211 airframes (which included 2 S.1 airframes converted to S.2). Some 62 of these were powered by the de Havilland Gyron Junior as NA.39 or S Mk.1 airframes. The remaining 149 were Rolls-Royce Spey-powered S Mk.2 or S Mk.50 airframes. Production ran from January 1962 to October 1977.

A full Buccaneer production list can be found in Appendix 1 on page 176.

Tanking Buccaneers

At this stage of proceedings I have to nail my colours to the mast; I have always held a soft spot for the lovely old Buccaneer. During the 1980s and early 1990s, Lossiemouth-based Buccaneers were regular customers of the Victor K.2, as well as VC10 K.2 and K.3 aircraft of the RAF tanker fleet. I was fortunate to have been invited to fly on board these tanker aircraft on various occasions and to photograph a variety of RAF assets,

ABOVE During the 1980s and early 1990s, Lossiemouth-based Buccaneers were regular customers of the VC10 K.2 and K.3 aircraft of the RAF tanker fleet. On one late January afternoon in 1990, a formation of four Buccaneers from 12 Squadron (including XX900, XZ431 and XW532) took their turns behind the hoses, tanking in pairs, before gathering on the port side of the VC10 for a quick photocall. Shortly afterwards they departed back on to their operational duties. *(Keith Wilson)*

BELOW During a flight aboard 8 Squadron Shackleton AEW.2 WL757 on 15 February 1990, the author was able to photograph a pair of 12 Squadron Buccaneer S.2B aircraft that joined alongside for a brief photoshoot. Nearest the camera is XX894 in 12 Squadron's special 75th anniversary colour scheme, which the squadron had celebrated at RAF Lossiemouth the previous day. XX900 was in standard camouflage and completed the formation. *(Keith Wilson)*

including Buccaneers, on the hoses. On one late January afternoon in 1990, a formation of four Buccaneers from 12 Squadron took their turns behind the hoses, tanking in pairs, before gathering on the port side of the VC10 for a quick photocall. Shortly afterwards, they departed back on to operational duties.

Special colour scheme air-to-air from a Shackleton AEW.2

When No 12 Squadron celebrated its 75th anniversary at RAF Lossiemouth in February 1990, one of their aircraft – XX894 – was painted into a special commemorative grey and green colour scheme. Around that time I was visiting Lossiemouth and the day after 12 Squadron's celebratory party I found myself working inside a No 8 Squadron Shackleton AEW.2 off the coast of Scotland. Thankfully, a hasty photo opportunity had been arranged and a pair of 12 Squadron Buccaneers – including the specially painted XX894 – found their way alongside WL757, with me working happily from the starboard observation window. Once again, images from that brief but enjoyable shoot are included in this book.

Back-seating in the Buccaneer

My affection for the venerable old Buccaneer was significantly increased after I spent a week with 12 Squadron at RAF Lossiemouth in December 1992. Here, I was able to observe and photograph the squadron at work, train in the simulator and eventually fly in the back seat of XX885. I was able to witness and photograph a four-ship low-level NAVEX around some of

the beautiful Scottish landmarks, engage in buddy-buddy air-to-air refuelling, perform a simulated attack on a splash target using Sea Eagle missiles before arming and dropping 28lb practice bombs on to the range at Rosehearty, then watch them splash into the sand, close to the target, with immense pride!

A number of images in this book were obtained during my visit to 12 Squadron and I am immensely grateful to Squadron Leader Norman Browne, my escort officer for the visit as well as the designated Simulator Instructor. Here, I tested his patience until he eventually got me operating the fuel transfer and weapons release systems effectively before I was allowed to actually fly with the squadron. Norman also provided me with some excellent time and experience in the front seat too, where I quickly learned about the Buccaneer's amazing handling capabilities, culminating in my attempts to 'land' the simulator on to an aircraft carrier flight deck.

Then there was Squadron Leader Rick Phillips to whom I must express my heartfelt thanks for accommodating my aspirations and answering my endless questions; and to Flight Lieutenant Glenn Mason who demonstrated his superb flying skills and placed the aircraft and my camera exactly where it was required. A few years later, I had the pleasure of flying with Glenn, this time in a 100 Squadron Hawk T.1 during an air-to-air photoshoot with three Victor K.2 aircraft from 55 Squadron over The Wash. Once again, Glenn's excellent flying skills provided some amazing photo opportunities with the three Victor K.2 aircraft.

BELOW An advertisement for the new Blackburn Buccaneer on the front cover of the 15 June 1961 edition of *The Aeroplane and Astronautics* magazine. *(BAE SYSTEMS)*

On a very sad note, I had hoped to include some words of wisdom on flying the Buccaneer from Glenn but before I could interview him, he suddenly and very sadly passed away. However, Rick Phillips very kindly stepped into the breach and I am most grateful to him.

Farewell to the Buccaneer

On Wednesday 22 September 1993, the UK's media were invited to a special event at RAF Lossiemouth to mark the impending retirement of the Buccaneer from RAF service. No 12 Squadron were to cease flying on 30 September, while 208 Squadron would continue until the spring of 1994. I was lucky enough to be invited to the event and later joined a Hercules camera platform for an air-to-air photographic sortie with four Hunters and four Buccaneers – two each from 12 and 208 Squadrons – flying neatly alongside and behind the cameraship around some of the beautiful Scottish scenery in the region. The event provided a fitting farewell to a wonderful aircraft and a number of images from that event have been included in this book.

BELOW The farewell four-ship Buccaneer S.2B formation at RAF Lossiemouth on 22 September 1993, comprising two 12 Squadron aircraft (XX885 and XV359) nearest the camera, in formation with a pair from 208 Squadron (XV352 and XX895). They were photographed at low level along the Scottish coastline.
(Keith Wilson)

Any left flying?

Following the Buccaneer's removal from RAF service, three former Royal Aircraft Establishment (RAE) Buccaneer S.2B aircraft – XW986, 987 and 988 – found their way to South Africa where they operated in civilian hands at Thunder City, providing back-seat rides to people with deep pockets. Following maintenance and administrative issues with the South African CAA, all three were later grounded and placed up for sale by auction. Their current status is not known, although it is throught that at least two of them may still be capable of flight.

Aircrew Association and social media

During the course of my research for this volume, I had reason to contact the Buccaneer Aircrew Association as well as The RAF Buccaneer Groundcrew Forum (12, XV, 16, 208, 216, 237) via social media. I was amazed at their continued enthusiasm for the venerable Buccaneer; their camaraderie for the old Buccaneer squadrons; and their willingness to help with

the project. I received messages of support from more than a dozen members and some have actually contributed their Buccaneer memories to this volume.

Another group to provide help and assistance was the Buccaneer XX900 Facebook page. As the name suggests, this small group of volunteers helps to maintain Buccaneer S.2 XX900 in a 'live' running condition at Bruntingthorpe.

The Buccaneer Aviation Group (TBAG)

Finally, I cannot close without mentioning The Buccaneer Aviation Group (TBAG) at Bruntingthorpe. Led by the Chairman Dave Webber and 'encouraged' by his son Andrew Webber, this amazing group of enthusiasts are keeping the Buccaneers in prominent view of visitors to Cold War Events at Bruntingthorpe. Their passion for all things Buccaneer is absolutely amazing. They maintain two aircraft (XW544 and XX894) in a 'live', running condition and the group show them both off to the public whenever opportunities permit, allowing visitors to witness the spectacular Buccaneer smoke and noise at Bruntingthorpe.

In addition, the team are regular visitors to the Shannon Aviation Museum where they have revitalised the hydraulic systems on the aircraft, allowing it to demonstrate its wing-folding capabilities at museum events.

More on The Buccaneer Aviation Group can be found in Appendix 4 on page 183.

Terms of affection

Towards the end of their operational career, when both aircrew and groundcrew alike were asked 'what was the best aircraft to replace the venerable old Buccaneer', the unanimous answer was 'a new Buccaneer!'. Sadly, that wasn't to be, and the Tornado took on some of the roles previously performed by the multiple-capability Buccaneer. The withdrawal of four squadrons of Tornado aircraft from RAF Germany created an immediate surfeit of these aircraft and the replacement of the anti-ship Buccaneer by Tornado GR.1B aircraft was an inevitable decision. Although the Navigation/Attack system of the Tornado was generally superior to that of the Buccaneer, there were many notable disadvantages including a lower range, reduced radar range in over-water operations, initial limitations on the firing of Sea Eagle missiles and the ability to carry just two of the missiles as a meaningful weapons load as opposed to four on the Buccaneer. Was this 'upgrade' to the Tornado GR.1B really progress?

The Buccaneer was much loved by both its RAF aircrew and groundcrews alike, who fondly remember her as 'The Banana Jet'; and by members of the South African Air Force as 'Easy Rider'.

Keith Wilson
Ramsey, Cambridgeshire, May 2018

ABOVE A pair of 'live' Buccaneer S.2 aircraft at Bruntingthorpe on 28 May 2017, after completion of their high-speed runs up and down the main runway. To the left is TBAG's S.2B XW544/O in XV Squadron colours, while to the right is XX900/900 of the Cold War Jets Collection.
(Keith Wilson)

Chapter One

History and development of the Buccaneer

Although its design dated back to the early 1950s, the Buccaneer entered service in May 1961 with the Royal Navy's Intensive Flying Trials Unit, 700Z NAS, and after switching services remained in RAF service until March 1994 when 208 Squadron finally withdrew the remaining airframes in use. Seldom has a military jet aircraft enjoyed this level of longevity, especially in such demanding roles.

OPPOSITE The fifth development Blackburn NA.39 – XK490 – on display at Farnborough in September 1959. At the time of the show, Blackburn was still an independent company but that was about to change and a slight clue may have been offered when XK490 was parked alongside two Hawker Siddeley products – Gloster Javelin FAW.8 XJ125 and Avro Vulcan B.2 **XH536.** *(BAE SYSTEMS Image 7 2426)*

The Buccaneer was specifically designed as a low-level strike aircraft in an era when high-altitude manned bombers reigned supreme. However, through the 1960s and 1970s, when the military doctrine became more about penetration beneath the enemy radar systems and not setting off a wave of retaliatory anti-aircraft missiles, the Buccaneer's low-level capabilities became a crucial factor.

The second factor was the Buccaneer's performance. Although not so when powered by the early Gyron Junior, the latter S.2 examples powered by the economical and efficient Spey turbofan could fly lower, faster and longer than any comparable aircraft.

The third factor was the aircraft's incredible strength, a reflection of the role it was to undertake in turbulent air at very low level. The wing panels were manufactured from solid metal on special milling machines designed and constructed for the task by the engineering team at Blackburn Aircraft. Then there was the 'heavy duty' undercarriage, designed to absorb the shock of each and every controlled crash that represented a touch-down on to aircraft carriers' flight decks.

The final factor was the Buccaneer's advanced design featuring both 'area rule' as well as a blown air system. The design team at Blackburn Aircraft Limited used every available technology to eke performance from what was – in the early Gyron Junior-powered S.1 aircraft – a seriously underpowered aircraft.

Requirements of NA.39

The first gleanings of a forthcoming Royal Navy requirement for a new aircraft were obtained by the design team at Blackburn Aircraft in the late summer of 1953, with the first drafts of NSR NA.39. By the autumn of 1953 almost a dozen companies were involved in discussions with the Ministry of Supply. At Blackburn Aircraft, under the leadership of Barry Leight, design work commenced in earnest with the expectation of the issue of a specification and invitation to tender in early 1954.

However, during the autumn of 1953 the following specific requirements of the NA.39 were known:

1 A take-off weight not to exceed 40,000lb, with overload up to 45,000lb.
2 A landing weight of between 30,000 to 35,000lb.
3 The folded dimensions of 51ft in length, and 20ft in width.
4 A normal design weapons load of 4,000lb.
5 Catapult and arrester gear limitations defined.
6 The primary role to be the attack of ships at sea or on large shore-based installations, all of which could be described as 'radar discrete targets', which should be identifiable at long range.
7 Primary weapons were listed as 'Green Cheese' – a large anti-ship homing bomb, along with a tactical nuclear bomb.
8 A large range of secondary weapons were also listed, and the aircraft was to have the capability of operating as a flight-refuelling tanker.
9 The operational profile envisaged descent from cruising altitude to very low level just beyond anticipated radar detection range, and a high-speed low-level dash to and from the target.
10 An ambitious radius of action was also specified.

Carrier-borne aircraft have traditionally been the stuff of compromise, given that their take-off, landing and hangarage facilities have always been severely limited.

According to Roy Boot:[1]

The problem was therefore, within the severe carrier constraints of weight and dimensions, to produce an aircraft with the stipulated radius of action with a high-subsonic performance with strong emphasis on high-speed low-level characteristics and with a large weapons bay capable of use at much higher speeds than had previously been practicable.

1 Roy Boot joined Blackburn Aircraft in 1949, initially leading the Future Projects Office. It was from this office that the NA.39 (later Buccaneer) emerged as an ongoing project. He was promoted to Assistant Chief Designer in 1962, Chief Designer in 1966 and Executive Director and Chief Engineer in 1968. From 1978 to 1984 he was Executive Director New Aircraft at British Aerospace, Warton, heading their activities of AST403 (the proposed Jaguar/Harrier replacement), the early collaborative studies for a multinational European fighter, a light combat aircraft and next-generation STOVL designs.

Basically, the specification for NA.39 was a very tough ask!

Thankfully, Roy Boot had already anticipated the needs and drawn up the initial B.103 design, and also had a low-speed wing tunnel model constructed. This design featured a pair of Armstrong Siddeley Sapphire engines, each producing 11,000lb of static thrust. The wing design featured a straight swept trailing edge and two different angles of leading-edge sweepback, while the thickness/chord ratio decreased from root to tip. A high T-tail with a fin-tip mounted tailplane was selected, although problems with such tails, in particular on the Javelin, had hardened opinion against this configuration.

In order to keep the weight down, while easing carrier hangar stowage, there was a strong case for maintaining the wing area and span as low as possible. A span of 45ft and wing area of 650ft^2 were to be the maximum if a heavy and cumbersome double wing-fold were to be avoided. B.103 featured a single wing-fold while the nose cone was also foldable, permitting the aircraft to travel up and down the aircraft carrier lifts.

Results of the Jet-Deflection Trials on the Meteor had become available and this seemed to offer a plausible solution to reducing landing speeds by 25 knots with a 60° deflection. However, it could not be utilised during catapult launching, and the asymmetric problems of a single-engine landing placed a large question mark against the jet-deflection principle.

Engine and technology development

With details of the requirements now known, work on what was now also known as 'NA.39', began in earnest in November 1953. The Blackburn engineering team of just one was significantly increased to three designers, two aerodynamicists, one stressman and one weights engineer. Within three months, this team had increased to ten designers, five aerodynamicists, two stressmen and the weights engineer; who, with the wind tunnel team, saw the tender submission through to the end. Eventually, more than 1,000 technical staff were employed on the Buccaneer.

By early 1954, interest was being shown in a lightweight engine in the 7,000–8,000lb thrust category. Parametric studies at Blackburn had shown that such an engine could be well suited to the NA.39 design. What was of particular interest was a weight saving of almost 5,500lb compared with the twin Sapphire arrangement and this could bring the NA.39 inside the stated carrier limitations, provided that sufficient lift could be generated for take-off and landing. The eventual adoption of the de Havilland engine would provide the design with a 35% increase in range, which would give the Blackburn design a decisive advantage over its competitors. A wing area of 535ft^2 and span of 42ft seemed to be the minimum which could be contemplated, so design work proceeded on this assumption.

Boundary-layer control

A major breakthrough occurred when data on blowing engine bleed air over wing flaps, pioneered by Dr John Attinello in the USA, became available. This boundary-layer control (BLC) principle was strongly advocated by Lewis Boddington, whose responsibilities at the Ministry of Supply included the NA.39. The system had already been tested on a Grumman Panther in the USA and would soon be tested on the Supermarine Scimitar. Eventually, design work suggested that BLC would reduce both catapulting and landing speeds by 15 knots. Then further design work was undertaken between Roy Boot and Blackburn's Technical Director, N.E. 'Nero' Rowe, which showed that if the blow was extended over the whole of the span while the ailerons were drooped, it showed an even more significant impact – a reduction in take-off and landing speeds of around 25 knots. The design went ahead in this manner.

Area rule

Another piece of advanced technology adopted on the project was that of 'area rule'. Once again, the feature was based upon pioneering NACA research undertaken in the USA where the work of Richard Whitcomb showed the advantages of the total cross-sectional area of high-speed aircraft forming a smooth 'streamlined' curve all the way from nose to tail, with no bulge resulting from the wing. With conventional aircraft, the wing adds a significant peak to the curve. However, with 'area rule', this peak is smoothed out by reducing the area of the fuselage in line with the wing while increasing it aft of the wing.

The US research was aimed primarily at supersonic aircraft designs but Blackburn established that the principle could usefully reduce the drag of an aircraft designed to cruise at or around Mach 0.85. When 'area rule' was applied to the B.103 design, the result showed it to be a rather crude design. Particularly evident were problems in the areas of the wasp-waisting and bulged tail. However, with the principles of 'area rule' being applied, significant reductions in drag were provided, which in turn meant that the amount of thrust required for the maximum cruise was also reduced. The modified design provided a large amount of useful extra space in the rear of the fuselage for equipment, which proved to be a significant bonus.

When designing a new aircraft, the selection of the engine is always a major decision. It was of particular importance in B.103, on which valuable thrust would be required to operate the boundary-layer control. The adoption of area rule made a further, and crucial, contribution to the final choice of the powerplant.

The Royal Navy requirement was always going to be particularly difficult to meet in an aeroplane where the physical size was dictated by carrier operations. In order to achieve the maximum range it was essential to use the smallest possible engines. Originally, B.103 was designed with two Sapphire engines, providing plenty of thrust for take-off, including providing the required thrust into the blown air system, and would facilitate the design maximum cruise of Mach 0.85 to be met.

However, the Sapphire engines were both heavy and thirsty.

Calculations completed by the design team now indicated that with the area rule principle applied, a thrust of a little over 14,000lb would provide the desired maximum cruise speed. De Havilland offered Blackburn the 'PS43' (Project Study 43) version of the Gyron Junior engine; a two-fifths scale version of their 20,000lb Gyron turbojet. This smaller development featured an added compressor

stage and two rows of variable stators, and developed a modest thrust of 7,000lb. Fortunately for Blackburn, the PS43 version of the engine eventually selected had been de-rated to 7,000lb from an original design rating of 8,000lb in order to reduce the maximum jet pipe temperatures and to obtain an improved specific fuel consumption. By allowing the jet pipe temperature to rise to the original design figure, the thrust with BLC was held at 6,500lb. However, with the addition of air cooling to the turbine, the full 7,000lb of thrust could be obtained with the BLC system in operation.

At the time it was appreciated that this amount of thrust would be marginal, and subsequent events proved this to be the case. However, it was also assumed that natural engine evolutions and development would result in increased thrust, and this was later achieved with the Rolls-Royce Spey 101.

Initial development order

The adoption of the Gyron Junior engine saw a 35% increase in range and gave the Blackburn project a decisive advantage over competing projects. This resulted, in July 1955, with B.103 being chosen by the Admiralty, and the Ministry of Supply placing an order for 20 development aircraft, the first of which was due to fly in April 1958.

This large order for development aircraft was something of a change from the normal process, when the Ministry of Supply usually placed an order for just one or two prototypes. However, it may have been acceptable in the days of relatively simple piston-engine aircraft, but when advanced jet aircraft such as the Supermarine Swift and Hawker Hunter were involved, it had resulted in unacceptably long development periods. The order for a large number of aircraft also went some way to mitigating any aircraft losses in a programme, while enabling several aspects of the flight trials to be conducted simultaneously.

Wind tunnel testing

The NA.39 was fully tunnel-tested up to its design Mach number and well beyond. Initially, the then recently opened high-speed tunnel at the RAE Bedford was utilised before the company's own supersonic tunnel was opened in 1958 by Earl Mountbatten, then the First Sea Lord.

Construction of the prototype NA.39

Construction of the prototype NA.39 aircraft – allocated the serial XK486 – commenced and proceeded swiftly. The centre section was removed from its jig on 6 July 1957, less than three months after work commenced. XK486 was to be built as an empty shell, without folding wings or any operational equipment. However, production of the second prototype was running just behind the first and featured thicker wing skins. The aircraft was to be subjected to an exhaustive flutter and airframe resonance test to prove the fatigue life of a representative productive aircraft.

With an originally specified date of April 1958 for the first flight, design, build and testing proceeded apace at Brough. By March 1958, the resonance tests were completed, as were the initial engine runs. XK486 was then painted in a smart colour scheme of glossy white below the centreline and royal blue above, before being photographed by the Brough marketing team ahead of the first flight.

Brough runway unsuited to NA.39 operations

With the relatively small runway at Brough proving totally unsuitable to operations of the NA.39 programme, arrangements were made for the lease of the necessary parts of the disused airfield at Holme-on-Spalding-Moor, located 10 miles from Brough as the crow flies, but 18 miles by road.

The main 6,000ft runway, taxi tracks and buildings on the main site for offices and laboratories were refurbished, equipped with the necessary services and brought up to operational status; together with the large J-type hangar. Later in the programme the adjoining pair of T2-type hangars was added to the programme, one for aircraft and the other as a store.

The Ministry of Supply required emergency arrester gear to be fitted to the runway. Initially, this was of the nylon pack type, but later this

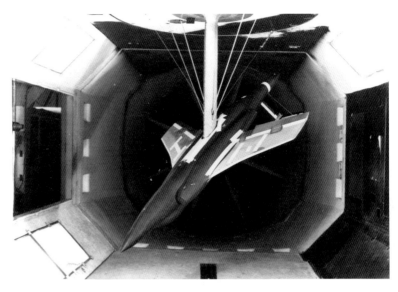

ABOVE The NA.39 was fully wind-tunnel tested up to its design Mach number and beyond. Initially, these were conducted at the then recently opened high-speed tunnel at the RAE Bedford, before the company's own supersonic tunnel was opened in 1958. *(BAE SYSTEMS Image YWT2140)*

was replaced by the more efficient and effective water-squeeze type. Both were to prove very useful during the programme.

First flight at Bedford Thurleigh

Even with the additional safeguard of the arrester gear, the risk of using Holme-on-Spalding-Moor for the initial flight trials was considered unacceptable. The choice was between the two great test airfields at Boscombe Down and Bedford Thurleigh; in the end the latter was chosen due to its closer proximity to Brough.

BELOW The first engine runs were completed on the NA.39 prototype XK486 outside the factory at Holme-on-Spalding-Moor on 26 February 1958. *(BAE SYSTEMS Image BAL11246)*

Subterfuge on the road

The prototype NA.39 was due to be transported by road to the RAE site at Bedford ahead of its maiden flight. It was painstakingly dismantled by withdrawing precision-ground steel bolts from reamed holes, and by disconnecting numerous hydraulic lines and electrical connections.

During this stage, significant attempts were made to avoid giving away too much information to any Soviet agents or sympathisers, which one can assume would have congregated near the Blackburn factory at Brough. For the entire road journey to the RAE at Bedford, the aircraft was covered in shrouds. To further confuse the enemy the roundels on the aircraft were not the 'standard' size and those on the second and third aircraft were different again. The Blackburn team went to great lengths to ensure that early photographs

did not contain objects from which the aircraft could be scaled. Similarly, photographs of the wing planform were not permitted.

Within a few days of its arrival at the RAE, the aircraft was reassembled, checked and ready to make its first flight. With three weeks still to go before its scheduled maiden flight, there appeared to be plenty of time for taxiing trials.

With the aircraft declared 'ready', chief test pilot Lieutenant-Commander Derek Whitehead, a former Royal Navy pilot who had recently left Boscombe Down in January 1958 to join Blackburn especially for the flight test of the NA.39, climbed into the front seat of XK486. He was joined by his observer, Bernard Watson, who occupied the rear seat, and they commenced the taxiing trials.

All went smoothly until, after one high-speed run, heavy braking severely overheated the brakes and one of the main wheel tyres burst. Normally, this would have only been a minor mishap, but when the tyre burst, the point of rupture in the high-pressure tyre happened to be pointing straight up into the wheel well. The violent blast of air severely damaged the skinning of the engine nacelle on the inner wing. It was not a particularly good advertisement for what was considered to be the strongest wing ever built in Britain! A major effort was required to repair the wing and this work was completed on 29 April 1958, when the taxi trials could recommence.

Today, this type of incident is prevented by using special fusible plugs fitted in the wheels. If the temperature rises dangerously high, the plugs melt, permitting the tyre to deflate safely. This fusible tyre modification was later incorporated into the Buccaneer aircraft in use with both the FAA and RAF.

First flight of the NA.39

On 30 April 1958, with Derek Whitehead and Bernard Watson on board, Blackburn NA.39 XK486, resplendent in its royal blue and white colour scheme, thundered down the runway before lifting off and heading skyward. Things were taken relatively gently on this flight, although the aircraft did climb up to 17,000ft before landing 39 minutes later. Both the take-off and landing were flown unblown, although the airbrakes were tested and were deployed

for the landing. The first flight was reported as 'a real success'. It was far too early to be certain, but Whitehead was clearly convinced that the latest Blackburn project was going to be a winner.

The first flight took place just 33 months after the contract had been placed. To have met all of the target dates during the design and construction phases of such an advanced design was an achievement of which the Blackburn Aircraft Company was justifiably proud.

Flight trials commence

The following flights, all undertaken from Bedford, concentrated on the blown air high-lift system configurations. Generally, all the tests – flown by Derek Whitehead and G.R.I. 'Sailor' Parker – went well. Initially, flap, aileron droop and tailplane droop were all selected separately, allowing for flexibility in experimenting with different settings of each, until an integrated system was eventually fitted to the eighth aircraft onwards.

The aircraft were restricted to 350 knots while operating at Bedford due to the requirement to complete a canopy jettison test under full flight load. The only place this could be done on the aircraft was at Holme-on-Spalding-Moor.

The spell at Bedford lasted longer than the Blackburn design team wanted – three months – as it took time to convince the authorities regarding the move to Holme-on-Spalding-Moor.

Holme-on-Spalding-Moor

A flight operations team was set up under flight test manager John Stamper. A team of six pilots and seven flight test observers was assembled, with the pilots headed by Derek Whitehead.

The second and all subsequent aircraft were towed from Brough to Holme-on-Spalding-Moor on their own wheels and were almost ready to fly upon arrival. The folding wings were an obvious advantage for the road journey. Eight aircraft were constructed and flown in the first 16 months, in accordance with the terms of the contract drawn up some four years earlier.

During the trials the aircraft under test were accompanied by a Meteor NF.12 or a Hunter F.4 acting as a 'chase' aircraft. The NA.39

programme was one of the first in Britain where this commonplace US procedure, obviously worthwhile, was adopted.

By September 1958 XK487, equipped with strain gauges, flutter exciters and instrumentation, was active in the programme. This aircraft was vital to the extension of the flight envelope, which it did efficiently over a period.

The third prototype, XK488, made its first flight in October 1958 and after conducting its clearance trials, was handed over to de Havilland Engines. It completed most of its much-needed Gyron Junior development flying from Hatfield and Filton. XK489 made its first flight on 31 January 1959 and joined the flight trials programme shortly afterwards where it was employed on navalisation (folding wings, arrester hook, etc.) and stores-carrying trials.

From March to July 1959, there was a rapid expansion of the fleet with XK490, XK491 and XK523 all being added. Having demonstrated the satisfactory rotation of the bomb door in flight and played its part in flight-control development, XK490 went – as planned – to RAE Bedford for arresting and catapult

ABOVE **Derek Whitehead (left) and Bernard Watson (centre) chat with an official from the Royal Navy immediately after the successful first flight of XK486 on 30 April 1958.** *(BAE SYSTEMS Brough Image BAL11609)*

BELOW **A nice air-to-air study of three of the pre-production NA.39s – XK486, XK487 and XK490. Production aircraft would later feature distinctive fairings forward and aft of the junction of the fin and all-moving tailplane.** *(BAE SYSTEMS Image BAL13079)*

proofing and clearance; all of which was completed satisfactorily.

XK490, intended for arming carriage and release trials, found itself short of role equipment and was subsequently deployed to Malta for handling and cooling system trials. As a result, a new and improved cold-air unit was required, along with a new control system. In addition, the trials identified the requirement of an entirely new distribution of cooling air in the radio bay.

XK491 was slated for autopilot trials, as well as being the first aircraft to be fitted with the air turbine alternator and its standby inverter, all previous aircraft having been fitted with just the two 6kW generators with inverters supplying AC.

Around this time, XK523 emerged from the factory ready for initial flight trials. Up until now, wheels, brakes and tyres had all been supplied by Dunlop, but someone decided that an alternative source of supply should be investigated. Accordingly, XK523 found itself with a trial installation of Goodyear equipment, which included a new type of anti-skid system. With memories of the taxiing incident involving XK486 still fresh in the mind, a cautious approach was adopted with the taxi-runs up to ever-increasing speeds. On the very first run, up to a relatively low speed, the aircraft porpoised wildly as soon as the brakes were applied. Further tests were made and even the Goodyear designer was unable to resolve the problem. With the scheduled first flight date approaching, it appeared that this aircraft would be the first to miss its target. Thankfully, Goodyear solved the problem; the aircraft was duly modified and met its first flight target.

Engine problems aside, the first three aircraft flew perfectly well up to a maximum speed and Mach number. However, XK489 and XK490 both showed a tendency towards directional tramping above 520 knots (Mach 0.9). At the time, this was accepted but, when XK491 exhibited severe tailplane-shake at similar speeds, investigation could not be delayed. The problem was diagnosed as a shock-induced separation in the fin/tailplane junction and that a large tailplane-fin junction bullet, along with a detailed aerodynamic clean-up in

this area, would improve the situation. Design changes were made and the modifications were eventually improved in time to be fitted to the first aircraft delivered to the Royal Navy.

Carrier trials

Carrier trials were due to commence in October 1959, with XK489 and XK523 operating from HMS *Victorious*. Unfortunately, these were postponed when XK490 crashed into the New Forest on 12 October 1959 while on an evaluation flight from Boscombe Down. Sadly, the American pilot and Blackburn observer were both killed. Investigators eventually decided the accident had been caused by a stall at low speed, with insufficient height to recover. Both crew members had ejected from the inverted aircraft but were too low to survive.

It was not until January 1960 that the carrier trials were able to commence aboard HMS *Victorious* in Lyme Bay. The task of making the very first deck landing was bestowed upon Derek Whitehead, who flew XK523 from Holme-on-Spalding-Moor and carried out a number of touch-and-goes before completing an uneventful landing on to the carrier.

Two days later, XK489 arrived on to the carrier for a series of trials which were to last a week, often in miserable weather

RIGHT The NA.39's very first carrier launch was performed from HMS *Victorious*. During the launch, the Gyron Junior engines were run at a temporary high jet pipe temperature to ensure sufficient air for the blown air system, as well as enough thrust for the take-off. *(BAE SYSTEMS Image BAL14606)*

conditions. Launches were made at increasing weights, with a total of 31 flights eventually being achieved. No major problems were encountered, although some changes were later made to the arrester hook and undercarriage as a result of the trials. It did provide an excellent opportunity for the NA.39's compatibility to be checked with the Royal Navy's carrier, especially the refuelling and servicing methods employed; and the all-important aspect of being able to fit on to a standard deck lift.

New standard NA.39

The eighth NA.39 was built to a new standard, incorporating a number of changes found necessary or desirable during the trials programme. As a consequence, XK524 did not make its maiden flight until 4 April 1960, almost eight months after XK523. Visually, XK524 differed little from its predecessors but included a number of structural modifications and changes to the cockpit layout and

RIGHT This dramatic view of XK523's first launch shows the aircraft throwing off the launch bridle – which drops into the sea – as the aircraft staggers into the air. *(BAE SYSTEMS Image BAL14608)*

instrumentation. As such, it was the first NA.39 built to production standards. Unfortunately, as a result of some of these changes, several of the qualification trials had to be repeated.

XK525 followed on 15 July 1960 and was the first aircraft with the complete navigation and weapons system. By the end of 1960, XK526–XK528 had all joined the test programme, with all three spending much time with the A&AEE at Boscombe Down in an effort to meet the planned date for Controller Aircraft (CA) Release date of April 1961.

NA.39 named 'Buccaneer'

During the early years of the flight trials the NA.39 design had remained nameless but on 26 August 1960 the name 'Buccaneer S Mk.1' was formally adopted; the 'S' indicating strike, that is, nuclear capability. Blackburn chose to mark the event by releasing an image of six development aircraft on the ground, taken at Holme-on-Spalding-Moor a few weeks earlier.

Two more losses

A second crash was suffered by the programme when XK486 was lost on 5 October 1960 while undergoing autopilot trials. G.R.I. 'Sailor' Parker was flying the aircraft manually in cloud when he suffered an instrument malfunction and the aircraft started to roll. Parker and his observer managed to eject safely, but the aircraft crashed at Little Weighton, near Brough. The cause was later found to be a failure of the artificial horizon instrument and, thankfully, the crash had no significant impact on Blackburn's test schedules.

Another aircraft was lost on 31 August 1961. At the time of the incident, XK529 was involved in deck trials from HMS *Hermes* when the aircraft crashed in Lyme Bay, with the loss of both of the crew. At the time, the aircraft was being operated by the A&AEE Boscombe Down's 'C' Squadron.

CA Release

In July 1961, on schedule, an effective CA Release was obtained. This enabled the Royal Navy to get to grips with their new aircraft with the remaining four Buccaneer S.1 aircraft being delivered to the Intensive Flying Trials Unit (IFTU) to bring them up to full strength.

BELOW During the early years of the flight trials the NA.39 had remained nameless but on 26 August 1960 the name 'Buccaneer S Mk.1' was formally adopted. To publicise the naming, Blackburn released this image of six development aircraft (XK488, XK487, XK523, XK489, XK524 and XK525) taken at Holme-on-Spalding-Moor, 7 August 1960. *(BAE SYSTEMS Image BAL15505)*

RIGHT An early Royal Navy Buccaneer S.1, XN929, was displayed by Blackburn Aircraft at Farnborough in September 1962. The aircraft is fitted with the 'first standard' retractable flight refuelling probe, trialled with dry contacts only, but which proved completely unsatisfactory. As the nozzle approached the tanker drogue, a bow wave effect from the Buccaneer caused the drogue to move suddenly so that engagement of the drogue was something of a lottery. (BAE SYSTEMS Image FAS 37-62)

RIGHT An early proposal submitted to the Royal Navy was for an AEW variant of the Buccaneer, which was offered in model form around September 1963. Utilising the rotating bomb bay, the proposal is seen in this view with the equipment retracted . . . (BAE SYSTEMS Image B2227-1)

RIGHT . . . while in this view the AEW sensor is seen deployed. This option was not pursued by the Royal Navy. (BAE SYSTEMS Image B2227-4)

All 20 of the development batch of aircraft had flown by the end of 1961, with the final six aircraft incorporating virtually all of the features of production aircraft.

First deliveries to the Royal Navy

No 700Z Flight had been commissioned at Lossiemouth (HMS *Fulmar*) on 7 March 1961. Its role was simply stated as 'to get as many hours with the Buccaneer as possible'. The first two Buccaneer S.1 aircraft (XK531 coded LM/680 and XK532 coded LM/681) were delivered in August 1961. XK533–XK536 – the final four aircraft of the 20-aircraft pre-production batch – were delivered to 700Z by early 1962. These aircraft were coded LM/682 through to LM/685.

Rolls-Royce Spey 101 for Buccaneer S.2

As early as 1959, Blackburn were actively seeking an alternative powerplant to the de Havilland Gyron Junior. The lack of power was very much the Achilles heel of the Buccaneer, both as a shipboard aircraft as well as a land-based one.

The most promising option was the Rolls-Royce RB.163 Spey turbofan, which was being developed for production in a civilian form to power the three-engine de Havilland DH.121 Trident airliner for British European Airways (BEA).

ABOVE Three Buccaneer S.1 aircraft of 800 NAS at Lossiemouth on 13 August 1964. The nearest aircraft displays a selection of armament and weapons available. After having completed a maiden short tour with the S.1 variant aboard HMS *Eagle* in home waters and the Mediterranean (December 1964–May 1965), 800 NAS made one major Far East cruise aboard the same carrier (August 1965–August 1966), which included operations off Aden and on the Beira patrol. *(BAE SYSTEMS Image B2221-2)*

BELOW Some of the development aircraft – as well as early front-line squadron aircraft – were finished in an all-white 'anti-flash' paint finish, recognising the aircraft's potential nuclear role. In this image from April 1965, the trials S.2 XN975 provides fuel from its underwing Mk.20 pod to S.1 XN923, which had been 'borrowed' from 700Z NAS to test a new fixed in-flight refuelling pod. *(BAE SYSTEMS Image BAL20828)*

ABOVE To further speed up the development of the forward-looking radar system under development for the TSR-2, the second fixed-wing, pre-production aircraft, XK487, was loaned to Ferranti and flown to Turnhouse Airport, Edinburgh, on 8 May 1963. The aircraft was used by Ferranti for around three and a half years before being returned. *(BAE SYSTEMS Image Ferranti 2250)*

In a military form, it offered 11,380lb of thrust and an improved specific fuel consumption for a modest increase in installed weight. However, a growth in air mass flow would require changes to both intakes and jet pipes. These design changes were refined during 1960, by which time the Spey Mk.101 had effectively been selected for the Buccaneer S.2.

The thrust of the non-afterburning Spey was so much higher than that of the Gyron Junior that the extra loss of engine thrust when the blown air system was selected was no longer of any great significance. The BLC system was redesigned on the S.2 to take advantage of the engine's high mass flow, with the result that a reduction of 8 knots on launch (take-off speed) and 2 knots on landing speeds, was required compared to the earlier S.1.

The S.2 programme became public during 1961, before the S.1 had even reached squadron service. Later, on 8 January 1962, Hawker Siddeley announced that a production order for the Spey-engined S.2 had been received for the Royal Navy. Unfortunately, no S.1 could be released from the S.1 development programme that year, although both XK526 and XK527 were earmarked for conversion to S.2 configuration.

XK526 was the first aircraft converted to S.2 specifications and made its maiden flight at Holme-on-Spalding-Moor on 17 May 1963, followed by XK527 on 19 August of the same

year. Production S.2 aircraft rolled off the line at Brough in the early summer of 1964, with a batch commencing with serial number XN974.

Hawker Siddeley P.145 Project

In the hope of selling a land-based version of the Buccaneer, either to the RAF or for export, Hawker Siddeley announced Project P.145 in October 1966. It took advantage of work already completed on the Martel anti-ship missile wing store carriage, the rocket-assisted take-off of the Mk.50 together with its 430-gallon wing tanks, the bogie undercarriage design and the Improved Weapons Systems studies.

A new feature of the P.145 was a large reconnaissance pack, picking up with the airframe attachments for the bomb door. This pack contained a range of cameras, infra-red linescan and sideways-looking radar, similar to that fitted to the Phantom.

P.145 offered a maximum take-off weight of 62,000lb on a typical operational profile, could carry 4,000lb of bombs for a radius of operation exceeding 1,400 miles; or 10,000lb of bombs over 800 miles; with a maximum bomb load of 16,000lb over a radius of 400 miles. All of these were offered with a take-off run of less than 4,000ft. It would have provided any operator of the type with a potent weapons platform.

At this stage of proceedings, the RAF was politically committed to an order for 50 F-111A aircraft and, once again, rejected the P.145 proposal. However, within a few years – when politics once again reared its ugly head – some aspects of P.145 would eventually come into play.

Orders forthcoming for the RAF

On 6 April 1965, the budget speech from the then Labour Government announced the cancellation of the revolutionary BAC TSR-2, which had flown for the first time just a few months earlier. A decision was taken to replace the TSR-2 with an order for 50 F-111A swing-wing supersonic nuclear strike aircraft.

In early 1968, sweeping defence cuts were introduced by Harold Wilson's Labour Government. These included the cancellation of the 50 F-111A aircraft mentioned above. The government's solution to the problem was an order for Buccaneer S.2 aircraft – a type that the RAF had rejected on previous occasions as not being suitable! That said, it would have been a very rare occurrence if the RAF *had* ordered an aircraft type that had been designed specifically for a Royal Navy shipboard application.

Initially, an order for 26 new-build Buccaneer S.2B aircraft was placed. The RAF requirement was to accommodate a larger range of weapons, including Martel, while maintaining the reconnaissance capability involving the bomb bay-mounted reconnaissance pack.

Along with the decision to acquire new-build Buccaneer aircraft, it was further agreed to hand over to the RAF all of the remaining Fleet Air Arm's inventory of Buccaneer S.2 aircraft. The era of the aircraft carrier was over and all of the ships would be withdrawn from service in the following years.

Buccaneer longevity

The Buccaneer had successful Royal Navy, Royal Air Force and South African Air Force careers. RAF aircraft fought in the First Gulf War and eventually remained in service until 1993, when they were finally replaced by surplus Tornado GR.1 aircraft that had become available after their withdrawal from service in RAF Germany.

The following chapters will examine in more detail the Buccaneer's career with all three services.

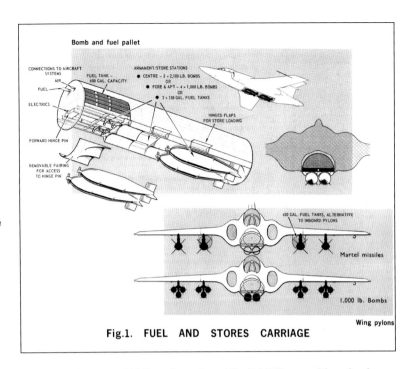

Fig.1. FUEL AND STORES CARRIAGE

ABOVE In October 1966 Brough produced the P.145 Proposal for a land-based version of the Buccaneer, either to the RAF or for export. Realising the importance of range, and knowing that since the original design of the Buccaneer most stores had been adapted to withstand the environmental conditions of external carriage at the relevant speeds, a fuel and store pallet was proposed. Sadly, at this stage, the RAF was committed to the F-111K. *(BAE SYSTEMS)*

BELOW The first aircraft officially handed over to the RAF was XV350, a former FAA airframe which was transferred to the RAF on 1 January 1969, although it did not make its first flight, after modification, until 11 February. Interestingly, XV350 spent its entire life on trials work, either at Holme-on-Spalding-Moor or Boscombe Down, and is shown here undergoing manufacturer's trials with four Martel missiles. *(BAE SYSTEMS Image CN1781D)*

Chapter Two

Anatomy of the Buccaneer

'The NA.39 is ahead' proclaimed an advertisement placed by Blackburn Aircraft Limited. The advert went on to extol the virtues of the area rule principles which *'minimises drag because it allows the airflow gradually to contract and expand over the total cross section of the aircraft. This has special virtues for high-speed, low-level flying because it ensures good control response and a smoother ride for the crew.'*

OPPOSITE 'Jackal 3', an unmarked 12 Squadron Buccaneer S.2, XV332, photographed while setting up for an approach to land at RAF Lossiemouth on 3 December 1992. The effects of the technically advanced boundary layer control (BLC) system can be seen to good effect on the tailplane and wing trailing edges in this image. *(Keith Wilson)*

Advanced aerodynamics including 'blown air'

The aerodynamic evolution of the Blackburn NA.39 (later Buccaneer) was a long one. The basic wing design finally chosen for the aircraft utilised ideas that had been developed at Brough over a considerable period. The wing embodies two angles of sweepback, with a change of wing section from inboard to outboard in order to provide a near-constant critical Mach number spanwise, while at the same time ensuring that initial stalling occurs inboard of the wing. Under low-speed conditions this requires additional assistance at the outer leading edge. This could have been provided with the use of leading-edge flaps or slats, but instead, leading edge blow was used. Extensive detail development was required by the design team at Brough in order to achieve the absolute maximum performance as there was always a tendency for one area of the wing to stall earlier than the rest.

The general configuration of the aircraft suggested a high tail, although this particular design element was unpopular at the time. There had been a number of incidents on other aircraft designs due to stable stall conditions, tailplane flutter, as well as unexplained structural failures. However, by using blown air and preventing the wingtip stall, the heavy inboard downwash – which would normally cause a stable stall – was avoided.

Blown air and BLC

In 1954, while the Brough design team were working on their B.103 proposal for the NA.39 requirement, the data on blowing engine bleed air over wing flaps, pioneered by Dr John Attinello in the USA, had just become available. The Attinello flap had been flown on a modified Grumman Panther, and plans were afoot to test the principle on a Supermarine Scimitar jet, which would provide the UK with actual data on the advanced technology. According to Roy Boot:

The breakthrough which occurred to enable flap-blowing to succeed came with the availability of the necessary quantity of air at a high enough pressure to choke the slits, and hence automatically to get an even spanwise distribution.

Having become aware of the beneficial effects of 'flap blowing' – blowing engine bleed air over wing flaps to re-energise the airflow and to improve lift – the Brough design team were keen to incorporate it into their project B.103. The potential was far too good to miss and they adopted BLC into their proposal. They estimated that around 10% of the mass airflow of each engine would be redirected through ducts along the leading edge of the wing and tailplane; and over the wing trailing edge, ahead of the flaps and ailerons. Then, by incorporating drooped ailerons, the wing effectively had full-span flaps and the boundary-layer control could reduce the landing speed by 17 knots, with the BLC blow automatically activating when the surface extension exceeded 10°.

The same BLC system also provided hot air for airframe de-icing – another Royal Navy requirement for the NA.39 – and proved a most elegant solution to the problem.

BLC was not, however, a magic panacea as it led to a significant pitch change which became evident on the selection of flaps. This was overcome by the Brough design team by incorporating an innovative tailplane flap.

BELOW The prototype Blackburn NA.39 photographed in the experimental shop at Brough in January 1958, as the aircraft nears completion. *(BAE SYSTEMS Image BAL11074)*

Area rule

The principle of area ruling became available while the B.103 design was being finalised. Area rule suggested that the cross-sectional area of an aircraft must be kept constant. The Brough design team once again adopted the principle with enthusiasm and the design of the B.103 was subtly altered to include some fuselage waisting along with the area rule bulges in the rear fuselage behind the wing trailing edge.

Although their inclusion into the design was on the grounds of aerodynamics, both to delay the drag rise at speeds close to Mach 1.0, and to improve the flying qualities at high speed and low level, they had a significant secondary impact. Their inclusion added additional stowage space for avionics into an already crowded fuselage.

Choice of engine

When the original design submission was initially made to the Ministry of Supply, the choice of engine had not been finalised. The Brough design team was still considering both the Bristol BE.33 producing 11,400lb of static thrust and the de Havilland Gyron Junior of 7,100lb static thrust. In the end, the Gyron Junior was chosen for the project, as it weighed considerably less than the proposed Bristol engine and just met the stated carrier limitations. Initially, the airframe was designed to accept both engines but later in the process, when a heavy emphasis on weight saving became paramount, the spar rings were tailored exactly to meet the Gyron Junior jet pipes.

However, this engine would always prove to be the Achilles heel of the Buccaneer S.1 and it wasn't until later in the programme, when the Rolls-Royce Spey 101-powered Buccaneer S.2 became available, that the design met – and often exceeded – its design criteria.

Machine tool manufacturing problems

In order to provide the structural strength required for the high-speed, low-level attack role, the B.103 required a long fatigue life in what was to be a very demanding environment, with 3,000 hours being the design aim of the airframe. Accordingly, the design team made extensive use of integrally machined skin panels, spars and ribs. However, the manufacture of these posed difficult problems, not least of which was the almost complete lack of any UK-manufactured machine tooling available on which to produce them. Meanwhile, companies such as High Duty Alloys strove to manufacture production quantities of high-strength steel for key components in grades that had been unobtainable just a year earlier, except in small quantity test quantities.

In the United States the trend towards integral machining had been studied from 1948 onwards and the USAF had funded a special research programme to aid the machine tool industry to produce large-scale skin mills, stretch-presses and other very large machine tools. However, such support in the UK was non-existent!

Accordingly, when Blackburn wanted to

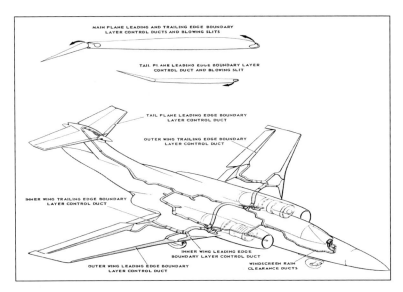

ABOVE Diagram of the BLC system of the Buccaneer S.2. *(BAE SYSTEMS)*

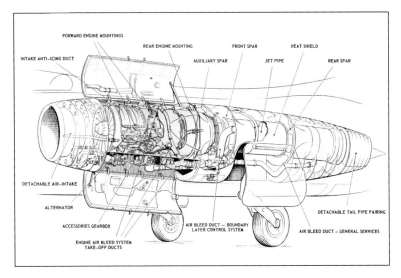

BELOW Diagram of the engine installation in the Buccaneer S.1 featuring the de Havilland Gyron Junior engine. *(BAE SYSTEMS)*

Blackburn/BAE Buccaneer S.2B. *(Mike Badrocke)*

1 Glass-fibre radome
2 Radome latches
3 Fixed flight refuelling probe
4 Hinged radar equipment module
5 Radar scanner
6 Ventral weapons recorder/camera
7 Ferranti Blue Parrot multi-mode search and fire control radar
8 Pressurised radar housing
9 Ice detector probe
10 ADF antenna
11 Windscreen rain dispersal air duct
12 Front pressure bulkhead
13 Cockpit pressurisation valve
14 Radar module hinge arm
15 VHF homing antennae
16 Landing/taxiing lamp
17 Total pressure head
18 Levered suspension nosewheel axle
19 Steerable nosewheel, aft retracting
20 Nosewheel leg door
21 Leg pivot mounting
22 Rudder pedals
23 Canopy emergency release
24 Control column handgrip
25 Instrument panel shroud
26 Pilot's head-up display
27 Windscreen wiper
28 Windscreen panels
29 Ejection seat headrest and face blind firing handle
30 Pilot's Martin-Baker Mk 6 MSB zero-zero ejection seat
31 Side console panel
32 Engine throttle levers
33 Cockpit internal pressure shell
34 Fuel system electrical equipment bay, cockpit air conditioning pack on starboard side
35 Port engine air intake, thermally de-iced
36 De-icing air spill duct
37 Ventral radar altimeter antenna
38 Hydraulic equipment bay
39 Artificial feel control unit
40 Navigator's instrument consoles
41 Radar display
42 Blast screen
43 Starboard engine air intake
44 AN/CPU-123B Paveway II 1,000lb (454kg) laser-guided bomb, normally carried on starboard inboard stores station
45 430 Imp gal (1,955 lit) slipper tank, carried for LGB designator role
46 Sliding cockpit canopy cover
47 Navigator's Martin Baker Mk.6 MSB ejection seat
48 Circuit breaker panel
49 Cockpit rear pressure bulkhead
50 Fuel system recuperator (2)
51 Forward fuselage integral fuel tanks, total capacity of fuselage tanks 1,560 Imp gal (7,092 lit)
52 Canopy electric drive motor
53 Canopy centre arch
54 Miniature detonating cord (MDC) canopy breakers
55 Starboard wing blowing air ducts
56 Inboard stores station pylon mounting
57 Wing fold hinge joint
58 Outboard stores pylon
59 AN/SLQ-101(V)-10 ECM pod
60 Martel TV-guidance data-link pod, maritime strike role
61 ARI 18228 radar warning receiver and wide-band homing antenna fairing
62 Outer wing panel vortex generators
63 Inboard leading edge blowing duct
64 Outboard leading edge blowing duct
65 Starboard navigation light
66 Wing tip fairing
67 Starboard formation light
68 Aileron hydraulic actuator
69 Starboard 'blown' drooping aileron
70 Wing folded position
71 Trailing edge blowing air duct
72 AN/ALE-40 chaff/flare launcher, also beneath jet pipes or rear fuselage

73 Starboard blown flap
74 Wing fold hydraulic jack
75 UHF antenna
76 Anti-collision strobe light
77 Wing spar attachment fuselage main frames
78 Weapons bay roof structure
79 UHF standby antenna
80 Rear fuselage integral fuel tanks
81 Dorsal spine fairing
82 Cable ducting, fuel vent piping on starboard side
83 Fuel tank bay rear bulkhead
84 Radio and avionics equipment compartment
85 Flush HF antenna
86 HF variable capacitor
87 Rear equipment bay conditioning air intake
88 ILS localiser antenna
89 Fin spar attachment joints
90 Tailplane blowing air duct
91 Three-spar fin box construction
92 Tailplane control rod
93 All-moving tailplane hydraulic actuator
94 Moving tailplane sealing fairing
95 ARI 18228 RWR antenna fairing
96 Tailplane leading edge blowing air duct
97 Starboard tailplane
98 Tailplane flap
99 IFF antenna
100 Tailplane flap dual electric actuators
101 All-moving tailplane pivot mounting
102 Tailplane flap operating linkage
103 Tail navigation light
104 Position light
105 Rear ARI 18228 RWR antenna fairing
106 Tailplane flap rib construction
107 Port tailplane multi-spar and rib structure
108 Tailplane blown leading edge
109 Rudder rib construction
110 Split tailcone airbrakes
111 Airbrake strake
112 Airbrake rib construction
113 External honeycomb doubler
114 Airbrake drag link
115 Hydraulic jack
116 Rudder hydraulic actuator
117 Yaw damper mechanism
118 Sloping fin-spar attachment frames
119 Fuel vent

120 Runway emergency arrester hook
121 Hook hydraulic jack and damper
122 Tail bumper hydraulic jack
123 Retractable tail bumper
124 Ventral access hatch
125 Electrical distribution panels
126 Engine fire bottle (2)
127 Jet pipe fairing
128 Exhaust nozzle
129 Rotary weapons bay door hinge point
130 Weapons bay door hydraulic jack
131 Internal weapons bay, 4 x 1,000lb (454kg) bomb maximum capacity, more normally used for long range fuel tank
132 Engine exhaust duct
133 Exhaust duct machined ring frames
134 Stub wing spar bolted joint
135 Port flap hydraulic jack
136 Flap blowing air duct
137 Port flap construction
138 Blowing air duct wing fold coupling
139 Port blown drooping aileron
140 Aileron hinge point
141 Aileron rib construction
142 Port formation light
143 Crash trip switches
144 Remote compass transmitter
145 Port navigation
146 Pitot head
147 Machined wing skin/stringer panels
148 Machined wing ribs
149 Port aileron hydraulic actuator
150 Aileron control rod linkage
151 Port ARI 18228 RWR and wide-band homing antennae

152 AIM-9L/M Sidewinder air-to-air missile
153 Missile launch rail
154 Outboard stores pylon
155 Pylon hardpoints
156 Port wing blown leading edge
157 Machined wing spars
158 Wing fold hinge joint
159 Spar latch
160 Port mainwheel
161 Mainwheel door
162 Shock absorber leg strut, leg shortens on retraction
163 Port, wing blowing air ducting
164 Main undercarriage leg pivot mounting
165 Hydraulic retraction jack mounting
166 Stub wing front spar joint
167 Engine bay ring frame/fuselage mainframe bolted joint
168 Bleed air cross-over duct
169 Rear engine mounting
170 Engine bleed air ducting
171 Main engine mounting

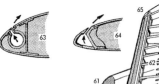

172 Rolls-Royce RB 168-1A Spey Mk 101 non-afterburning turbofan engine
173 Intake compressor face
174 Engine accessory equipment
175 Hinged cowling panels
176 440 Imp gal (1,000 lit) weapons bay long-range fuel tank, door-mounted
177 Weapons bay rotary door integral fuel tank, capacity 425 Imp gal (1,932 lit)
178 Rotary weapons bay door forward hinge point
179 1,000lb (454kg) freefall HE bomb
180 Pylon adaptor
181 AN/AVQ-23E Pave Spike laser designator pod

182 Optical head and hinged protector
183 Laser designator on-board heat exchanger
184 Radar Martel seeker head
185 Missile pylon adaptor
186 TV Martel anti-shipping missile, maritime role
187 BAe Dynamics Sea Eagle long-range anti-shipping missile

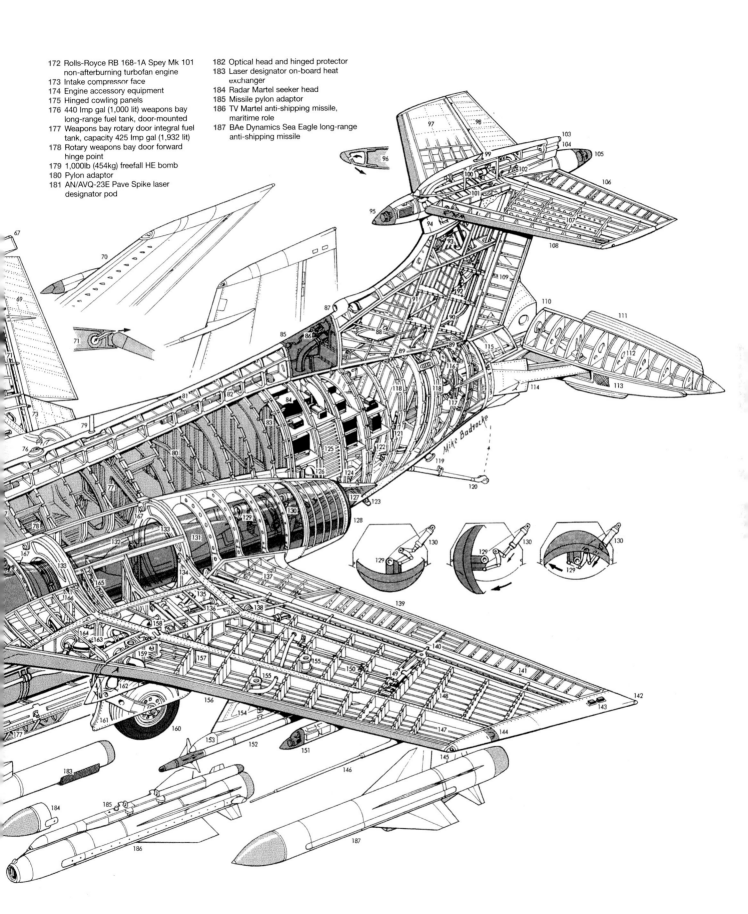

Mike Badrocke

RIGHT Diagram
of the port outer
wing section of the
Buccaneer. (BAE
SYSTEMS)

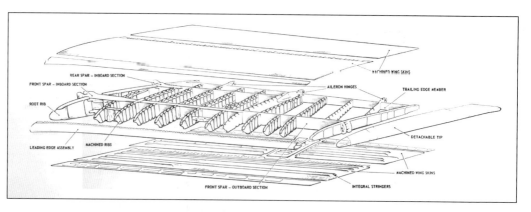

ABOVE As with many of the main structural components used on the NA.39, the wing outer panels were machined from solid metal. The port bottom forward wing skin was photographed on 21 August 1956. (BAE SYSTEMS Image BAL8760)

BELOW The Buccaneer test rig at Brough on 6 November 1958. (BAE SYSTEMS Image BAL12472)

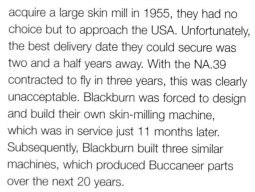

acquire a large skin mill in 1955, they had no choice but to approach the USA. Unfortunately, the best delivery date they could secure was two and a half years away. With the NA.39 contracted to fly in three years, this was clearly unacceptable. Blackburn was forced to design and build their own skin-milling machine, which was in service just 11 months later. Subsequently, Blackburn built three similar machines, which produced Buccaneer parts over the next 20 years.

A similar situation occurred with the proposed acquisition of a stretch-press. Blackburn even considered the design and manufacture of one of their own before the Ministry of Supply relented and allowed the import of a large Hufford stretch-press from the USA to manufacture Buccaneer parts. Numerous problems were encountered with the machining of the major skin panels and structural members machined from solid billets, and these took Blackburn a long time to overcome. As every aircraft structural designer knows, it is one thing to design an airframe that is initially strong enough, but quite another to design one that will continue to remain so after many years of service.

Fatigue testing

The airframe was intended for a service life of 3,000 hours using a high-low flight profile. It was designed from the outset to operate in the very demanding primary role of low-level strike, which required the aircraft to be capable of high speed at low level through dense and turbulent air. These requirements called for a very robust construction, which later earned the aircraft another of its nicknames – the flying brick outhouse!

The 3,000-hour life was confirmed by a full-scale test programme, with the complete wing assembly being tested to 30,000 equivalent flying hours (see image on page 40) and the tailplane specimen to 15,000 hours. These tests included simulation of 15,000 and 7,500 hours of low-level runs of 250 miles each with turbulence levels representing the worldwide average, while also denoting combat manoeuvres up to and including 5g.

Structure of the fuselage

The fuselage is of skin and stringer construction, with stretch-formed panels. Two heavy longerons run the length of the centre fuselage to act as closing members for the weapons bay and to contain the substantial catapult and arrester loads. The upper centre fuselage is double-skinned, and contains the integral fuel tanks.

Major equipment is cleverly housed in three main areas: the lower forward fuselage, on either side of the nose wheel bay; the lower centre fuselage, between the forward end of the weapons bay and the rear of the cockpit (known as the accessory bay); and the rear fuselage (known as the radio bay). Both of the latter two bays are accessible with entry through a door in the fuselage to a man standing on the ground.

The front fuselage contains the pressurised cockpit with accommodation for a crew of two in tandem under a single electrically operated rearward-sliding Perspex canopy. Another clever innovation is that the two seats are staggered, with the rear (observer's) seat being higher and to the right of the pilot's, thereby permitting the maximum forward view for the back-seater.

LEFT The layout of front and rear cockpits of the Buccaneer gave both crew members the best possible view forward, as seen here on S.2B, XW544. The front, pilot's, cockpit is slightly offset to the left, while the raised rear, observer's, cockpit is offset to the right, permitting a good view over the pilot's shoulder. In addition, a windscreen was added to the front of the observer's position in case of a high-speed seat ejection and for protection in the event of a bird-strike. *(Keith Wilson)*

Martin-Baker zero-zero ejection seats are fitted to both crew positions.

Crew comfort was of particular importance during the design phase, especially for an aircraft designed to fly at high speed at low level, where the incidence of turbulence is significant. Furthermore, many roles require long endurance flights, possibly in poor weather conditions. The cockpit pressurisation provides a pressure

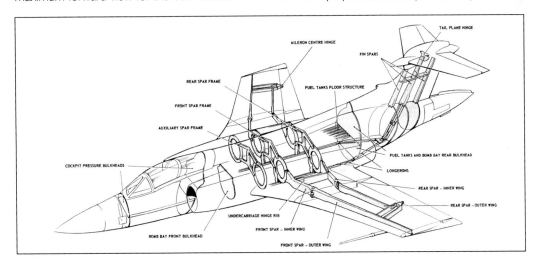

LEFT The primary structure of the Buccaneer. *(BAE SYSTEMS)*

ABOVE Many of the major fittings on the Buccaneer were machined from solid metal to provide additional structural strength. In this image, from left to right are: the inner wing rib, inner wing front spar, outer wing front spar and the inner wing rear spar. *(BAE SYSTEMS Image BAL12392)*

BELOW Buccaneer front and rear spar frames, port side inner-wing spar members, and outer-wing hinge fittings, seen here in the folded position. *(BAE SYSTEMS)*

differential varying from zero at 8,000ft, to 4lb/in^2 at 25,000ft and constant at higher altitudes. A liquid oxygen system provides oxygen to both crew members from a single container with a capacity sufficient for 9–12 hours' supply, depending upon the type of sortie.

The centre fuselage is double-skinned alongside the engine and extends to aft of the wing trailing edge. The top half of the fuselage accommodates eight integral fuel tanks. The forward part of the bottom half of the centre fuselage is an accessory bay for hydraulics along with electrical control gear.

The rear fuselage extends to the tail and embodies the distinctive area rule bulge which contains the bulk of the electrical equipment and has its own cooling system. Below floor level is the Doppler aerial, the 'hold back' attachment for catapult launching and the heavy-duty arrester hook. At the rear end of the fuselage is a support structure and the operating jack for the enormous airbrakes.

Fuel system

The eight fuselage fuel tanks have a total capacity of 1,560 gallons. The fuel was transferred to the proportioners (pumps) by air pressure and two recuperators which provided fuel flow under negative-G conditions for a limited time. The bomb-door fuel tank (RAF and SAAF only) contained 450 gallons fed by two electric pumps. Overload tanks containing 250 gallons (RAF and FAA) or 430 gallons (SAAF) could be fitted to the inner wing stations and a 440-gallon tank into the bomb bay – these transferred fuel by air pressure. The air-to-air refuelling pod carried a further 140 gallons of fuel. All tanks could, in addition to feeding the engines, feed the refuelling pod and the jettison outlet through individual valves on a separate

LEFT The arrester hook designed for its Royal Navy aircraft carrier operations was retained on the purely ground-based RAF examples later ordered. These were used on many occasions, when emergency landings were performed on to runways equipped with arrester gear, usually after a hydraulic failure, or if a take-off was aborted at high speed. *(Keith Wilson)*

outlet from each proportioner. Air-to-air refuelling and fuel jettison were both at 1,200lb (150 gallons) per minute. Fuel jettison float switches in two of the main tanks stopped this process at 4,000lb (500 gallons) of fuel remaining.

Flying surfaces

With the exception of the inner wing, all flying surfaces are of integrally machined skins and ribs. From wing fold to wing fold most of the loads are carried by machined steel forgings, with spars in the wings, rings around the jet pipes which attach to spiders extending across the fuselage and over the weapons bay.

The wing is a two-spar structure with thick integrally stiffened skins machined from solid billets. The inner wing embodies two main spars of steel along with a further, auxiliary aluminium alloy spar. The spars pick up with strong steel rings, through which the jet pipes pass. The rings are joined by steel spider-like frames running across the fuselage.

The outer wings, which fold upward hydraulically for storage (while also permitting the aircraft's transition on Royal Navy aircraft carrier lifts) feature two aluminium-alloy spars. To obtain the necessary contour and stiffness, the ribs and spars are also machined from solid billets and the skins are bolted to them. The slits, through which the BLC air passes, vary from 0.025in to 0.057in wide.

The flying controls feature conventional ailerons, rudder and an all-moving tailplane, wing trailing-edge flaps and the fuselage airbrake. The main flying controls are all hydraulically operated with the control column projecting from the pilot's instrument panel, while rudder control is with conventional rudder pedals.

The powered control units are of the tandem ram type with each ram being powered by one of the two independent systems, thereby providing redundancy in the event of one system failure. Should this occur, the power would be of a reduced rate, although the output would still be sufficient to hold the maximum moment of the control system.

Tailplane and fin

The Blackburn design team had a significant problem to solve with the tailplane. Blowing

ABOVE The clever wing-folding mechanism seen here on Buccaneer S.2B, XW544, at Bruntingthorpe. *(Keith Wilson)*

air over the flaps would increase the pitching moment by 80%, and with blown flaps and drooped ailerons on a swept wing, the pitching moment is trebled compared with a conventional unblown part-span flap. This caused two problems: the peak lift to be generated by the tailplane is greatly increased; and there is also the need to deal with the large trim change associated with selection of the flaps. A trailing-edge flap on the tailplane geared to flap and droop selection could counteract the trim change, but, as the tailplane load increases with decreasing speed, it would raise the tendency for a leading-edge stall on the 5% thick tailplane. This stall problem was dealt with in a similar manner to that of the outer-wing leading edge. The tailplane anti-icing duct was modified to form a blowing slit, but in this case, because of the direction of the load, was positioned on the under-surface.

At the conclusion of the design and testing process, the tailplane is all-moving to provide good control at high speeds. Its surface area is, however, minimised to avoid over-sensitivity at high speeds as well as to minimise drag and weight. For take-off and landing it has trailing-edge flaps and ailerons. The overall tailplane trim change due to flap deflection and aileron droop is negligible.

ABOVE **The large and very effective airbrake designed for the Buccaneer. Aside from providing significant handling improvements while in the landing configuration, it also reduced the overall length of the aircraft by 4ft, allowing it to fit into the standard Royal Navy aircraft carrier lift.** *(Keith Wilson)*

ABOVE RIGHT **The high T-tail and airbrake on Buccaneer S.2B, XW544. The original design of the tail for the NA.39 did not feature the bullets at the front and rear of the tailplane, but these were later added to prevent severe shaking of the tailplane caused by the shock-induced separation of the airflow in the fin/tailplane junction. Similarly, the airbrake on the NA.39 was originally a clean design but a later reconfiguration eliminated some handling difficulties.** *(Keith Wilson)*

BELOW **Another requirement for the NA.39 was to be able to fit inside a 'standard' Royal Navy deck lift as fitted to all aircraft carriers. One of the space-saving features of the aircraft to achieve that requirement was a neatly folding nose radome, as seen here on Buccaneer S.2B, XX894.** *(Keith Wilson)*

The highly swept fin construction is of machined skins with internal stiffeners bolted to machined ribs and three spars, each of which is attached to strong frames in the rear fuselage. The tailplane, mounted on top of the fin, is of a similar construction to the outer wings.

To meet both the deck landing engine failure and crosswind landing cases, the rudder is very powerful and features artificial 'q-feel' capabilities.

Airbrake

The extreme rear of the fuselage is split into two petals which can, after significant development during the extensive flight trials, can be extended over the complete speed range to form a most effective speed brake. On the approach to land, it is used to reduce the minimum drag speed to well below the approach speed. This provides a satisfactory control of speed and descent path without the requirement of auto-throttle.

However, as clever as the design of the speed brake is, it has a major secondary benefit as along with the folding nose cone, it reduces the overall length of the aircraft by 4ft, to a dimension that permits its transition in aircraft carrier lifts!

Folding nose cone

Primarily designed for stowage purposes on aircraft carriers, the resin-bonded fibreglass nose cone hinges sideways to port. However, the benefit of this hinging design also provided

ABOVE Although virtually devoid of equipment on this test aircraft, the folding radome is shown to good effect in this image of NA.39, XK523, taken during carrier acceptance trials on board HMS *Victorious* in early 1960. The Buccaneer only just squeezed into the deck lift and hangar deck. *(BAE SYSTEMS Image BAL14559)*

ABOVE These two images demonstrate the in-flight rotating bomb bay, or in this case, the bomb-door tank (BDT) design on board Buccaneer S.2B, XW544. In the first image, the bomb door is starting to rotate and open . . . *(Keith Wilson)*

LEFT . . . until the bomb bay is fully open and able to dispense its ordnance. *(Keith Wilson)*

excellent access for the engineers to the systems installed in this area of the aircraft.

Weapons bay and hardpoints

Located just aft of the accessory bay is the large, rotating weapons bay. The stores are carried on the door that rotates through a full 180° for attack, resulting in a shallow bay providing the

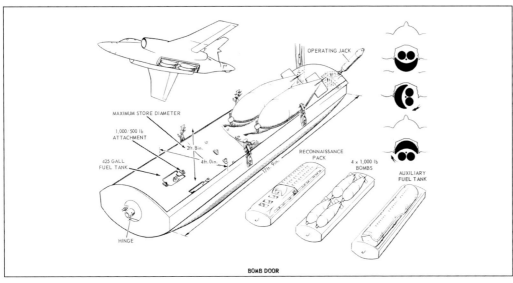

LEFT Diagram of the Buccaneer bomb bay which, aside from conventional ordnance, had alternative capabilities including a reconnaissance pack and an auxiliary fuel tank. *(BAE SYSTEMS)*

RIGHT Preserved at Bruntingthorpe in its former Gulf War colours is Buccaneer S.2B, XX889. It is fitted with a reconnaissance pack in the bomb bay which includes markings from its previous life with 208 Squadron. *(Keith Wilson)*

best possible aerodynamic characteristics. The rotating door permits operations at the highest possible speeds and was a very successful and innovative design feature.

BELOW Buccaneer S.2B, XX901, is owned by the Buccaneer Aircrew Association who have loaned the aircraft to the Yorkshire Air Museum at Elvington, where it is preserved in its former Gulf War colours. The aircraft includes the optional 440-gallon bomb bay fuel tank and is shown with the rotating bomb bay door open. *(Lee Barton)*

If required, the bomb bay door was also designed to embody an integral 450-gallon fuel tank, without any detriment to the aircraft's bomb-carrying capacity. Provision was also made for the installation of a 440-gallon fuel tank in the weapons bay.

Undercarriage structure

The undercarriage, having been designed for carrier operations (which demanded a maximum vertical velocity of descent of 18ft/sec) is very robust! Consequently, for land-based operations, it permits touchdowns at high weights where the 'normal' velocity of descent demanded is a mere 12ft/sec.

The tricycle gear has a single nose wheel along with single main wheels. The units are of the levered suspension type and incorporate a liquid-spring shock absorber. The steerable nose wheel retracts rearwards into the main fuselage while the main wheels retract sideways into the undersides of the engine nacelles. During the retraction process, the trailing arm is lifted up, effectively shortening the landing gear in order to minimise the space required.

Double-disc hydraulic brakes are fitted to the

FAR LEFT The port main undercarriage leg of Buccaneer S.2B, XX894, clearly shows its aircraft carrier design origins. The wheel retracts neatly into the adjacent bay. *(Keith Wilson)*

LEFT Similarly, the steerable nose wheel leg was designed and constructed to withstand the rigours of use on board Royal Navy aircraft carriers. The nose wheel and leg retract rearward into the bay. *(Keith Wilson)*

main wheels along with the Maxaret anti-lock braking system. Interestingly, Dunlop's Maxaret – which was developed in the UK – was the first anti-lock braking system (ABS) to be widely used. Introduced in the early 1950s, Maxaret was rapidly taken up in the aviation world, after testing found a 30% reduction in stopping distances, and the elimination of tyre bursts or flat spots due to skids.

Flying Controls and General Services hydraulics

Two hydraulic systems are fitted, one powering the aircraft General Services and the other the Flying Controls. Fluid pressure is provided by four engine-driven pumps, two on each engine.

Pressure from the General Services system operates the undercarriage, wing flaps, airbrakes, weapons bay door, fuel proportioners, wheel brakes, nose wheel steering, wing-fold mechanism, arrester hook and tail skid. The General Services system operates at $4,000lb/in^2$ and is powered by two pumps, one on each engine, which supply

fluid pressure for both normal and emergency operation. In the event of loss of fluid in normal operation the pressure lines from the pump are isolated. Emergency selection then connects the pump to the emergency pressure line and fluid from the emergency reservoirs permits operation of the services to ensure, for example, a safe landing.

In contrast, the Flying Controls system operates at $3,300lb/in^2$ and powers the ailerons, tailplane and rudder, the autostabiliser and autopilot system, the tailplane and rudder artificial feel units and the approach yaw damper for the rudder. Once again, there are two independent hydraulic systems each taking power from a pump on one engine. In an emergency on this system, power from the General Services hydraulic system can be supplied to the Flying Controls.

Electrical power

Electrical power is supplied from an AC generation system. On the Buccaneer S.1 constant-frequency AC, vital for much of the avionics, was provided by a 10kVA air turbine alternator with a standby inverter for essential services. Two 6kW engine-driven generators provided power for the main airframe services,

ABOVE Despite initial trials with a removable in-flight refuelling probe that would have minimised external drag, in-flight trials showed a bow-wave effect from the Buccaneer that moved the basket away from the probe. Eventually, the successful final design was this fixed (but removable, if required) version that did not suffer with the earlier handling issues. *(Keith Wilson)*

although the air-turbine alternator was a constant source of problems.

With the introduction of the S.2, each engine drives a 30kVA alternator through a constant-speed drive unit providing a 200V AC supply. Each alternator normally supplies a separately fused distribution system while a step-down transformer is used to provide a 115V AC supply required for certain onboard equipment. Some systems need a 28V DC supply and this is provided by rectification of part of the AC output.

In the event of a total failure of the generating system, the S.2 introduced automatic 'load shedding' of non-essential services. An emergency battery provides power for up to 80 minutes to the essential services through independent circuits.

In-flight tanker

The Buccaneer could be quickly converted to the tanker role with the installation of a Flight Refuelling Mk.20B or 20C hose and drogue unit positioned on a special starboard inner wing pylon – usually on the starboard wing. In addition to the in-flight refuelling equipment, the pod contains a 140-gallon

tank, which is continually replenished by the transfer of fuel from the aircraft's fuel system during refuelling operations. When operating with the in-flight refuelling pod fitted, in Royal Navy service it was normal for the aircraft to carry a 250-gallon slipper tank on the port inner wing pylon, along with a 440-gallon tank in the weapons bay, providing a total fuel capacity of 2,390 gallons. The FAA Buccaneers were not fitted with the bomb-door fuel tank (as on the RAF aircraft) because the clearance with the deck on landing was too small. The average transfer rate is 150 gallons per minute and refuelling can be conducted at speeds down to Mach 0.5 and at heights up to 36,000ft.

This refuelling capability was not restricted just to the in-flight refuelling of other Buccaneer aircraft; in its Royal Navy service, the Buccaneer tanker could also support the in-flight refuelling of Phantom, Sea Vixen and Scimitar aircraft, and any aircraft fitted with the NATO-standard refuelling probe, providing a significantly versatile asset.

Rolls-Royce Spey 101 engine for S.2

The earlier Blackburn B.103, NA.39 and Buccaneer S.1 had been powered by the de Havilland Gyron Junior. While the engine was lighter than other alternate contemporaries, it only provided a modest thrust of just 7,000lb making its performance – especially on take-off – somewhat 'marginal'. As a consequence, the aircraft never possessed a sparkling performance, nor did it fulfil its full potential. But all that was to change!

The Buccaneer S.2 was powered by the Rolls-Royce RB.168-1A Spey Mk.101 axial flow, two-spool, bypass turbofan engine. The engine had been developed for use in the de Havilland Trident and BAC One-Eleven airliners. In military form it has also been used in certain marks of the Phantom. Thrust was originally quoted as 11,380lb but later reduced to 11,100lb static thrust, although the most striking aspect of the engine was its low specific fuel consumption, something which provided the Buccaneer with a longer-range capability originally estimated at around 80%. The additional 8,200lb of static thrust provided by both engines certainly allowed the Buccaneer S.2 to achieve its full potential.

The engines are mounted inboard adjacent to the fuselage sides, with pitot-type intakes with external BLC bypass. To minimise structural problems, the engines are mounted forward of the wing spars to the extent that the ring spar rings encompass the smaller diameter of the jet only. This position of the engine had originally been arrived at when the Brough design team were considering jet deflection, but was retained when this principle was abandoned in favour of the blown air system. The configuration results in a very long jet pipe which needed very careful design to avoid losses. However, one advantage of the long jet pipe is that cooling air passes outside it, which ultimately minimises the temperature on exit, making detection by heat-seeking missiles more difficult. The jet efflux is angled outward and downwards to lessen interference with the fuselage and airbrakes. The whole jet pipe is curved and installed into the airframe on tracks and rollers.

An innovative use of new technology

It is necessary to reiterate the importance of the Blackburn design team's forward-thinking attitude and the clever and enthusiastic use of new technologies, as they became available. Both BLC and Area Rule had significant impacts on the eventual capabilities of the B.103, although the design innovations did not stop there. The very clever and aerodynamically efficient rotating bomb bay, hinged wings, folding nose cone and rear fuselage 'brake petals' all contributed to make the Buccaneer what it finally became – a highly effective high-speed, low-level and later, medium-level weapons delivery platform.

That said, the early S.1 would always be held back by its underpowered de Havilland Gyron Junior engines, but once the Rolls-Royce Spey 101-powered S.2 variant became available the Buccaneer would prove its credentials in both Royal Navy and Royal Air Force use and would serve the latter until eventually being replaced by the Tornado GR.1B aircraft.

BELOW Installation of the Rolls-Royce Spey 101 engine in Buccaneer S.2B, XW544, at Bruntingthorpe. This engine is regularly run inside XW544, allowing the aircraft to both taxi around the airfield and occasionally to demonstrate the Buccaneer roar with high-speed runs up and down the Bruntingthorpe runway. (Keith Wilson)

Chapter Three

Royal Navy Buccaneers

━━━━●━━━━

Every aircraft entering service with the Royal Navy undergoes a period in an Intensive Flying Trials Unit (IFTU); the more complex the aircraft and its role, the more varied and lengthy is the task of the unit. The Buccaneer definitely fell into the 'Complex and Varied' category.

OPPOSITE HMS *Ark Royal* at sea with seven Buccaneer S.2 aircraft from 809 NAS, five Phantom FG.1 aircraft (892 NAS), two Gannet AEW.3 aircraft (849B NAS) and a single Sea King HAS.2 helicopter (824 NAS) on deck. The image was taken in the mid-1970s before the vessel was finally withdrawn from service on 4 December 1978. *(Crown Copyright/Air Historical Branch Image TN-1-7079-6)*

ABOVE XK531 was the 15th development aircraft produced and made its first flight on 18 May 1961. Initially employed as a trials aircraft, XK531 was the first Buccaneer S.1 delivered to the Royal Navy's 700Z Flight at RNAS Lossiemouth in 1961, where it assumed the code 'LM-680'. *(BAE SYSTEMS Image BAL17269)*

BELOW Initially, 700Z Flight had just two aircraft on strength – XK531, coded 'LM-680', and XK532, coded 'LM-681'. Both aircraft were photographed at Lossiemouth, known as HMS *Fulmar*, shortly after delivery to the Flight in 1961. *(FAA Museum)*

On 7 March 1961, while the manufacturer's trials were continuing, No 700Z Flight was formed – under the command of Lieutenant Commander A.J. Leahy – at NAS Lossiemouth, known as HMS *Fulmar*. The task of the unit was to assess the operational characteristics of the Buccaneer and to ensure it met the original requirements, while formulating operating procedures for future squadron operations. However, this work was to be seriously hampered until the end of the year by the fact that Blue Parrot radar-equipped aircraft were unavailable – instead, the nose cone merely contained a lump of lead, to ensure the CofG (centre of gravity) of the aircraft was within limits.

The job of the Flight was put simply by Commander Leahy at the time: 'to get in as many hours with the Buccaneer as possible', with a target of 40 sorties a month.

Another task for the unit was to provide sufficient trained crews for the formation of the first front-line Buccaneer unit – No 801 NAS – which was to be recommissioned on 18 March 1964.

First aircraft delivered

Interestingly, the first aircraft delivered to the Flight on 2 May were not Buccaneers, but a pair of Meteor T.7 aircraft (WS116 and WS104). They were followed shortly afterwards by the first of four navalised Hunter T.8 aircraft. These were to provide the pilots the opportunity to continue training until the first Buccaneer S.1 aircraft were delivered in August 1961.

Initially, 700Z Flight had just two aircraft on strength – XK531 and XK532. Both were pre-production machines, but by the end of 1961 the number had increased to five, including XK533, XK534 and XK535, all three being

LEFT XK534 was the 18th pre-production NA.39 ordered and made its first flight at Holme-on-Spalding-Moor on 19 August 1961. Shortly afterwards the aircraft was flown to Schleswig for demonstration to West German officials. In November 1961, the aircraft was issued to the Royal Navy's Intensive Flight Trials Unit (IFTU) – 700Z Flight – at NAS Lossiemouth when it was allocated the code 'LM-683'. *(BAE SYSTEMS Image BAL17339)*

equipped to production standards. Ultimately, by early 1962, the Flight had six aircraft on strength with three of the aircraft being delivered and operated in the all-over white anti-flash nuclear radiation livery. Once delivered, the aircraft were coded in the LM-680 through to LM-685 range.

The unit evaluated five primary aspects of the Buccaneer performance and equipment, these being: range, at heights from sea level up to 40,000ft; airframe and engines; weapons systems; tactical capability; and servicing requirements.

In order to meet these evaluation targets, the unit flew the available Buccaneers long and hard, both by day and at night. During this period some serviceability problems were encountered, but no more than would be expected for such a new aircraft. These problems did not prevent the first two aircraft logging 340 flying hours up to the end of December 1961, a total that approached that of all the other Buccaneer aircraft flying from Holme-on-Spalding-Moor and Boscombe Down during the same period.

From a servicing perspective, the Buccaneer represented a significant forward step over previous aircraft. Members of the groundcrew with experience on other aircraft soon developed a liking for the aircraft. The turnaround time to refuel a Buccaneer, recharge with oxygen and to check the batteries was just 20 minutes. An engine change required around three hours, an advantage in this aspect being that the port and starboard Gyron Junior engines were interchangeable.

After deck trials on HMS *Hermes* and extensive weapons trials, No 700Z Flight was eventually disbanded on 20 December 1962, having been in existence for 21 months instead of the 12 originally envisaged, with a total of 1,258 hours having been flown on the Buccaneer.

First front-line Royal Navy squadron

No 801 Squadron had the honour of becoming the first front-line Royal Navy Buccaneer unit. The squadron, under the command of Lieutenant-Commander E.R. Anson, was commissioned at Lossiemouth on 17 July 1962, having been formed around a nucleus of personnel from 700Z Flight. At the time it re-formed, the squadron had no aircraft, but soon built up to a strength of five S.1 aircraft, commencing with XN925. By the end of 1962, the squadron had eight aircraft on strength.

On 19 February 1963, 801 Squadron made its first carrier deployment aboard HMS *Ark Royal*, for a four-week cruise. Most of the aircraft were painted in the standard Navy colour scheme of grey top and white undersides and carried the *Ark Royal* codings starting with 'R-115'. The remaining aircraft were in the all-over white anti-flash colour scheme and also carried *Ark Royal* codings.

Later, the squadron was transferred to HMS *Victorious* when it sailed from Portsmouth on 14 August 1963 for a tour of the Far East. During the cruise, the squadron was disembarked for a two-week period to Embakasi, Nairobi, in February 1964, as a

BELOW Buccaneer S.1, XK536, operated by the A&AEE at Boscombe Down, undergoing trials aboard HMS *Hermes* in 1962. Note the Blackburn Air Starter Pod being used to start the aircraft. This pod could be carried by the Buccaneer on a weapon pylon, if and when required. *(FAA Museum)*

BELOW XN974 the first production-specification Buccaneer S.2 photographed during a low-level sortie on 10 June 1964. *(BAE SYSTEMS Image BAL19991)*

ABOVE Buccaneer S.1 XN930 was the 9th production aircraft ordered in a batch of 40. It was delivered to the Royal Navy in February 1963 and issued to 801 NAS at Lossiemouth. Coded '121/V', the aircraft embarked on HMS *Victorious* for carrier trials in 1964 and was photographed undergoing barrier tests. *(FAA Museum)*

ABOVE No 801 NAS had the task of bringing the Buccaneer S.2 aircraft into full squadron service. Initially based at Lossiemouth, where this image was taken, the squadron was embarked upon HMS *Victorious* in May 1966. Shortly afterwards, the vessel undertook a cruise in home waters and in the Mediterranean. *(FAA Museum)*

LEFT The Martin-Marietta AGM-12 Bullpup was the initial precision attack capability of the Buccaneer, although it was also used by the Sea Vixen. Buccaneer S.1 airframes were converted to carry the Bullpup under Mod 5031. In this image, probably taken in 1963/64, a Bullpup was photographed being fired from 801 NAS Buccaneer S.1 XN935 coded 'V-118' operating from HMS *Victorious*. The Bullpup failed to prove its accuracy and reliability and did not figure in the day-to-day operations of the Buccaneer. *(BAE SYSTEMS)*

show of force during a period of local unrest in neighbouring Tanganyika. The Buccaneers returned to the ship on 22 February, when their presence was no longer required, and the cruise continued. Eventually, HMS *Victorious* returned to Portsmouth in July 1965 – marking the end of the ship's commission. No 801 NAS returned to Lossiemouth on 22 July 1965 but it marked the end of their S.1 operations as the unit was disbanded five days later, on 27 July 1965.

809 Squadron

The second front-line squadron was No 809 NAS, also known as the Strike Headquarters Squadron, which was commissioned on 15 January 1963. It consisted essentially of the remaining aircraft and crews of 700Z Flight, which had been disbanded a month earlier. However, 809 NAS's very first aircraft – Buccaneer S.1 XN924 coded 'LM-220' – was a new airframe. The squadron was shore-based, at Lossiemouth, where it continued Buccaneer operational development until the end of the S.1 production run in 1965.

At the time of its formation, it utilised five former 700Z Buccaneer S.1 airframes (XK531, XK532, XK533, XK534 and XK535) as well as a single Hunter T.8 (WW664), and the number of aircraft on strength grew as the re-equipment effort got into full swing.

In addition to trials work, 809 NAS's primary task was the training of pilots and observers. The first course commenced the day after formation and the training task was eased considerably with the arrival of a Buccaneer simulator in November 1963.

In January 1965, 809 NAS began the training

ABOVE No 801 NAS Buccaneer S.2, XV162, releases a '2,000lb shape' – a correctly weighted and balanced casing of a Red Beard free-fall tactical nuclear weapon – in level flight; probably during trials at West Freugh. Level bomb-drops were tested at a variety of speeds, although the preferred delivery technique was a 'toss'. Red Beard was carried on a special bomb door with aerodynamic fairings as attaching the weapon to the standard bomb door had resulted in a serious level of aerodynamic buffet. *(FAA Museum)*

RIGHT An 800 NAS Buccaneer S.2 – XT278, coded 'E-102' – launches from HMS *Eagle* while the Wessex 'plane guard' looks on. *(FAA Museum)*

ABOVE No 800 NAS made one major cruise aboard HMS *Eagle* with the Buccaneer S.1 aircraft and this included operations off Aden as well as on the Beira Patrol along the coast of Mozambique while enforcing the blockade against Rhodesia. Buccaneer S.1 coded 'E-108' was photographed landing on to HMS *Eagle* while a Wessex helicopter stands guard. *(Crown Copyright/Air Historical Branch Image TN-1-7163-8)*

of South African Air Force (SAAF) crews, including Commander Rogers, the prospective CO of the SAAF Buccaneer squadron.

No 809 NAS continued to produce high-quality crew right up until the squadron was renumbered as 736 NAS on 26 March 1965. During its relatively short existence as the Buccaneer training unit, 809 NAS had lost three Buccaneer S.1 airframes.

800 Squadron

The third and final front-line Buccaneer S.1 squadron was 800 NAS, which was commissioned on 18 March 1964. The squadron took part in the Fleet Air Arm Jubilee

RIGHT An 800 NAS Buccaneer S.1 – XN971, coded 'E-102' – prepares to take on fuel from an unidentified Scimitar F.1 of 800B Flight. At the time of the image, both aircraft were operating from HMS *Eagle*. Interestingly, the Scimitar F.1 was the Buccaneer's predecessor in the Royal Navy's attack squadrons. *(FAA Museum)*

Review on 28 May before embarking on HMS *Eagle* on 2 December for duties in the Far East.

While in the Far East, the squadron participated in Exercise Showpiece Malaysia off Singapore early in 1965. From 15 March, HMS *Eagle* took over the responsibilities of *Ark Royal* in the Mozambique Channel, when its Buccaneers were employed on the enforcement of the oil embargo off Beira into the seaport terminal of the oil pipeline to Rhodesia.

No 800 NAS remained with HMS *Eagle* throughout its Buccaneer association. On 14 August 1966, 800 Squadron disembarked to Yeovilton and Lossiemouth to bring to an end its period of active service with the Buccaneer S.1.

Beira Patrol

Rhodesia's mostly white minority government, led by the country's elected prime minister, Ian Smith, unilaterally declared the former colony's independence on 11 November

1965, after rejecting British preconditions for independence that involved racial equality and rule by the black majority. The United Nations Security Council reacted by passing Resolution 217, calling for sanctions on Rhodesia. The resolution was later used by the British as legal justification for the blockade.

Britain imposed its own national sanctions, including an oil embargo, but ruled out invading Rhodesia. The British Government was initially opposed to military action, instead relying on UN sanctions to pressure the Rhodesian Government.

In October 1965, the Joint Intelligence Committee estimated that even a full trade embargo would fail to cripple Rhodesia's economy, but suggested that prolonged and severe economic pressure could induce the white electorate to overthrow the government. In early 1966, Prime Minister Harold Wilson made statements that sanctions were working, predicting that the Rhodesian Government would soon fall. At the same time, the Foreign Office was looking into the possibility of a maritime blockade.

During the first week of February 1966, it became clear that Rhodesia continued to import oil by land from South Africa, and Prime Minister Wilson was warned that black African states could push for more urgent sanctions and raise the matter at the United Nations. On 24 February, the Chiefs of Staff Committee warned that tankers with oil bound for Rhodesia could arrive in the port of Beira in Mozambique, the terminus of a pipeline going to Rhodesia, unnoticed, and began preparing a maritime surveillance plan.

Following reports of Rhodesia defying the oil embargo by sea, the British felt pressure to take action and thus prove their commitment to sanctions. On 1 March, the Royal Navy

BELOW Photographed during a cruise in the Indian Ocean in 1971, an 800 NAS Buccaneer S.2 – XT273, coded 'E-113' – provides fuel to a rocket-equipped Sea Vixen FAW.2 of 899 NAS while both aircraft were operating from HMS *Eagle*. *(FAA Museum)*

LEFT Both the S.1 and S.2 versions of the Buccaneer were tested by the A&AEE's 'C' Squadron at Boscombe Down. An S.2 (thought to be XN976) was photographed while refuelling a Vulcan B.2 – XM606 – of the Cottesmore Wing. Both the Flight Refuelling Ltd Mk.20C or Mk.20E tanking pods were used by the Buccaneer, and normally with a slipper tank on the opposite wing. Note the airbrakes being used by the Vulcan to stay on station. *(FAA Museum)*

established the Beira Patrol and stationed the frigate HMS *Lowestoft* off Beira, directing it to prepare for intercept operations starting on 4 March. On 6 March, Gannet AEW aircraft from the carrier HMS *Ark Royal* began search operations in the Mozambique Channel. The frigate HMS *Rhyl* and a logistical support ship were soon added.

On 28 February 1966 HMS *Eagle* sailed from Singapore en route to Beira. It remained on station until 31 April 1966 when relieved by *Ark Royal*, before returning to Singapore on 10 May 1966. In just 71 days, HMS *Eagle* flew a total of 1,070 sorties.

The Beira Patrol lasted until 1975. At any time, two British frigates or destroyers, with the support of both land- and carrier-based surveillance aircraft and auxiliary vessels, were committed to the patrol. Various British warships cruised the Mozambique Channel 20–45 miles from Beira, checking on oil tankers heading for the port.

Initially, Royal Navy ships were to shadow and question Beira-bound tankers, and were only allowed to forcibly divert a tanker away after Britain obtained permission from its flag state. However, in the event that permission was granted, British warships were only permitted to demand it change course in the name of its flag state, and fire a shot across the bow if it did not work. The use of force was not authorised, and if the tanker absolutely refused to comply, the shadowing warship could take no more action and only follow it to within Mozambique's 6-mile territorial limit – effectively letting the tanker proceed unhindered into port.

After an incident where the Greek tanker MV *Joanna V* freely sailed into Beira even after Greece refused to grant the vessel permission to continue, the British lobbied for UN authority to use force. The UN Security Council subsequently passed Resolution 221. However, this resolution confined the blockade to Beira and authorised only the Royal Navy to use force. As a result, the Royal Navy alone had to enforce the blockade without assistance, and tankers with oil for Rhodesia could freely dock at other Mozambican ports. The resolution also empowered the British to seize the *Joanna V* upon its departure from Beira if it had discharged its oil cargo there.

The rules of engagement were subsequently liberalised, but use of force was limited 'to the very minimum', and Defence Ministry approval was required for the diversion of vessels. British warships also had to remain outside Mozambique's territorial waters. After an embarrassing incident involving the French tanker *Artois*, the rules of engagement were further modified, allowing the use of disabling fire.

Britain never managed to obtain UN authority enabling other navies to participate. Rhodesia continued to receive oil shipments and was also able to withstand the blockade by strictly rationing oil. In September 1966, it was estimated that Rhodesia received 220,000 gallons of oil daily, when it only required 200,000 a day under its rationing policy.

In March 1971, new Prime Minister Edward Heath allowed the Royal Navy to commit one warship at a time, rather than two. Three months later, the patrol lost its air component when the Malagasy Republic (now Madagascar) asked the RAF to eliminate its detachment at Majunga. After an overall drop in the number of frigates in the fleet, the Royal Navy was allowed to make the patrol intermittent before it was finally eliminated on 25 June 1975, when Mozambique gained independence from Portugal and assured Britain that it would not allow the transhipment of oil into Rhodesia.

The operation had cost an estimated £100 million, and 76 Royal Navy ships had taken part. A total of 47 oil tankers were intercepted, of which 42 were allowed to proceed.

ABOVE HMS *Eagle* **assumed responsibilities for the Beira Patrol from HMS** *Ark Royal* **on 15 March 1965 and one of its Buccaneer S.1 aircraft (possibly XN980) was photographed while 'inspecting' the Greek-registered tanker MV** *Joanna V* **in the Mozambique Channel in 1966. The patrol was necessary for enforcing the oil embargo into the Beira seaport terminal of the oil pipeline to Rhodesia. This particular ship caused a political storm between the British and Greek Governments at the time when the captain of the vessel 'declined' the Greek Government's instructions not to proceed into the port of Beira with 18,700 tons of oil.**
(FAA Museum)

Torrey Canyon

The SS *Torrey Canyon* was an LR2 *Suezmax*-class oil tanker with a cargo capacity of 120,000 tons of crude oil. She was shipwrecked off the western coast of Cornwall, on 18 March 1967, causing an environmental disaster. At that time she was the largest vessel ever to be wrecked.

On 19 February 1967, *Torrey Canyon* left the Kuwait National Petroleum Company refinery, at Mina (later Al Ahmadi), Kuwait, on her final voyage with a full cargo of crude oil. The ship reached the Canary Islands on 14 March. From there the planned route was to Milford Haven in Wales. *Torrey Canyon* struck Pollard's Rock on the Seven Stones reef, between the Cornish mainland and the Isles of Scilly, on 18 March.

It became grounded and, several days later, began to break up.

In an effort to reduce the size of the oil spill, the British Government decided to set the wreck on fire, by means of air strikes from both the FAA and RAF. It provided an interesting opportunity for the Buccaneer aircraft to demonstrate their anti-shipping abilities!

On 28 March 1967, eight Buccaneers from Nos 736 and 800 NAS, operating from RNAS Lossiemouth, dropped 1,000lb free-fall bombs on the ship. Of the 42 bombs dropped, 30 hit the *Torrey Canyon*, but the oil proved hard to ignite and burn. Afterwards Hunter aircraft from RAF Chivenor dropped cans of kerosene on to the wreckage in an attempt to fuel the blaze. However, the fire was put out by high tides, and further strikes were needed to reignite the oil.

Following two more Buccaneer attacks from aircraft at RNAS Brawdy, supported by incendiary bomb-equipped Sea Vixen FAW.2s from RNAS Yeovilton and Hunter FGA.9 aircraft from the RAF's 1(F) Squadron dispensing napalm, all ensured the ship finally succumbed and sank beneath the waves.

A total of 161 bombs, 16 rockets, 1,500 tons of napalm and 44,500 litres of kerosene were used against the ship in an operation in which the Buccaneer did all that was asked of it. Unfortunately, the operation was ultimately unsuccessful as not all of the oil burned as expected and a significant spill from the vessel caused considerable ecological damage around the British coastline.

An inquiry in Liberia, where the ship was registered, found the shipmaster was to blame, because he took a shortcut in an attempt to save time en route to Milford Haven. Additionally, a design fault meant that the helmsman was unaware that the steering selector switch had been accidentally left on autopilot and as a consequence, he was unable to carry out a timely turn to go through the shipping channel.

Today, the wreck of the *Torrey Canyon* lies at a depth of 30m (98ft).

Deliveries of the S.2

Perhaps somewhat surprisingly, the Royal Navy placed a production order for the Spey-engined Buccaneer S.2 even before the

S.1 variant had entered service. Following the procedure adopted for the earlier S.1 version, a newly formed Intensive Flying Trials Unit – 700B Flight – was commissioned on 9 April 1965 at Lossiemouth. Eventually, it operated a fleet of eight Buccaneer S.2 aircraft. This time around, only a few months were required to prove the new aircraft for Royal Navy use and the unit was disbanded on 30 September 1965.

To initiate the plan to re-equip all the Royal Navy squadrons with the new S.2 variant, all of the older S.1 airframes were transferred to 801 NAS, which had been commissioned at Lossiemouth on 9 April 1965.

809 NAS forms on the S.2

Next up was No 809 NAS, which was recommissioned with Buccaneer S.2 aircraft on 27 January 1966. The first of the new aircraft – XT278 and XT280 – arrived on 3 January 1966 and by the end of the month three more – XT277, XT279 and XT281 – had been delivered.

After a successful work-up on the new aircraft 809 NAS was assigned to HMS *Hermes* for the first of two Far East tours. During the first of these, HMS *Hermes* sailed to Gibraltar where it patrolled when unilateral restrictions were first placed on airspace by the Spanish authorities – particularly for aircraft landing at Gibraltar's North Front airfield.

Between February 1968 and May 1970, 809 NAS remained shore-based, but when it did return to sea it was aboard HMS *Ark Royal*. Initially, all operations were conducted in home waters, the Mediterranean or the Atlantic. HMS *Ark Royal* and 809 NAS were to become regular visitors to the USA, with the first visit being made in June/July 1971, with shore calls to Cecil Field NAS, Florida. It was followed by similar visits in February 1972, June 1973 (shore calls at Fort Lauderdale in Florida and Cecil

ABOVE LEFT In the conventional attack role the Buccaneer could carry up to eight 1,000lb bombs, with two on each wing pylon and four stowed internally within a closed rotating bomb bay. Here, the bomb bay is open, just ahead of the planned drop from an 800 NAS Buccaneer S.2, XT283 coded 'E-111'. *(FAA Museum)*

ABOVE Bombs gone! Seven 1,000lb bombs have been dropped from XT283 while the final one on the starboard wing pylon is about to leave the aircraft. *(FAA Museum)*

Field NAS), February/March 1975 (shore calls to Oceana (Virginia) and Cecil Field NASs), March–May 1976 (also shore calls to Cecil Field and

BELOW A Buccaneer S.2 and Royal Navy crew with the wide range of weaponry that the aircraft was capable of carrying, including bombs, air-to-ground missiles, long-range tanks, starter and in-flight refuelling pods and camera pack. Prominent in the foreground is the Red Beard nuclear weapon. *(BAE SYSTEMS Image BAL21702)*

LEFT No 801 NAS remained assigned to HMS *Victorious* until the ship's demise in late 1967, when the squadron transferred to HMS *Hermes*. Here, an 801 NAS Buccaneer S.2 (XT270, coded 'LM-237') takes on fuel from a VAH-2 KA-3B Skywarrior of the US Navy. It is thought that this image was shot while HMS *Victorious* was operating with the USS *Enterprise* in the Far East between July 1966 and June 1967, when a number of Buccaneer crews were able to gain experience of refuelling from the Skywarrior. *(FAA Museum)*

Oceana NASs), April–June and August 1978 (with shore calls at Roosevelt Field (New York), Cecil Field and Oceana NASs).

Jet Strike Training Squadron – 736 NAS

Also formed in 1966 was No 736 NAS, a Buccaneer training unit based at Lossiemouth, which came about by the renumbering of 809 NAS. The role of the unit was to train pilots and observers for the front-line Buccaneer force, its alternative title being the Jet Strike Training Squadron.

Initially, its aircraft were S.1 airframes relinquished by 801 and 809 NASs including XK534, XN924, XN950, XN957, XN961, XN965 and XN967 along with a single Hunter T.8, WV322. It spent time at the RNAS at Yeovilton where it carried out deck-landing practices (DLPs) aboard HMS *Ark Royal* off South Wales in June 1966.

On 9 May 1966, the squadron's first S.2 airframe arrived when XT284 flew in to Lossiemouth. Deliveries of the S.2 version continued and by 1970 736 NAS was operating eight S.1s and twelve S.2 aircraft. Both marks were operated together until December 1970 when two S.1 aircraft were lost in crashes and soon afterwards the S.1 variant was grounded before being withdrawn from service. The last S.1 was returned to the Naval Air Servicing Unit (NASU) in January 1971.

In 1969, 736 NAS was allocated the task of training RAF Buccaneer crews, the first course of which began in June after a familiarisation course on the Hunter. Number 1 RAF Course left for RAF Honington in September of that year. Later, when the Royal Navy usage of the Buccaneer

ABOVE A pair of 809 NAS Buccaneer S.2 aircraft form an air-to-air refuelling 'daisy chain' in company with an 892 NAS Phantom FG.1 and a US Navy A-7E Corsair II (thought to be 157552). This demonstration may well have been staged in April 1975 during a shore visit to either NAS Cecil Field or NAS Oceana while HMS *Ark Royal* was cruising in the Atlantic during the period January–June 1975. *(FAA Museum)*

BELOW Among interesting company while aboard the US Navy aircraft carrier *Roosevelt* in April 1972 is Buccaneer S.2, XV152 coded 'R-024'. The image was taken while its parent aircraft carrier, HMS *Ark Royal*, was exercising in the Atlantic with the US Navy carrier. In the foreground on a cluttered deck is an F-4J 157274/AE-204 of VF-84 Squadron. This activity was known as 'cross-decking', which occurred on both Royal Navy and US Navy aircraft carriers. *(FAA Museum)*

RIGHT **RIGHT** An interesting Balbo! A pair of 892 NAS Phantom FG.1s, along with a single Buccaneer S.2 – XT286, coded 'R-022' – were photographed in a tight formation with three A-7E Corsair II aircraft from the US Navy's VA-46 Squadron, along with a two-seat TA-4J Skyhawk, probably from VA-45. The image was taken when 809 and 892 were operating from NAS Cecil Field in spring 1976, while HMS *Ark Royal* was engaged on a cruise in the Atlantic from February to July that year. *(FAA Museum)*

was winding down while that of the RAF was increasing, the training function for both services was transferred to 237 OCU although carrier qualifications were handled by 809 NAS, the Royal Navy's very last Buccaneer squadron.

No 736 NAS conducted its last flying on 22 February 1972 and were officially disbanded just three days later, on 25 February.

800 NAS recommissioned on S.2

No 800 NAS was recommissioned on the Buccaneer S.2 variant in early September 1966 and the first aircraft – XV156 – was delivered shortly afterwards. By 10 February 1967, the squadron had worked up to operational standard, initially with eight aircraft, although this would later increase to twelve. The following month, 800 NAS were given the slightly unusual task of bombing the grounded tanker SS *Torrey Canyon*.

In August 1967, 800 NAS joined HMS *Eagle* for a tour of the Far East where the squadron was placed on alert while the Malayan Federation talks were being held in November. No 800 NAS stayed with HMS *Eagle* and enjoyed a number of tours in both home waters and the Mediterranean before one final tour of the Far East in 1971. After two shore calls at Tengah and one at Kai Tak, the tour ended on 23 January 1972. A month after its return, on 23 February 1972, 800 NAS was disbanded at Lossiemouth.

803 NAS – the fourth Buccaneer S.2 squadron

No 803 NAS was the final Buccaneer S.2 squadron to be commissioned, having been formed at Lossiemouth on 3 July 1967 as the Headquarters Squadron. It was initially allocated two S.1 aircraft – XN959 and XN971 – which

ABOVE In addition to its regular strike/attack duties, the Buccaneer S.2s of 809 NAS were regularly employed as tanker aircraft to extend the endurance of their HMS *Ark Royal* deckmates. Here, a Buccaneer S.2, coded 'R-027', was photographed while refuelling an 892 NAS Phantom FG.1 XV587/'R-010'; while another 892 NAS Phantom FG.1, coded 'R-002', looks on. *(PRM Aviation)*

BELOW A nice air-to-air study of 809 NAS Buccaneer S.2, XV863 coded 'R-020', from HMS *Ark Royal*. The white ring in the roundel was deleted by 1975, during which time 809 NAS was based at RAF Honington – its assigned shore base while not deployed aboard HMS *Ark Royal*. At this time, the Royal Navy Buccaneers of 809 NAS shared the facilities at RAF Honington with the Buccaneers of the RAF. *(Crown Copyright/Air Historical Branch Image TN-1-7163-4)*

BELOW Test pilot Don Headley flies Buccaneer S.2, XK527, fitted with four Matra Martel air-to-ground precision tactical strike missiles. These manufacturer's trials were conducted from the airfield at Driffield.
(BAE SYSTEMS Image BAL22912)

were joined by two further S.1 aircraft in September. The first of four S.2 aircraft – XV165 – was delivered to the squadron on 24 January 1968 and a conversion programme was soon under way. The last of the S.1 airframes left the squadron by the end of July 1968.

In its role of Headquarters Squadron, 803 NAS was involved in the ongoing trials of new weapons and avionics. The first of these began with the trials of air-to-air TACAN for refuelling rendezvous, a system that was later used extensively by the RAF. The squadron also tested various weapons with two of the final tasks being the testing of Lepus flares and the dropping of the '600lb Shape' – a correctly weighted and balanced dummy WE177 nuclear weapon.

When the Royal Navy's force of Buccaneers was set to reduce to just one squadron, the need for a Headquarters Squadron became redundant and 803 NAS was disbanded on 18 December 1969.

Royal Navy S.2 losses

On 9 June 1966, the first Buccaneer S.2 was lost when XN979 crashed into the sea off The Lizard in Cornwall. The aircraft was recovered from 360ft of water, which significantly assisted the subsequent investigations into the cause of the accident. Shortly afterwards, another S.2 was lost

and the Royal Navy suspected that something might be wrong. However, in view of the success of the flight trials, the test pilots were convinced the accidents were down to pilot handling errors when not adhering to the approved techniques.

To prove this point, a test pilot was sent to demonstrate how it should be done. The demonstration flight lasted just 18 seconds! It convinced everyone that something really was wrong. The cause was eventually traced to a combination of underwing stores and slipper tanks, which had not been evaluated during the trials. The combination caused the centre of drag to be raised, thereby pitching the nose up and into a stall. The problem was rectified by modifying the wing tanks, altering the tailplane settings at take-off and by revising the S.1 take-off procedure whereby the landing gear was selected 'Up' before take-off. The drag of the extended gear now reduced the tendency for the nose to pitch up.

Martel missile introduced

The Royal Navy had already decided to introduce the Martel on its Buccaneer S.2 aircraft, and a programme to provide the necessary airframe and avionics changes had been instigated in September 1966. Martel, which was available in both TV-guided and anti-radar versions, met the Navy's requirements for stand-off attack and radar suppression, respectively. Despite the relatively short service life remaining with the S.2 Buccaneer, the missile was adopted for service.

A number of significant airframe modifications had to be incorporated to allow the carriage of the Martel – which were completed under Modification 1188. The wing pylon arrangement was changed while the wing-folding mechanism was strengthened to permit the added weight. The observer's cockpit was also modified to incorporate the new display screen required for the TV version.

Two- and four-Martel schemes were considered and although the two-Martel system would have meant a significantly lower cost per airframe, the final decision favoured the four-Martel option. This had an added advantage that the new pylons could, with triple ejector racks, permit the carriage of three 1,000lb bombs on each station. Buccaneer S.1 XK527 was used to clear the pylon

arrangements and to perform initial test firings, while S.2 airframes XN974 and XV350 – both of which spent their entire lives on trials work – took part in trials of the Matra anti-ship missile and other weapons with the new pylons.

Royal Navy S.2 airframes reworked to be Martel-capable were designated S.2D; other Navy aircraft received a more basic avionics upgrade and became S.2Cs.

Politics intervenes as carrier operations come to an end

Soon after the Labour Government came into power in 1964, a remarkable change in the fortunes of the Royal Navy occurred. Following the appointment of Denis Healey as Minister of Defence, economic cuts on a massive scale were initiated. In response, the First Lord of the Admiralty and the First Sea Lord resigned and many high-ranking officers were replaced. The political decision to phase out aircraft carriers and fixed-wing aircraft was taken. As a direct consequence, Britain was to be deprived of her traditional ability to defend her sea routes with decades of naval strategy being consigned to the scrap heap.

During its Royal Navy career, the Buccaneer saw service with four aircraft carriers. HMS *Victorious* was the first to be retired, having suffered a major fire during a refit in 1967. *Hermes* was converted into a commando carrier in 1970 leaving the two *Ark Royal*-class vessels to operate into the 1970s.

HMS *Eagle* survived until being paid off on 26 January 1972 and eventually being scrapped, with HMS *Ark Royal* continuing until it suffered a similar fate on 4 December 1978.

Royal Navy bids farewell to the Buccaneer

With the winding-down of the Royal Navy's Buccaneer force from three front-line squadrons to just one, and with the disbandment of both the Headquarters and Training units, it was decided to relocate 809 NAS to a new shore base at RAF Honington, where the RN aircraft could operate alongside the RAF Buccaneers. They moved to their new base on 18 October

1972, following the end of a short home-waters cruise aboard HMS *Ark Royal*.

Having been established with standard S.2 airframes, 809 NAS became the recipient of fresh equipment in the course of 1973, beginning in July with the receipt of S.2C airframes. Martel-capable S.2D airframes continued in October, and by the end of the year the standard S.2 had been phased out.

No 809 NAS soldiered on as the only remaining FAA Buccaneer squadron, undertaking carrier qualifications training in addition to its front-line commitments.

The decision to retire HMS *Ark Royal* and its entire air wing meant that when 809 NAS disembarked from her carrier after its final cruise in home waters and the Mediterranean in December 1978, all of its aircraft were flown off to RAF St Athan for disposal or reassignment to the RAF. The squadron itself was disbanded at Lee-on-Solent on 15 December 1978, along with 892 NAS (Phantom FG.1s) and 849 NAS 'B' Flight (Gannet AEW.3s), bringing to a close the Royal Navy Buccaneer adventure.

BELOW A superb view of HMS *Ark Royal* taken in the 1970s, with six Buccaneer S.2 aircraft located on the forward deck.
(FAA Museum)

Chapter Four

South African Air Force Buccaneer operations

―(●)―

In spite of the Buccaneer's undoubted qualities, export success for the aircraft was distinctly limited. Sadly, this is probably due to having been labelled a 'naval' aircraft and in part to the British Government's somewhat ineptitude in negotiating with foreign governments! Had Blackburn been able to negotiate directly with the US Air Force or West German military authorities, things *may* have been different.

OPPOSITE The South African Air Force's first Buccaneer S.50, serial number 411, was photographed while operating in Class B markings as G-2-1 in 1965. *(BAE SYSTEMS Image CN2541A)*

65

SOUTH AFRICAN AIR FORCE BUCCANEER OPERATIONS

ABOVE A view of the Brough 'B' Shed with SAAF Buccaneer S.50 aircraft numbered 413, 414 and 415 in an advanced stage of construction. *(BAE SYSTEMS Image BAL20656)*

ABOVE RIGHT The first SAAF Buccaneer S.50 undergoing flight clearance trials for the Nord AS30 missiles on 17 February 1966. *(BAE SYSTEMS 2143826)*

After all, the NA.39 was carefully studied by American authorities in 1957 under the terms of the Mutual Weapons Development Program (MWDP) treaty, and they later declared the project 'sound'. Unfortunately, it was not to be and instead the US Government placed significant orders for the Grumman YA2F (later A-6) Intruder aircraft for their navy.

Similarly, negotiations had been conducted by British Government officials with West German military officials for an aircraft to replace the British-built Sea Hawk Mk.100 and 101 then in service with the Bundesmarine. It seems that the negotiations were not conducted in a suitably professional

manner and the large order went to Lockheed for their F-104 Starfighter.

Thankfully, negotiations between Britain and the South African Government fared a little better, although it proved to be the one and only export success for the Buccaneer.

Simonstown Agreement

In 1962, discussions with the South African Government regarding a possible order for the South African Air Force (SAAF) became detailed. The subject of the negotiations was the S.2 variant, which at that time had not yet taken to the air. However, it did include a significant number of changes to meet the country's 'hot and high' airfield operations. The contract was signed in January 1963 for 16 Buccaneer Mk.50 aircraft, as the SAAF variant had become known.

At the time of the negotiations, Britain and South Africa were operating under the Simonstown Agreement – whereby Britain offered South Africa maritime equipment and weapons to defend the vital trade routes around the Cape of Good Hope. Following the closure of the Suez Canal in 1956, these routes had become of great importance to Britain and Europe. In addition to the defence of the trade routes, Britain was also granted base facilities at Simonstown, near Cape Town.

Rocket powered

The SAAF Buccaneer S.50s were basically similar to the Royal Navy S.2 aircraft, but

BELOW Trials of the Bristol Siddeley BS605 single-chamber, retractable auxiliary motors located in the rear fuselage to improve take-off performance in 'hot and high' situations were completed in the first aircraft when marked as 'G-2-1'. These rocket motors were powered by a mixture of kerosene drawn from the aircraft's standard fuel supply and HTP (high-test peroxide). This image was taken on 14 March 1965. *(BAE SYSTEMS Image 2071135)*

were fitted with a pair of Bristol Siddeley BS605 single-chamber, retractable, auxiliary motors in the rear fuselage to improve take-off performance in 'hot and high' situations. These rocket motors were powered by a mixture of kerosene drawn from the aircraft's standard fuel supply and HTP (high-test peroxide), held in plastic tanks. The rocket motors developed 8,000lb of thrust for 30 seconds. As a result, the total thrust installed was over 30,000lb – significantly better than the 14,200lb thrust of the Gyron Junior-powered Buccaneer S.1.

The main innovation introduced on the S.50 was the enlarged slipper tank, which could accommodate 430 imperial gallons of additional fuel.

The first S.50 – serial number 411, which operated under Class B markings as 'G-2-1' – made its first flight on 9 January 1965. Trials with the new rocket motors were soon completed satisfactorily, as were the trials with the underwing armament of four Nord AS30 guided missiles. The S.50 did not feature hydraulic wing-folding capabilities, but was able to fold its wings manually.

It had been decided that all 16 Buccaneers would be allocated to 24 Squadron, to be based at Waterkloof Air Force Base, south of Pretoria, located 4,914ft above sea level. It was because of this factor that the installation of the rocket pack was deemed necessary by the SAAF. The runway at Waterkloof was long enough for the Buccaneer, even operating at maximum permitted weights, although it was considered that under certain conditions it *might* be necessary – as a safety precaution – to utilise the additional thrust; not just during take-off but also soon afterwards while trying to gain the necessary flying speeds in the climb. What must be remembered is the amount of effective thrust that was utilised by the bleeding of air for the BLC system on the Buccaneer. That all said, the success of the booster rockets will remain a matter for debate as they were removed from the aircraft during the fleet modification programmes in 1976.

Politics rears its ugly head – again!

Following the signing of the original contract in 1962, a Labour Government was elected to

power in the 1964 general election. The new Prime Minister – Harold Wilson – indicated his intentions to rigidly enforce the United Nations arms embargo against South Africa. The South African aircraft were affected as none of the aircraft had been delivered.

The Labour Government's reason for refusing to supply the Buccaneers to South Africa was because it was considered immoral to supply weapons which might be used to enforce South Africa's apartheid policy in a counter insurgency role against the black population of the country. It is difficult to believe, particularly with the benefit of hindsight, that this ludicrous explanation was accepted by many supporters of the government. The Buccaneer was designed – and purchased by the SAAF – primarily to destroy well-defended major targets, mainly of a maritime nature. By complete contrast, the Wilson Government was strangely silent about the 'suppression' value of helicopters then being purchased by South Africa from France.

At some time it was even reported that the British Government was ready to sell the SAAF Buccaneers to the Indian Air Force. Early in November 1964, the Indian Minister of Defence visited Britain, apparently to purchase maritime weaponry for his country.

Eventually, after severe pressure from the South African Government, Britain agreed to supply the first 16 Buccaneers ordered, although an option that was held for the purchase of a further batch of 20 aircraft was cancelled.

ABOVE An unidentified SAAF Buccaneer S.50 (although thought to be 411) undergoing flight testing of the SAAF-specific long-range tanks on 12 April 1965. The pilot at the controls is Blackburn's chief test pilot, Derek Whitehead. *(BAE SYSTEMS Image BAL2082745)*

No 24 Squadron formed at Lossiemouth

No 24 Squadron, SAAF, was formed at RAF Lossiemouth on 1 May 1965, initially utilising S.1 airframes borrowed from the Royal Navy until the new S.50 aircraft became available for training and work-up. No 24 Squadron's first commanding officer – Commandant 'Bob' Rogers – and three other aircrew had already

trained on the Buccaneer, under conditions of considerable secrecy, with 809 NAS from January 1965. Rogers would eventually go on to become the Chief of the Air Force.

With the eight aircraft having been delivered to the unit (serial numbers 412–419), the work-up proceeded well. A date was set for delivery of the first eight airframes to South Africa, in two groups of four aircraft. They started their long journey from Lossiemouth on 27 October 1965, routing to Yeovilton, Las Palmas, Cape Verde and Ascension Island. It was on this leg that aircraft 417 stalled and entered a spin at around 35,000ft, and suffered a double engine flame-out as a result. Captain Martin Jooste and Lieutenant Anton de Klerk ejected, before being picked up out of the sea the following morning by the Dutch cargo vessel RMS *Randfontein*. This rescue followed a significant search effort by a Portuguese Air Force Douglas DC-6 along with two 35 Squadron, SAAF, Shackleton aircraft in locating the airmen. The remaining seven Buccaneer aircraft made it safely to South Africa.

Delivery by sea

Because of the loss of Buccaneer 417 on the ferry flight, it was decided to deliver the remaining eight SAAF aircraft by sea, routing from Hull to Cape Town. During the journey, the wings were folded and the aircraft completely cocooned in a protective covering so they could travel as deck cargo. The first four aircraft (421, 423, 424 and 426) arrived in Cape Town aboard the SA *Van der Stel* on 5 August 1966, followed by the remaining four aircraft (411, 420, 422 and 425) aboard the SA *Langkloof* on 17 October that year.

Under normal circumstances the lost aircraft would have been replaced but, strangely, this was not permitted under the Labour Government's strict arms embargo. This embargo coincided with a somewhat peculiar and sinister period in Labour Party politics when

BELOW Having 'lost' one of the first Buccaneer S.50 aircraft when serial number 417 crashed into the sea on its delivery flight, the decision was taken to deliver the remaining eight aircraft by ship, in two batches of four. In this image, aircraft number 421 was photographed while being moved by road from the Brough factory to Hull Docks. The wings were folded and a protective cocoon added in order that the aircraft could travel as deck cargo. *(BAE SYSTEMS Image BAL21764)*

LEFT The SA *Van der Stel* with four Buccaneer S.50 aircraft (421, 423, 424 and 426) secured on the deck ahead of its voyage to Cape Town. They arrived on 5 August 1966. *(BAE SYSTEMS Image 21776)*

the government seemed hell-bent on cancelling all of Britain's aircraft projects and replacing them with American-purchased products. This period saw the cancellation of the Hawker P.1154 (a supersonic Harrier) which was replaced with the Phantom; the HS.681 V/STOL transport that was replaced with an order for the C-130 Hercules; and the most famous aviation cancellation of all – the TSR-2 – which was replaced with the F-111. Sadly, the latter never actually made it to these shores as it too was subsequently cancelled and eventually replaced with an order for Buccaneers!

Joint exercises

Royal Navy and SAAF Buccaneers often participated in the combined Anglo-South African naval Capex exercises which were held annually off the South African coast. The last of these joint Royal Navy/South African Navy exercises, organised under the terms of the Simonstown Agreement, was held off the Western Cape coast in November 1973. In addition to six Buccaneer S.50s from 24 Squadron SAAF, Mirage IIICZs and IIIEZs from Nos 2 and 3 Squadrons SAAF, along with Wasp helicopters and Shackleton maritime reconnaissance aircraft joined a pair of RAF Nimrod aircraft, and Sea King and Wasp helicopters from HMS *Tiger* and HMS *Rhyl*. Sadly, it also saw the loss of two 24 Squadron Buccaneers when they crashed into the sea off Danger Point, near Cape Agulhas, with both crews being lost.

Shortly after this exercise, Britain severed the Simonstown Agreement and as a consequence, no further Capex exercises were held.

Sinking the *Wafra*

SAAF Buccaneers were called into action in March 1971 to lend a hand in the destruction of a stricken tanker in much the same way that the Royal Navy had assisted with the *Torrey Canyon* (see Chapter 3, page 58). On 27 February 1971, the Monrovian-registered tanker *Wafra* sent out a Mayday signal reporting that its engine room was flooded. On board was 60,000 tons of crude oil en route from Ras Tannara in the Persian Gulf to the Caltex refinery near Cape Town. Shortly afterwards, the Soviet tanker *Gdynia* took the *Wafra* in tow

towards Mossel Bay on the South African coast but the towline snapped just two hours later. The small African coaster *Pongola* then took over, but heavy seas progressively forced the *Wafra* further inshore. At 17:30hrs, the anchor was lowered, but even this did not prevent the relentless movement towards the shoreline.

The crew abandoned ship and shortly afterwards the stern of the *Wafra* grounded and oil began leaking out. It was imperative to refloat the ship and tow her away to deeper waters for an eventual transfer of cargo oil to avoid a major pollution catastrophe. On 8 March, after several attempts, the powerful tug *Oceanic* succeeded in pulling the stricken vessel off the sandbank. However, by this time, the owners had written the vessel off and it was considered far too dangerous to attempt to transfer the cargo to another tanker. The only way to avoid a major ecological disaster would be to tow the vessel out to sea and then sink her. By the time the *Oceanic* had towed the vessel around 90 miles offshore, the weather had deteriorated and the risk that the heavy seas would break the vessel in two and spill all of the oil was becoming very real.

The best option was, with the help of the South African Air Force, to sink the *Wafra* as quickly as possible. It was decided to use the Buccaneer for the task and on 10 March two aircraft were despatched from Waterkloof to AFB Langebaanweg, near Cape Town, to prepare for the attack. The deployment was supported by a Transall C-160, along with the required groundcrew. Later that evening, the Buccaneers were airborne.

At the time, the SAAF's sole Viscount transport aircraft, with South African Minister of Defence P.W. Botha on board, was circling the stricken vessel, as were a pair of SAAF Shackleton aircraft – this time with a number of journalists on board.

The weapon selected for the task was the Nord AS30 air-to-surface guided missile, the use of this being considered valuable practice as, at the time, it was only the third time this type of rocket had been deployed. For attacks of this nature, the aircraft approaches the target at around 3,000ft and at a speed of 450 knots; the missile is fired from about 4 miles out. As a target, the *Wafra* was floating with just 10–15ft showing above the waterline and was drifting and turning in winds up to 50mph. It was not going to be an easy target!

The first missile was aimed at the ballast tank. A little too high, it skimmed the deck just above the tank, and struck the water 60ft past the target and exploded. The second missile was deliberately steered away from the tanker when one of the observing aircraft flew too close to the ship. The third missile missed the ballast tank but hit the ship further forward, just above the waterline. It penetrated the ship and blew a 15ft-diameter hole, which was insufficient to sink the vessel. The fourth missile, fired at the bow, passed above the target. The Buccaneers returned to base with the *Wafra* still afloat.

A second attempt was made the following day but the *Wafra* refused to sink. At this point it was decided to try depth charges dropped from a Shackleton of 35 Squadron. The attack, made on 11 March, once again failed to sink the ship. Another attempt was made later in the day but very poor light made the target almost impossible to see.

However, the Shackleton remained airborne right through the night, cruising in the vicinity of the vessel. Early the following morning, flying at an altitude of 100ft, it dropped six depth charges only 20ft from the port side of the ship. A few minutes later and a second attack was made with three depth charges being dropped just 10ft from the side of the ship. The *Wafra* began to burn fiercely and 40 minutes after the first attack, the ship disappeared beneath the waves.

After an onslaught of twelve AS30 missiles, of which seven struck the ship, plus nine depth charges, the unsinkable ship had finally been sunk and a major pollution catastrophe had been averted. Later, P.W. Botha stated that he hoped Harold Wilson took note of Operation *Wafra* and the use to which the SAAF Buccaneers had been put.

Another tanker attack

While en route from the Persian Gulf with a full load of 18,000 tons of crude oil, the Liberian vessel *Silver Castle* collided with the South African cargo vessel SA *Pioneer* in thick fog on 20 April 1972, around 6 miles from the mouth of Bushman's River.

The stern of the *Silver Castle* was severely damaged in the collision and caught fire. With six of her 22 tanks damaged, the vessel was towed out to sea and most of her oil was successfully transferred to another tanker. However, the collision and subsequent fire had damaged the vessel beyond economic repair and on 29 April, it was decided to scuttle her. After several attempts by conventional methods, the SAAF was requested to sink the ship, now lying 170 miles south-east of Cape St Blaize.

Once again, Buccaneers were selected for the task and six aircraft, led by Commandant Pierre Gouws, were despatched from their base at AFB Waterkloof to the Flying Training School at Langebaanweg on 15 May.

The first five aircraft took off at first light the following morning, armed with 1,000lb bombs. The sixth aircraft took off later to provide air-to-air refuelling duties. The attack on the *Silver Castle* lasted just ten minutes, during which time 27 bombs were dropped, of which 19 struck their target.

Just six minutes later, a Shackleton of 35 Squadron, SAAF, reported that the only evidence remaining of the *Silver Castle* was an oil slick on the water.

SAAF Buccaneer operations

South Africa has used aircraft in support of two distinct but related campaigns; both concerned with internal security. The most extensive action was against nationalists in South West Africa (now Namibia), the other against banned nationalists in South Africa itself.

South West Africa was a German colony until 1915, when it was conquered by South Africa, which was given a mandate to administer the territory. However, since then, South Africa had refused to relinquish control of the territory. In 1958, the South West Africa People's Organization (SWAPO) was formed and two years later it spawned a military arm, the People's Liberation Army of Namibia (PLAN). Secure bases for these operations were provided in newly independent Zambia. The first PLAN insurgents entered Namibia in September 1965, and the first clash occurred when SAAF helicopters lifted police to a camp in Ovamboland. Initially, the police were easily able to control these activities, but in January 1973, a police station in the Caprivi Strip was attacked. From that point on, the security of the region passed to the armed forces. By August 1976, there were 12,800 combat troops and 5,000 reservists in the territory, with a supporting Air Commando detachment of one Impala and one Mirage squadron, plus a range of helicopters.

When Angola was granted independence from Portugal in 1975, it was ruled by the People's Movement for the Liberation of Angola – Labour Party, later the People's Movement for the Liberation of Angola (MPLA). The MPLA fought against the Portuguese army in the Angolan War of Independence of 1961–74, and defeated the National Union for the Total Independence of Angola (UNITA) and the National Liberation Front of Angola (FNLA), two other anti-colonial movements, in the Angolan Civil War of 1975–2002.

Following the Angolan expedition of 1975–76, the South Africans formed 32 Battalion, partly from Angolans, as a key counter-insurgency force. This unit was to operate outside South Africa's borders, being infiltrated, exfiltrated and resupplied by both ground transport and helicopters. It was involved in a clash with the MPLA on the border on 18 February 1977, but more significantly in Operation Reindeer, which began in May 1978. Furthermore, two major PLAN camps had been identified in Angola: 'Moscow' at Cassinga, 155 miles into Angola, and 'Vietnam' at Chetequera just across the border. Both conflicts ran for many years and involved considerable South African military forces; in many cases, the Buccaneer aircraft was involved.

In the mid-1970s, skirmishes between SWAPO insurgents from southern Angola and combined South West African/South African forces were steadily increasing as the void following Portugal's withdrawal from Angola drew in militarised support from the Soviet Union, along with its satellite Cuba and the now-independent Angola. In May 1975, a force of four Buccaneers was launched in a show of force but resulted in the loss of one aircraft – serial number 426 – following a mid-air collision near Grootfontein AFB in South West Africa.

In April 1978, a full-scale military operation – codenamed Operation Reindeer – was

launched against the two PLAN camps. The operation included the use of six of the SAAF's remaining eight airworthy Buccaneer S.50 aircraft. One of the Buccaneers went unserviceable just before take-off and four attacked the complex at Cassinga with 450kg bombs, while a fifth was armed with four rocket pods and an internal fuel tank in the bomb bay for extra range; to provide close air support for the troops on the ground.

After a swift turnaround at Grootfontein, the Buccaneers were back in the fray, this time providing cover to ground troops at Cassinga and also attacking a target near Ruacana.

Further engagements followed a similar pattern as 24 Squadron participated in cross-border strikes including Rekstok (March 1979), Rekstok II (July 1979), Daisy (November 1981) and Weldmesh (September 1985). Sandwiched in between was Protea, one of the largest South African Defence Force (SADF) efforts of the conflict, aimed at neutralising military complexes in southern Angola near the towns of Xangongo, Ongiva, Peu-Peuamd and Mongua. The 13-day

ABOVE A striking air-to-air view of SAAF Buccaneer S.50, serial number 421, photographed along the South African coastline. After retirement, serial number 421 was preserved with the SAAF Museum at Swartkop AFB. *(via Johan Conradie)*

BELOW An early image of Buccaneer S.50, serial number 423, as the aircraft is still painted in its original (as delivered) colours. No 423 was later destroyed when it crashed seaward of Scottburgh on 3 August 1978. *(via Johan Conradie)*

BELOW Buccaneer S.50, serial number 416, at Rooikop on 1 October 1984. The aircraft is painted in toned-down markings and carries large slipper tanks. *(via Johan Conradie)*

operation opened on 21 August 1981 with the Buccaneers tasked to destroy radar sites at Chimemba and Cahama on 23 August. Five aircraft participated in the attack with four of them carrying eight 450kg bombs while the leader carried a mixture of four 450kg bombs along with a pair of AS30 missiles.

Having transited at low level, upon reaching his 'pitch-up' point around 20nm from the target at Cahama, the leader climbed to 15,000ft before settling into a 20° dive and firing a single missile from 13nm out. The projectile was guided to its target, which then removed the radar aerial with clinical precision at precisely 11:00hrs.

Seven minutes later, the second AS30 was fired and struck the radar at Chimemba, effectively blinding the air defences and providing freedom of movement for the balance of the remaining SAAF forces supporting ground operations. Sadly, the respite was short-lived. Such was the scope of the enemy's defence network that the radar was simply replaced by a new one within a few hours – no mean feat given southern Angola's logistical infrastructure.

It was similar determination that saw the Buccaneers attack the repaired site five times in the next five days. The efforts expended by the enemy to keep both Chimemba and Cahama radar sites functional highlights two key elements of the campaign: the first being the importance Cuban and Soviet 'advisers' placed on both facilities; and the second being the overall level of sophistication the latter was prepared to commit to the theatre.

UNITA troubles

Towards the latter part of the 1980s, efforts to broker a political deal to bring a ceasefire to the region were playing out against a broader, more global backdrop, with parties on both sides seeking to obtain a strategic advantage that would allow them to negotiate from a position of power. To this end, Angolan forces began massing for a decisive attack on UNITA (the National Union for the Total Independence of Angola) positions in south-east Angola in mid-1987. South Africa's initial involvement would look to halt the Angolan advance under the guise of Operation Modular, which began on

13 August. On 2 September, two Buccaneers were deployed to Grootfontein AFB for photo-reconnaissance operations utilising the LOROP (Long-range Oblique Photo) pod carried in the rotating bomb bay with a high-definition capability up to 18 miles. The Buccaneers investigated airfields at Menongue and Cuito Cuananvale, as well as the bridge over the Cuito River before returning to their home base near Pretoria.

Some 14 days later, four of the five Buccaneers remaining on SAAF strength were back at Grootfontein in preparation for strike operations. These began on 16 September with an attack on 46 Brigade using 250kg pre-fragmentation and 1,000lb HE bombs. Interestingly, it was on this raid that the enemy managed its only SAM-8 lock on a SAAF Buccaneer during the entire conflict. This lasted around eight seconds before being broken by a combination of the external ECM pod (known as Bikini) and the pilot's flying skills. The pattern of raids continued over the following weeks with raids against 16, 21, 47 and 59 Brigades and their mechanised support using a mix of 120kg and 250kg pre-fragmentation bombs, as well as conventional 120, 250, 450 and 460kg ordnance.

On 13 October 1987, 24 Squadron entered into a new era with the arrival of the Kentron H2 'Raptor' TV-guided glide bomb into the operational theatre, even though the weapon was still in its development stages. A product of the local armament industry, the H2 had been introduced into squadron training in late 1986, with trials yielding impressive results. The device was launched from an outer wing station on the Buccaneer following a low-level run-in and a pitch-up to 32,000ft. The navigator would then assume control of the glide bomb and guide it to its target from around 36 miles (60km) away via a passive TV seeker.

On 25 November, three Buccaneer aircraft took off from Grootfontein AFB and headed towards a rendezvous with their Mirage F-1AZ fighter escort before setting course for an attack on the runway at Menongue airfield. Unfortunately, as the Buccaneer approached the release area, technical issues with the device saw the first intended use of the weapon aborted.

Attention now turned to the bridge spanning the Cuito River, a vital supply route for the brigades located on the eastern side of the river during their push into the south-east of the country. Two attempts to attack the bridge were made on 8 December; the first was scuppered by a technical issue and the second by weather over the target. An attempt on 11 December yielded similar frustrating events. On 12 December, the H2 was finally launched but appeared to fall short of the bridge; the following day communications with the bomb was lost seconds before impact and the results were inconclusive.

On 3 January 1988, an early morning attempt was aborted with FAPA (Angolan Air Force) MiG-23 fighters reported over the area; an attack would have left the Buccaneers

BELOW Buccaneer S.50, serial number 414, at Grootfontein AFB on 16 October 1987 during Operation Modular. The external load consists of 12 × 120kg Mk.81 bombs. *(via Johan Conradie)*

BELOW Another view of Buccaneer S.50, serial number 414, this time at Grootfontein on 8 February 1988. The aircraft is armed with a Kentron H2 'Raptor' TV-guided glide bomb on each underwing inner pylon, with the H2 communications pod on the starboard wing and an ELT555 'Bikini' active ECM pod under the port wing. *(via Johan Conradie)*

ABOVE Buccaneer S.50, serial number 414, loaded with 16 × 250kg Mk.82 low-drag bombs during flight clearance trials of the new bomb system on 16 June 1986. *(via Johan Conradie)*

ABOVE Another view of 414 over the Roodewal bombing range in July 1986. This time the load is 12 × 120kg low-drag bombs on the underwing triple bomb carriers, while hidden in the rotating bomb bay are a further 8 × 250kg low-drag bombs. *(via Johan Conradie)*

ABOVE In this view of 414, it is seen carrying a full combat load of eight 250kg Mk.82 low-drag bombs in the rotating bomb bay, two 250kg Mk.82 low-drag bombs on a multi-bomb carrier under the starboard wing, while under the port wing it carries a 'Bikini' ECM pod. Chaff and flare pods were fitted on both sides of the square box housing the TANS navigation system which is located behind the bomb bay. *(via Johan Conradie)*

BELOW An unidentified 24 Squadron SAAF Buccaneer S.50 undergoing in-flight refuelling trials with a 60 Squadron Boeing 707 ELINT/tanker aircraft on 13 March 1987. This was the very first occasion a SAAF Buccaneer had refuelled from a SAAF Boeing 707. *(via Johan Conradie)*

vulnerable at a crucial time in the weapon's release and guidance. Later that morning, two Buccaneers took off again and climbed away for another attempt. This time a near-textbook launch was made by Buccaneer 414 and the weapon detonated effectively on the bridge with a section of around 20m near the centre of the bridge completely destroyed. A further effort was launched on 6 February to demolish the bridge completely but yielded inconclusive results. The bridge was subsequently repaired but could only be used for foot traffic, which proved to be a major blow against the enemy's supply efforts and his ability to wage war.

Operation Modular morphed into Hooper and eventually Packer; however, it was a military stalemate with both sides able to hold their own and progress no further. Elsewhere, the political climate was changing and a negotiated settlement became a reality. Further ground engagements occurred in the south-west of the country during Operation Excite in May/June 1988 but politicians managed to agree terms and on 30 August 1988, the last South African troops left Angola.

Mid-life upgrade

In 1974–75, the SAAF instigated what became known as the '600-series' mid-life upgrade to their remaining airframes. Packages of modifications were supplied by Hawker

Siddeley as any hope of acquiring the remaining 20 aircraft on which they held options was completely scuppered by Westminster. These included the fitting of the 450-gallon bomb-door fuel tank, along with capabilities to carry an underwing FR Aviation Mk.20 refuelling pod in order to function as buddy-buddy tankers to other SAAF Buccaneers, as well as the SAAF fleet of Mirage jets. Other improvements included an upgraded strike computer, new ejection seats, improvements to the Blue Parrot main radar and strike computer, as well as upgrades to the cockpit environment.

It has also been reported that 24 Squadron operated a pair of MB326 Impala Mk.1 aircraft as weapons system trainers for the systems uniquely used by the Buccaneer. Both Impala aircraft had modified rear cockpits, with the joystick removed. The aircraft carried electronic pods on wing hardpoints on each side of the aircraft.

Retired from service

In the rationalisation process that followed South Africa's withdrawal from South West Africa and the latter's independence in 1990, it was announced that 24 Squadron operations would be discontinued in March 1991. On 28 March, 24 Squadron flew its last official Buccaneer sortie in squadron service and on 30 June, the squadron was formally disbanded. The nature of its training and operations had taken its toll on aircraft numbers with only 5 remaining from the original order of 16.

In a tribute to an exceptional aircraft in both war and peace, it is fitting to note that all five survivors are preserved today in order to educate future generations of the part played by the incredible Buccaneer S.50 in SAAF history – affectionately earning the nickname 'Easy Rider' among SAAF crews in the process.

The best aircraft in SAAF service

According to Brigadier-General Richard 'Dick' Lord, DSC, 'the Buccaneer was perhaps the best aircraft in the SAAF arsenal in terms of a war in Africa. It could fly fast and low over great distances while carrying everything plus the kitchen sink.'

ABOVE Buccaneer S.50, serial number 414, on static display in the 24 Squadron hangar during the 25-year celebrations of the Buccaneer's service, 2 November 1991. A large selection of weapons for the aircraft is also displayed. *(via Johan Conradie)*

The author gratefully acknowledges the significant contribution provided by Steve McLean and SAAF Buccaneer aficionado Johan Conradie in the production of this chapter.

TABLE OF SOUTH AFRICAN AIR FORCE BUCCANEERS

Serial	Fate
411	Crashed 4 January 1973, near Ermelo
412	Displayed as gate guardian AFB Waterkloof (Pretoria)
413	Burned out after ground collision with MB326 on 27 May 1982 at AFB Pietersburg
414	On display at SAAF Museum, AFB Swartkop (Pretoria)
415	Crashed 16 October 1969, seaward of Eshowe
416	On display at SAAF Museum, AFB Ysterplaat (Cape Town)
417	Crashed into Atlantic Ocean on delivery flight, 30 October 1965
418	Crashed 14 October 1970 at De Wet bombing range near Bloemfontein
419	Crashed 24 November 1973 south of Danger Point during a training exercise with Royal Navy after colliding with Buccaneer 420
420	Crashed 24 November 1973 south of Danger Point during a training exercise with Royal Navy after colliding with Buccaneer 419
421	On display at SAAF Museum, AFB Swartkop (Pretoria)
422	On display, South African National Museum of Military History (Johannesburg)
423	Crashed 3 August 1978 seaward of Scottburgh
424	Crashed 9 January 1979 near Marble Hall
425	Crashed 1 March 1978 near Lydenburg
426	Crashed 15 May 1975 near Grootfontein, South West Africa

Chapter Five

RAF Buccaneer operations

In 1968, sweeping defence cuts were introduced into the RAF and her sister services; not so much of a planned defence policy, but forced upon the Labour Government as a result of the economic crisis which included a devaluation of sterling. RAF cuts meant the cancellation of 50 F-111A aircraft, which themselves were to have made up for the earlier cancellation of the TSR-2. At the same time, it was decided to speed up the withdrawal of forces from Malaysia, Singapore and the Persian Gulf and complete it by the end of 1971. All this would involve an accelerated run-down of RAF manpower.

OPPOSITE 'Jackal Formation' flying around the north-east coast of Scotland on 3 December 1992. Leading the formation are Squadron Leaders Rick Phillips and Norman Browne in XW527, with XV332 and XZ431 for company. *(Keith Wilson)*

The announcement, made by Harold Wilson, left the RAF procurement policy in complete turmoil. One magazine editorial at the time included the following: 'To lose one supersonic low-level strike aircraft is unfortunate. To lose two smacks of a lack of policy.'

An aircraft the RAF didn't want!

In April 1965, the Labour Government had cancelled the TSR-2 project. Among the many comments at the time was one made by Denis Healey, the Minister of Defence: 'We must see if TSR-2's strike role can be carried out by sea- or land-based Buccaneers. . . .'

This was not the first time the Buccaneer had been associated with the RAF. As early as 1957, when the RAF issued its original OR339 requirement for a Canberra replacement from which TSR-2 evolved, Blackburn had formally proposed a de-navalised version of the NA.39 to the Ministry of Supply, pointing out its stretch-range potential if used from land bases. Even stretched, it seems the NA.39 fell some way short of what the Air Chiefs required.

However, also playing a not-insignificant part in the lack of RAF interest in those early days was the traditional rivalry between the RAF and the Royal Navy. One high-ranking RAF officer was reported by a journalist as saying, 'My dear chap, the RAF has never bought a Fleet Air Arm aircraft.'

Undaunted by the continual knock-backs, Brough persevered and proposed a number of Buccaneer developments including the 'Mk.2*'. It had more powerful Spey engines, special RAF equipment – including many systems proposed for the TSR-2, a soft-field landing gear, optional fuselage gun pack and a take-off rocket. A further development of this variant featured even more TSR-2 systems and equipment.

The installation of such TSR-2 equipment presented few problems as one Buccaneer had, since 1963, been successfully engaged on test-flying the TSR-2 radar when the second fixed-wing, pre-production aircraft, XK487, was loaned to Ferranti and flown to Turnhouse Airport, Edinburgh, on 8 May 1963. The aircraft was used by Ferranti for around three and a half years before being returned. The effortless manner in which this aircraft flew at 500 knots

at 100ft over extended distances is said to have impressed some RAF officials. However, the Labour Government was not interested; instead it wanted the F-111.

Still undaunted, Hawker Siddeley offered a further-developed Buccaneer, designated 'S.2**'. The government, while seemingly admitting that this new proposal would meet many of the proposed requirements planned for the F-111, at half the cost, then went on to explain that it would not be cost advantageous because 'we should need twice as many'. Nor were they further swayed by the supersonic Buccaneer – the Labour Government was clearly sold on the F-111.

However, events in the USA were showing the F-111 was not quite the wonder aircraft that had been claimed. In fact, so far short did it fall from its promised specification and so far did it exceed its estimated cost price (even though in 1965 Prime Minister Harold Wilson had described it as a 'bargain') that in January 1968, the British options on the aircraft were cancelled. Its place was taken by an order for Rolls-Royce Spey-powered Phantom aircraft.

On 10 July 1968, less than six months later, the Ministry of Defence announced – with seemingly incredible disregard for its scorn over the past 12 years – that the Buccaneer was to be 'ordered for the RAF to replace the F-111 aircraft'.

Brough was delighted with the first contract for 26 aircraft which duly followed. The RAF aircraft were very similar to the Royal Navy S.2 aircraft, and retained the deck hook and folding wings – both of which would be used to advantage during RAF operations. The RAF aircraft featured a number of improvements over the naval version, including the fitting of a new underwing pylon that had been developed as part of the S.2* proposal.

The initial order was shortly followed by a contract for a further 17 aircraft, while the RAF would also receive a total of 64 former Royal Navy Buccaneer S.2 aircraft.

Navy training of RAF aircrew

In the latter years of the Royal Navy Fleet Air Arm operations, a significant proportion of aircrew was provided by the RAF, on a loan basis, although most only completed a single tour with a Navy squadron. Interestingly, some later returned to 736 NAS as instructors. Their early introduction to the aircraft and its operations were to provide an invaluable core of the RAF's Buccaneer operations.

While the RAF's new aircraft were under construction at Brough, the task of training the first RAF aircrews was perhaps unsurprisingly given to the Royal Navy and 736 NAS. The first RAF 'cell' was created within 736 NAS in the spring of 1969 – consisting of three pilots, two Pilot Attack Instructors (PAI, although the term QWI would come later), one QFI and three navigators. All were RAF officers who had previously operated the Buccaneer with an FAA squadron.

No 736 NAS was due to run eight courses, each with four aircrews, to convert pilots and navigators on to the Buccaneer, although later events were to conspire against these numbers being achieved.

Owing to a shortage of S.2 airframes, a number of S.1 aircraft were taken out of their recent retirement to supplement the S.2s. Crews arriving for conversion had an interesting variety of experience including Canberra, Hunter and V-bombers, while others were *ab initio* students. Initially, RAF courses used only the S.1 airframes, with the final three course sorties being used to convert students on to the S.2.

Sadly, in late 1970, the S.1's service career came to an abrupt end. On 1 December, with a student on his first solo, XN951 suffered an engine surge while in the circuit at Lossiemouth and the only option for both occupants was to eject. Just one week later, on 8 December, a student sortie in XN968 suffered an uncontrollable turbine failure which again left the crew with no other option than to eject. Sadly, one member of the crew did not survive the ejection. A closer examination of the remaining S.1 airframes showed the Gyron Junior engines to be in poor condition and the decision was taken to withdraw them from service. The last S.1 was flown out from Lossiemouth in January 1971 and all remaining training was conducted on the S.2 airframes.

This had a limited impact on 736 NAS as it was close to the end of its RAF training task, with course Number 7 due to graduate in March 1971. Some extra RAF Buccaneer S.2 airframes (including XV157 and XV349) were

flown into Lossiemouth to assist with the training programme from January to March 1971.

As it happened, course Number 7 was the last to run at Lossiemouth. Course Number 8 – a short course for experienced aircrew – was rescheduled to run concurrently with course Number 9 at RAF Honington in May 1971.

First RAF Buccaneer deliveries

The first batch of new-build aircraft for the RAF were designated S.2B and differed only in some details from the latest FAA Buccaneers, which were now designated S.2D. An order was placed for 26 aircraft with serials in the range XW525–XW550. XW525 made its first flight from Holme-on-Spalding-Moor on 8 January 1970.

Some carrier-specific details such as the catapult strop points were deleted on the S.2B, although the arrester hook and wing-fold mechanism were retained. For the rest, the differences were confined chiefly to items of equipment – especially avionics and communications – although further modifications, such as the fitting of the bulged bomb-door fuel tank, would be introduced during the Buccaneer's RAF service life.

The first aircraft handed over to the RAF was XV350, a former FAA airframe which was officially transferred to the RAF on 1 January 1969, although it did not make its first flight, after modification, until 11 February. Interestingly, XV350 never served with an RAF squadron; instead it spent its entire life on trials

BELOW XV347 of 12 Squadron, photographed at RAF Honington on 1 October 1969. XV347 was one of the first four aircraft delivered to the Buccaneer's first operational squadron on that day. *(Crown Copyright/Air Historical Branch Image TN-1-3633)*

ABOVE Two other
Buccaneer aircraft
delivered to
12 Squadron on
1 October 1969
included XV155
and XV348. *(Crown
Copyright/Air Historical
Branch Image
TN-1-4737)*

BELOW No 12
Squadron was
declared to NATO
shortly after its
formation and was
soon seen in its
maritime role. XN983
and XV348 were
photographed in June
1970. *(Crown Copyright/
Air Historical Branch
Image TN-1-6232-28)*

work, either at Holme-on-Spalding-Moor or
Boscombe Down.

A trickle of S.2 airframes permitted the
formation of the RAF's first Buccaneer
squadron – 12 Squadron – at RAF Honington
on 1 October 1969.

When 237 OCU (Operational Conversion
Unit) was formed in March 1971, the RAF
planning had envisaged the formation of six
frontline Buccaneer squadrons, including three
in the maritime role. Unfortunately, and despite
a follow-up order for a further 16 aircraft in
1971, this total was never achieved. The
RAF Buccaneer force peaked at five frontline
squadrons in 1979 when 216 Squadron was,
albeit briefly, formed.

The new batch of 16 S.2B aircraft were
ordered for the RAF and allocated the serial
block XX885–XX901. These were the first
airframes to include an RWR (Radar Warning
Receiver) installation within the fin/tailplane bullet
fairing, although most aircraft in the fleet were
retrofitted with this modification by 1975.

The batch of serial numbers noted above

actually covered 17 aircraft, with the 'extra'
aircraft – XX897 – being delivered to the RRE
(Royal Radar Establishment) at Pershore on 15
April 1976. XX897 served all of its service life on
radar trials work.

Aircraft of a final batch of three (XZ430–
XZ432) followed on, with XZ432 – the RAF's last
Buccaneer – being delivered on 6 October 1977.

In addition to the RAF orders and deliveries,
four further aircraft (XW986–XW989) were ordered
although this was later reduced to just three
when XW989 was cancelled. The remaining
three were specifically ordered for test purposes
by the Royal Aircraft Establishment (RAE) and
were all delivered during the first half of 1974.
Emphasising their 'non-combat' status, all were
initially finished in a high-visibility yellow, white
and dark green photographic paint scheme.
They were mainly engaged on weapons trials,
usually operating from West Freugh, although
they were officially on the strength of the RAE
at Farnborough. XW987 was later painted in
the red, white and blue 'raspberry ripple' colour
scheme. At the end of their test flying careers,
all were sold to civilian operators in the Cape
Town area of South Africa and were the very last
Buccaneer aircraft flying anywhere in the world.

12 Squadron

'Shiny Twelve' squadron disbanded as a
Vulcan B.2 squadron at RAF Cottesmore on
31 December 1967. It was then chosen to
be the RAF's first Buccaneer unit when it was
re-formed on 1 October 1969. It received its
first four aircraft that day, when they arrived
overhead RAF Honington in a formation
led by the Officer Commanding (OC), Wing
Commander G.G. Davies.

Among the first aircraft delivered were
XV155, XV157, XV347, XV348 and XV349, all
to 'interim S.2B' standard. Shortly afterwards,
12 Squadron was declared to SACLANT
(Supreme Allied Commander, Atlantic – one of
two Supreme Commanders of NATO) in the
anti-shipping role, using the Martel missile as its
primary armament.

The squadron remained at RAF Honington
until 1980, when the base was required for
the impending arrival of the TWCU (Tactical
Weapons Conversion Unit) Tornado GR.1
aircraft. Consequently, 12 Squadron moved

ABOVE Down where the Buccaneer belonged! XN983, a Buccaneer S.2B of 12 Squadron, was photographed at very low level in June 1970. *(Crown Copyright/Air Historical Branch Image TN-1-6232-34)*

RIGHT In early November 1970, 12 Squadron took eight of their Buccaneer S.2B aircraft to Luqa, Malta, for Exercise Lime Jug, a large-scale exercise held to practise procedures between RAF and Royal Navy forces. In the background are eight Phantom FG.1 aircraft from 43 Squadron, who also participated in the exercise. *(Crown Copyright/Air Historical Branch Image TN-1-6293-170)*

north to RAF Lossiemouth on 3 November 1980 where its role continued to be that of maritime strike and attack. From early 1988, the Sea Eagle missile entered the operational inventory of the squadron.

No 12 Squadron supplied aircraft and crews for Operation Granby in 1990–91 (see pages 93

LEFT An image taken off the coast of Luqa, Malta, on 4 November 1970 during Exercise Lime Jug, depicts a diamond-nine formation led by six Buccaneer S.2 aircraft of 12 Squadron followed by three Phantom FG.1 aircraft of 43 Squadron. *(Crown Copyright/Air Historical Branch Image TN-1-6293-3)*

LEFT This unique formation was flown on 5 November 1970 over the historical capital of Valletta during Exercise Lime Jug. Featured in the formation is Canberra PR.9 XH176 of locally based 13 Squadron; on either wing are Buccaneer S.2s XV347 and XV348 of 12 Squadron from RAF Honington; while at the rear of the formation are three Lightning F.6s – XS934/K, XS920/F and XR757/D – of 11 Squadron from RAF Leuchars. *(Crown Copyright/Air Historical Branch Image TN-1-6293-231)*

was initially equipped with all new-build S.2B airframes from the Brough production line and XW526, the second production S.2B, became the squadron's first Buccaneer.

The Buccaneers replaced Canberra B(I).8 aircraft which had provided the (nuclear) strike force within RAF Germany. In January 1971, after having completed its work-up at Honington, XV Squadron moved its five Buccaneer S.2B aircraft, along with a single Hunter T.7A (WV318), to RAF Laarbruch. Interestingly, XV Squadron was not fitted with the Buccaneer's distinctive nose-mounted in-flight refuelling probe. A lack of suitable air-to-air refuelling aircraft in the region, combined with the close proximity of the Inner German border, making the requirement unnecessary.

Sadly, the squadron lost its OC, Wing Commander D.A. Collins and his navigator, Flight Lieutenant P.A. Kelly, who were killed when Buccaneer S.2B XW532 crashed shortly after take-off from Laarbruch on 20 March 1971.

Despite the loss, the squadron pressed on with its re-equipment programme and throughout

ABOVE During an AAR training sortie for a 57 Squadron Victor K.2 – XL164 – on 8 August 1977, a pair of 12 Squadron Buccaneers provided the 'trade'. *(Crown Copyright/Air Historical Branch Image TN-1-7729-11)*

to 103) and finally retired the Buccaneer on 30 September 1993, re-forming the following day as a Tornado GR.1B unit.

XV Squadron

Exactly a year after the formation of 12 Squadron, XV Squadron became the RAF's second Buccaneer unit when it formed at RAF Honington on 1 October 1970. Unlike 12 Squadron a year earlier, XV Squadron

LEFT No XV Squadron formed at RAF Honington on 1 October 1970 and moved to RAF Laarbruch in early January 1971 as the first squadron to equip with the Buccaneer within RAF Germany. This image, taken during the winter of 1972/73, depicts four of their aircraft (including XW534) with the farthest pair painted in the old gloss markings and roundels, while those nearest have the toned-down matt finish low-vis markings. Later, the red 'XV' codes on the tails were painted in white. *(Crown Copyright/Air Historical Branch Image RAFG-15-010)*

RIGHT The transition from high-vis to low-vis markings is also apparent in this image from 30 May 1973, which depicts Buccaneer S.2 aircraft (including XT287 and XT270) from 237 OCU, RAF Honington. The nearest aircraft is seen in the old-style high-vis gloss paint and markings, while the remaining pair is in the new low-vis matt finish. *(Crown Copyright/Air Historical Branch Image TN-1-6779-2)*

the summer of 1971, XV Squadron continued to work-up in both the strike (nuclear) and attack (conventional) roles, while at the same time phasing out the 2in rocket projectile (RP) in September in favour of the 68mm SNEB RP. The same month also saw the squadron receive its first aircrew trained by 237 OCU at Honington.

The squadron worked up until it operated a fleet of ten Buccaneer aircraft alongside its full crew complement. The full complement of 12 aircraft was finally reached on 4 August 1972 – almost 18 months after the squadron arrived in Germany.

Finally, on 31 December 1972, XV Squadron was declared to NATO in both the strike (nuclear) and attack (conventional) roles, before it began to undertake QRA at Laarbruch. Initially, the aircraft were in 'soft' hangars but by 1976 the squadron operated from newly constructed Hardened Aircraft Shelters (HAS).

In keeping with the remainder of RAF Germany, the Buccaneer force began to tone down its aircraft markings during the winter of 1972/73 while the new-build aircraft were arriving painted in a matt camouflage finish, rather than the gloss of earlier aircraft. For XV Squadron, it also meant the toning down of aircraft code letters that had originally appeared in white near the top of the fin, which were later painted matt red.

Not being fitted with the air-to-air refuelling probe, XV Squadron's Buccaneers had operated in their overland role with the aircraft's internal and underwing tank fuel capacity (2,060 gallons) but from early 1973, this was significantly enhanced with the arrival of aircraft fitted with the ingenious bomb-door fuel tank which contained an additional 450 gallons of fuel. No XV Squadron continued to operate in its overland role, of which the strike alert was a major part.

On 1 July 1983, XV Squadron ceased

ABOVE No XV Squadron Buccaneer S.2, XT287/F, photographed at low level in the Mosel region, close to its base at RAF Laarbruch. The Buccaneers of both XV and 16 Squadrons were not fitted with the fixed in-flight refuelling probes, owing to the lack of available air-to-air refuelling tankers in the area, along with the relatively close proximity of the perceived enemy. However, by the mid-1970s all RAF Buccaneers were fitted with the bulged bomb-door fuel tank providing the RAF Germany aircraft with more than sufficient range to complete the operational profile. *(Crown Copyright/Air Historical Branch Image TN-1-9311-32)*

independent Buccaneer operations, and its Buccaneer element was absorbed by 16 Squadron. Meanwhile, No XV (Designate) Squadron began its work-up on the Tornado GR.1 which began arriving on 5 July.

237 OCU

With the RAF's training needs for the Buccaneer expanding, a full Operational Conversion Unit – No 237 OCU – was formed at RAF Honington on 1 March 1971. This formation signalled a reversal of the training roles between Royal Navy and Royal Air Force Buccaneer aircrews. On 25 February 1972, the Royal Navy's 736 NAS was disbanded, with the responsibility for

the training of Royal Navy Buccaneer aircrew being transferred to 237 OCU.

The first Buccaneer to arrive was an S.2, XT287, a former 809 NAS aircraft, which was delivered to Honington on 12 March 1971. The first long course (RAF Number 9) commenced in May 1971. For most of the 1970s 237 OCU ran a mixed fleet of 16 S.2, S.2A and S.2B aircraft. The S.2s were repainted but unmodified ex-RN aircraft which were eventually converted

to S.2B standard, along with the occasional S.2Ds. The OCU staff was a mixture of RAF and FAA aircrew in a 3:1 ratio.

The 237 OCU staff had a wartime role of providing augmentee crews for the front-line Buccaneer force, although in 1984 – with the disbandment of the RAF Germany units – the OCU was given the specific wartime tasking of laser designation for RAF Germany Tornado and Jaguar aircraft, utilising the Pave Spike equipment.

In October 1984, 237 OCU was the last Buccaneer unit to depart from Honington and move northwards to Lossiemouth where it remained until its disbandment on 1 October 1991. With the Buccaneer force still operating, the training function was continued by a dedicated flight within 208 Squadron.

16 Squadron

No 16 Squadron was also a long-term resident of RAF Laarbruch, having flown the Canberra B(I).8 on strike duties since 1958. It was selected to become RAF Germany's second Buccaneer unit, and training on the new type by No 16 (Designate) Squadron began in October 1972, with Canberra operations having ceased in June that year. The new Buccaneer unit officially took over the squadron number plate on 8 January 1973.

Having been formed later than XV Squadron, all of its new-build Buccaneer S.2B aircraft were delivered complete with the 450-gallon bomb-door fuel tank as standard. Initially delivered in gloss markings, they carried 16 Squadron's well-known crossed keys and 'Saint' markings high up on the tailfin. Even after the paintwork was toned down, the famous squadron badge continued to be carried.

Both RAF Germany Buccaneer squadrons had an identical overland primary role while both were assigned to SACEUR. Similarly to XV Squadron, 16 Squadron worked up to its NATO declaration in both attack and strike roles (with the QRA strike alert involving the holding of two armed aircraft at permanent readiness being the major commitment). This alert was shared by the two Laarbruch squadrons throughout their Buccaneer years and was only stood down after the general re-equipment of the RAF Germany strike/attack squadrons with the Tornado GR.1 aircraft.

RIGHT No 16 (Designate) Squadron began receiving new-build Buccaneer S.2B aircraft in October 1972 and officially re-formed at RAF Laarbruch on 8 January 1973, where it remained until disbanded on 29 February 1984. However, it also received a number of aircraft from 12 Squadron, including XV348 seen here, which was photographed while operating over the Rhine floodplain. *(Crown Copyright/Air Historical Branch Image TN-1-6939-29)*

As noted above, 16 Squadron absorbed the Buccaneer operations of XV Squadron when the latter transitioned on to the Tornado GR.1 on July 1983, and continued the QRA role until it too retired its Buccaneer aircraft on 29 February 1984.

The Tornado-equipped 16 Squadron, which had received its first aircraft on 13 December 1983, took over the number plate on 1 March 1984, drawing to a close 13 years of Buccaneer operations with RAF Germany.

208 Squadron

The fourth RAF squadron to be equipped with the Buccaneer was 208 Squadron, which from 1961 to 1974 had been based in the Middle East flying Hunter FGA.9 aircraft. No 208 Squadron was re-formed at RAF Honington on 1 July 1974 although initially it did not have any of its own aircraft, instead having to 'borrow' aircraft from 237 OCU. Its first aircraft (a non-Martel-equipped S.2A) arrived when XT275 was collected from the Sydenham, Belfast, yard on 6 September 1974, and was followed just a few days later by XT278, which was collected from Holme-on-Spalding-Moor.

Over the next 18 months, the squadron gradually replaced its S.2A aircraft with S.2Bs, eventually building to a full strength of 12. Initially, 208 Squadron was assigned to SACEUR, with an AFNORTH reinforcement role which would have taken the squadron to Norway in time of war.

ABOVE By the time that 16 Squadron was re-formed with the Buccaneer at RAF Laarbruch, the newly delivered aircraft were fitted with the bomb-door fuel tank as standard. In addition, the squadron was soon operating from HASs, which were coming into use at all RAF Germany airfields. The benefit of retaining the Royal Navy's wing-folding requirement is seen to good effect here. *(Crown Copyright/Air Historical Branch Image RAFG-DB-05)*

RIGHT A pair of Buccaneer S.2B aircraft (XV161 and XV354) of 208 Squadron photographed on 20 July 1975 while passing below the cliffs and alongside the Beachy Head lighthouse. *(Crown Copyright/Air Historical Branch Image TN-1-7326-17)*

With an overland role, the main weapons employed by 208 Squadron were the 1,000lb HE bomb and the BL755 Cluster bomb, although, like all RAF Buccaneer squadrons, WE177 nuclear weapons were also available in the strike role.

No 208 Squadron became the first Buccaneer squadron to deploy to Exercise Red Flag in Nevada when ten aircraft located to Nellis AFB in August 1977, these aircraft were then used by the RAF Laarbruch Wing for the second fortnight of the exercise.

On 1 July 1983, 208 Squadron moved to RAF Lossiemouth and became the second maritime strike-attack squadron, armed with Pave Spike laser designators and Paveway 1,000lb bombs and the anti-radiation (AR) Martel. The squadron was chosen to introduce the Sea Eagle anti-ship missile in 1986. Like 12 Squadron, 208 was chosen to supply both aircraft and crews for Operation Granby.

In October 1991, after the disbandment of 237 OCU, a Buccaneer Training Flight (BTF) was formed within 208 Squadron in order to meet the training requirements of the significantly reduced Buccaneer force. When 12 Squadron was disbanded in late 1992, 208 Squadron became the very last Buccaneer squadron in the RAF.

No 208 Squadron finally succumbed on 31 March 1994, with its place at Lossiemouth being taken by 617 Squadron and their Tornado GR.1B aircraft on 27 April. The 208 Squadron number plate was passed on to the Hawk advanced/weapons training unit as part of 4 FTS at RAF Valley.

BELOW No 208 Squadron Buccaneer S.2Bs lined up at RAF Honington, prior to their departure for Red Flag 1977. Some of the aircraft had a 'desert-style' sand and brown camouflage applied for the exercise. *(Crown Copyright/Air Historical Branch Image AHB-208Sqn-7708-2)*

Short-lived 216 Squadron

When the Royal Navy disbanded 809 NAS, their final Buccaneer squadron, the S.2C and S.2D aircraft all became available for conversion for the RAF. This permitted the formation of the RAF's fifth Buccaneer unit – 216 Squadron – although it was to prove a rather short-lived operation.

No 216 Squadron was probably best known as a transport squadron, having operated the Comet Mk.2 and later Mk.4, from 1959 until its disbandment in 1974. When 216 Squadron was re-formed at Honington on 1 July 1979, it was intended to be the second maritime Buccaneer unit and as such would be SACLANT-assigned. The intention was for 216 to have a maritime Pave Spike laser-designating capability, operating alongside and complementing the Martel-equipped 12 Squadron.

Following the grounding of the Buccaneer in 1980, and the subsequent aircraft-by-aircraft examination, the RAF found itself with fewer airframes than were required to effectively operate five squadrons. With 216 Squadron having not yet been declared operational, the decision was taken to lose one squadron. Having moved from Honington to Lossiemouth on 4 July 1980, the squadron's residual fleet of aircraft was absorbed into that of 12 Squadron on 4 August.

Interestingly, 216 Squadron was not officially disbanded in 1980; instead, it was reformed at Brize Norton on 1 November 1984 on the Tristar C.1 and K.1 aircraft.

Hunter trainers

There has never been a full 'twin-stick' dual control trainer version of the Buccaneer. However, the Royal Navy had cleverly pioneered the use of two-seat Hunter aircraft to fill this role. Consequently, two-seat Hunters became an essential part of Buccaneer conversion, including instrument flying and check rides. A number of RAF Hunter T.7A airframes, along with former Royal Navy T.8B aircraft, were fitted with the Buccaneer IFIS (Integrated Flight Instrumentation System) and replicated the Buccaneer's front cockpit in the Hunter's left-hand seat. Both variants had dual controls and the only major difference was that the T.7As had ILS (Instrument Landing System) fitted while the T.8B was equipped with a hook.

Initially, they were employed by the OCU at RAF Honington but all of the based squadrons were allocated hours on the type for dual instrument checks or currency flights.

Later, when the Buccaneer squadrons formed in RAF Germany, each squadron was allocated its own Hunter aircraft.

The value of these Hunter aircraft was emphasised when the Buccaneer was grounded while undergoing investigations after a fatal crash in Nevada. Without Buccaneers, all five squadrons were able to keep their pilots and navigators 'current' utilising the Hunter aircraft on strength in addition to further Hunter aircraft drafted into service. Six former 4 FTS Hunter T.7 aircraft were prepared and delivered to the Honington squadrons to supplement the two-seat Hunters already on the strength of 237 OCU. Other Hunter aircraft were 'borrowed' from the TWU at Brawdy, as well as from the RAE; and all proved invaluable during the six-month grounding period as most pilots at Honington managed seven or eight sorties per month.

Metal fatigue strikes the fleet

The stresses induced by continuous low-level operations finally took their toll on the Buccaneer aircraft far more than had originally been anticipated. The problem was violently exposed when XV345 disintegrated in mid-air when its front spar failed while participating in Exercise Red Flag at Nellis AFB, Nevada, in early 1980. The accident resulted in the grounding of all Buccaneer airframes for six months while fatigue tests were conducted by the manufacturers.

However, the Laarbruch Wing continued to mount nuclear QRA and all available aircraft would have been returned to service in the event of conflict. The eight remaining Laarbruch Buccaneers at Nellis AFB were inspected and two were found to be so damaged as to require returning to the UK by surface means. The remaining six were flown back to Laarbruch at high level, being limited to Mach 0.8, 2G and no turbulence. The formation left Nellis AFB on 19 May via Bergstrom AFB to Seymour Johnson AFB. They were led by OC XV Squadron, Wing Commander Trevor Nattrass and his navigator Flight Lieutenant Steve Parkinson in XN 983 – the aircraft with the greatest spar damage and cracks among the six. On 21 May they flew via Gander to Lajes, in the Azores, finally getting back to Laarbruch on 22 May.

According to Roy Boot:

At the time of the design of the Buccaneer basic structure in 1956, theoretical data on fatigue and fracture mechanics was, to say the very least, sparse. The aircraft specification called for a given fatigue life with flight conditions appropriate to the

ABOVE A 237 OCU Hunter T.7 XL614/O leading a pair of Pave Spike-equipped Buccaneer S.2B aircraft (XV352/FC and XZ432/HC) from the same unit, through the north-west Scottish coastline in March 1987. This image was taken during a visit by 237 OCU to the Strike Command Air-to-Air Missile Establishment at RAF Valley during their Missile Practice Camp. From 1984, 237 OCU had a wartime role as Pave Spike 'markers' for RAF Germany Jaguars and Tornados, as well as for F-16A aircraft of the (Royal Netherlands Air Force's) 311 Squadron. *(Geoff Lee/ Planefocus Image GHL8701395)*

hi-lo-hi sortie of that specification. During the design phase, stiffness rather than strength was found to be defining the scantlings – material thickness – and the application to the resulting structure of good engineering practices in relation to fatigue life was, on the evidence available, considered to produce the desired result.

An early Mk.1 development batch aircraft was allocated for fatigue testing, and this was eventually commissioned, taking advantage of loadings which had been measured in flight during the programme. Those fatigue tests continued over a number of years. They demonstrated, subject to minor repairs which had to be made from time to time, that the life of the airframe, in terms of damage rate and hours flown, was two to three times greater than the specification requirement. A good thing it was too! Experience has shown that the average damage rate per flying hour is double that deduced from the specification mission. In training units, where sorties are shorter with often more low-level flying, it is about treble. On some individual aircraft, operated without fleet management for fatigue life, the factor could be more than four. Nevertheless, based on the full-scale fatigue tests results, the life of the Buccaneer fleet appeared to be satisfactory.

It will not have escaped notice that the test airframe was an early Mk.1, whereas most of the operating was to be done with the Mk.2. At the time of the design of the Mk.2 an assessment of the structural changes was made, and the conclusion reached that the results of the tests under way would still be applicable.

In time, three things were to contradict this. First, the extended wingtip introduced during Mk.2 development had a greater effect on loading than had been anticipated. Second, there is always liable to be a corner in a complicated fitting where a stress complication sneaks in without being calculated, and which in the normal course of events never gets measured on test. Thirdly, changes in air-bleed ducting and powerplant fire zoning introduced on the Mk.2 were to have a most unexpected effect.

The first two matters mentioned were eventually discovered after the loss of two aircraft in Royal Air Force service, each of which caused major concern accompanied by flying limitations until the problem was resolved. In one case (XW526 on 12 July 1979), inspection and more frequent replacement of a pin overcame the crisis.

The second failure had more serious implications, as a main spar fitting had failed. One partial remedy was to remove the extended wingtips, and to restore the original square-cut ones, thereby reducing the loads. Detailed periodic inspection of the region of the component which had failed, and provisioning of a stock of new components for use as and when shown necessary from the inspection routines, all aircraft examined and modified found a place in returning to normal (operations). During the investigation of the failure the affected component had been inspected in situ in all aircraft, supplemented by a strip examination on a number of selected aircraft. To make absolutely sure of the long-term future, a relatively new aircraft, XN982, was removed from the fleet and positioned at Brough to become the subject of a new full-scale fatigue test. The problem with this is to run the test at a high enough rate to catch up with the fleet leaders in quick time.

Initially, it had been feared that aircraft may not be repairable – as had been the case with the earlier Valiant fatigue issues. However, this was not to be the case and a donor rework programme was initiated on the entire fleet. The least severely affected airframes were modified, often involving the cannibalisation of other airframes, and around 14 aircraft received inner wing replacements. Between 50 and 60 aircraft of the pre-crash RAF fleet of 90 were eventually returned to service, while a second batch of around 12 were placed into storage at the Maintenance Unit at RAF Shawbury as a reserve, capable of being rebuilt if necessary (or more importantly, if government funding would be forthcoming). The worst-affected airframes were placed into long-term storage or, in some cases, released for instructional use, after having been assessed as beyond economic repair.

Back into the air

The reworking of the airframes led to a reduction in available aircraft by around a third. The government made a statement on 28 July 1980 announcing the lifting of the grounding, and the rebuild programme continued while aircraft began returning to the squadrons in order that they could commence their work-up programmes in order to gain their operational capability. Priority was given to RAF Germany squadrons, as well as to 12 Squadron, as the only operational maritime squadron. However, with the recovery of more aircraft than had been feared, 208 Squadron's future with the Buccaneer was secured, although not so for 216 Squadron who were to fall victim to the fatigue problems.

A statement by the then Secretary for Defence reported that around half of the Buccaneer fleet had exhibited no signs of fatigue, or only minor cracks which had already been repaired, although admitting the RAF's Buccaneer declaration to NATO would have to be reduced. However, the somewhat fortuitous timing of the forthcoming service introduction of the Tornado IDS (GR.1) would entail a contraction of the Buccaneer force by 1983–84.

No 208 Squadron was the first to be declared operational, after a six-week work-up period. The remaining three squadrons followed shortly afterwards, although squadron strength took some time to build to the 'normal' level of 12 aircraft. Shortly afterwards, the OCU restarted its courses.

Fatigue monitoring became an ever more important task for the engineers on the Buccaneer squadrons from this moment on.

Exchange and loan service crews

Following the decision to withdraw HMS *Ark Royal* from service, the Royal Navy ceased training *ab initio* aircrew for the Buccaneer and the Phantom and relied more and more on loan-service aircrew from the RAF. By the time 809 NAS disbanded in 1978 half its aircrew were 'Crabs'. Some were quite senior flight lieutenants and displaced the more junior Royal Navy officers from the better cabins they had previously occupied on the basis of seniority. However, the Royal Navy refused to have a

squadron leader so the RAF posted Flight Lieutenant Phil Leckenby to 809 NAS and promptly promoted him! Phil ended up as 809 NAS's last Executive Officer; 809 NAS also had a US Navy Exchange crew.

For most of the Buccaneer's RAF service there was a USAF Exchange crew on 237 OCU with their RAF opposite numbers on the F-111 equivalent at Mountain Home AFB in Idaho. There was a navigator exchange between 12 Squadron and the US Navy A-6s at NAS Whidbey Island, Washington, and, right up to the end of the Buccaneer's service, a RAAF crew on the maritime squadrons with their opposite numbers on the F-111 at Amberley AFB, Queensland, Australia.

Operation Pulsator

In late 1983, following a situation in Lebanon, the British Government decided to send a force of six Buccaneer aircraft to RAF Akrotiri, Cyprus. They would provide Combat Air Support (CAS) to British Forces operating as part of the four-nation Multinational Force in Lebanon (MNF), should it be required.

A batch of 12 Lossiemouth-based Buccaneer aircraft received modifications for the operation. These included AN/ALE-40 chaff dispensers and the provision for AIM-9G or AIM-9L Sidewinder AAMs (on 11 of the aircraft). It was the first time that the Buccaneer had received a 'serious' self-defence missile capability. Previously in its Royal Navy career, the aircraft had provision for the earlier AIM-9B missile, but this had rarely been carried. Five live Sidewinder firings

ABOVE A XV Squadron Buccaneer S.2, XW546/L, photographed in the Mosel region of Germany while in close formation with an Upper Heyford-based F-111E 68-0028 from the USAF's 77th TFS, 20th TFW. This image was probably taken during a squadron exchange to Laarbruch.
(Crown Copyright/Air Historical Branch Image TN-1-9310-8)

were tested by 237 OCU in March 1987 ahead of the operation, with the trial taking place at the Strike Command Air-to-Air Missile Establishment (STCAAME) at RAF Valley.

The aircraft and crews chosen for this operation came from both 12 and 208

BUDDY-BUDDY TANKING

ABOVE During a sortie on 3 December 1992, 12 Squadron aircraft from 'Jackal Formation' were joined by another of the squadron's Buccaneer S.2B aircraft, XW530, call sign 'K2P18', in a buddy-buddy tanking fit, flown by Flying Officer Paul Binns and Flight Lieutenant Jim Maginnis. Here, 'Jackal 4', XZ431, takes on fuel in the vicinity of a number of cumulonimbus clouds that provide an interesting backdrop to the image. *(Keith Wilson)*

BELOW The view from the back seat of 'Jackal 2', XX885, as it takes on fuel at 18,000ft from buddy-buddy tanker XW530. Normally, the tanking would have been completed at low level but the weather during the sortie made it more comfortable (for the civilian passenger, at least) to conduct the refuelling at this height. *(Keith Wilson)*

Squadrons, although the crews selected were the more experienced ones who had previously flown in the overland role. The aircraft were configured with Pave Spike laser designators and Paveway 1,000lb LGBs along with ALQ-101 ECM pods. Somewhat interestingly, tactics were also developed to employ ground-based forward air controllers (FACs) to undertake the laser designation, this being considered a safer option should attacks needed to have been made on the city of Beirut.

In the end, no live attacks were made but the detachment remained in theatre until March 1984. Famously, two Buccaneers were despatched to fly at low level over Beirut in a show of strength – indicating the RAF presence, if such forces were ever required in theatre. Both aircraft were fitted with a single Sidewinder missile and an AN/ALQ-101(V)-10 ECM pod. One resulting photograph of a Buccaneer flying over the city rooftops at 100ft, with a Union Jack flying in the background, was widely published in daily newspapers across the world.

Thankfully, the Buccaneers were not called into action and all returned safely to RAF Lossiemouth in March 1984 when the MNF was withdrawn from theatre. However, the deployment to RAF Akrotiri did show the value of such deterrence, while also assisting with the morale of British troops in the region.

Terrorist attack

Two Buccaneers from 208 Squadron were at RAF Akrotiri on 2 August 1986 for a weekend Ranger from Lossiemouth when the airfield was subject to a mortar attack, the bombs missing the aircraft and dispersals (and the accommodation blocks where the crews were having a quiet beer), landing in the married quarters area. There was also a machine-gun attack on the families' beach area. Fortunately, these were in the early evening and there were no casualties.

Operation Granby

While Operation Pulsator was the nearest the RAF Buccaneer had come to a 'live' war, that was to change during the Gulf War of 1990–91. Details of the Buccaneers' considerable involvement in Operation Granby is covered in Chapter 6 on pages 93 to 103.

RIGHT During the last full year of RAF service, the Buccaneer Wing was honoured by being invited to lead the Queen's birthday flypast on 12 June 1993. They overflew Buckingham Palace in a 'diamond-sixteen' formation. *(Geoff Lee/ Planefocus Image GHL102927)*

Replaced by surplus RAFG Tornado GR.1s

By the early 1990s, the RAF was operating a significantly reduced size force of Buccaneer S.2B aircraft, all with the Lossiemouth-based Buccaneer Wing. It was clear by now that the airframes' age and fatigue life would require a major rework if suitable replacement aircraft were to be delayed for any length of time. A number of options were considered including a new-build maritime Tornado F.3 fitted with extra fuel tanks in order to provide the range required of the role. In the end, no 'new' aircraft would be required to fulfil the Buccaneer's role as the disbandment of four RAF Germany Tornado GR.1 squadrons under the Options for Change (the restructuring of British armed forces in 1990 after the end of the Cold War) provided sufficient airframes to allow the replacement of the Buccaneer fleet from 1993. These Tornado aircraft would be modified to carry the Sea Eagle and operate as the GR.1B variant.

Consequently, the Buccaneer was finally withdrawn from RAF service at Lossiemouth on 31 March 1994, 33 years after it had first touched down at the same airfield to enter service with the Royal Navy.

BELOW Farewell formation. On 22 September 1993, the UK's media were invited to a special event at RAF Lossiemouth to mark the impending retirement of the Buccaneer from RAF service. No 12 Squadron was to cease flying on 30 September, while 208 Squadron would continue until the spring of 1994. A special air-to-air photographic sortie with four Buccaneers – two each from Nos 12 (nearest the camera) and 208 Squadrons – were photographed against some of the beautiful Scottish scenery in the region. *(Keith Wilson)*

RIGHT A formation of seven Buccaneers flown especially to mark the aircraft's retirement from RAF service on 17 March 1994. The aircraft are painted to represent different squadrons of the Royal Navy and RAF. XX894 (nearest the camera) was painted in the markings of 809 NAS, to represent all the Royal Navy Buccaneer squadrons and was flown by OC 208 Squadron, Wing Commander Nigel Huckings. The aircraft are stacked in numerical squadron order – 12, XV, 16, 208, 216 and 237 OCU. *(Crown Copyright/Air Historical Branch Image DPR-771-54)*

Chapter Six

Buccaneers in the Gulf War

Despite earlier assurances that the Buccaneer would not be required in the build-up to the UK's Operation Granby in late 1990, 237 OCU accelerated its pace of overland Pave Spike training from November of that year. Once the conflict commenced and Desert Storm got under way, the Lossiemouth Wing was called upon – on 23 January 1991 – to deploy an initial batch of six Buccaneers to the Gulf. Their role was to provide laser-designation capabilities to the Tornado GR.1 force and 'to improve the standard for precision bombing'.

OPPOSITE **Buccaneer S.2 XV352/U** *Tamdhu* **of the Lossiemouth Buccaneer Wing photographed while refuelling from 55 Squadron Victor K.2 XL164. This image was taken during the latter part of Operation Granby as the normal 'defensive' AIM-9L Sidewinder missile on the port outer wing pylon has been replaced by a CPU-123 Paveway II laser-guided bomb.** *(BAE SYSTEMS)*

Over the next three days, six Buccaneer S.2Bs received Have Quick II secure radios, an improved IFF and the ARTF (Alkali Removable Temporary Finish) 'desert pink' paint applied. The first pair left RAF Lossiemouth for the transit to Muharraq, Bahrain, supported by a 216 Squadron Tristar tanker. All six aircraft – XX899/P, XX892/I, XW547/R, XW533/A, XX899/T and XW530/E – were delivered to Muharraq by the end of January.

The detachment was led by Wing Commander Bill Cope and styled itself as the 'Sky Pirates', emphasised by the code letters of the first batch of aircraft. Six further aircraft followed and, by 8 February, all 12 aircraft had names and suitable artwork applied, with all but one aircraft also receiving 'Jolly Roger' badgework to the side of the cockpit.

The detachment underwent a quick in-theatre work-up over the Saudi desert with RAF Tornado GR.1 aircraft. Their first mission was flown on 4 February and involved four Tornado and two Buccaneer aircraft, the latter pair led by Wing Commander Bill Cope, with Squadron Leader Norman Browne as 'Spike Leader' navigator in the second aircraft flown by Flight Lieutenant Glenn Mason. Their target was a bridge across the Euphrates River at As-Samawah, which was located, laser designated and destroyed by six LGBs with devastating accuracy. The second mission, once again against bridges, was equally successful, and the footage from the navigator's TV screen was shown nationwide across the USA on various evening news broadcasts. It went some way to recognising the RAF's – and the Buccaneer's – contribution to the war effort.

ABOVE Shortly after the modifications were completed, the first two aircraft left Lossiemouth for the nine-hour flight direct to Muharraq in Bahrain. The aircraft were met over the English Channel by a 216 Squadron Tristar K.1 ZD951 who escorted the pair all the way to their destination. In this desert colour scheme, the RAF Tristar fleet earned themselves the unfortunate nickname 'Pink Pigs'. (Squadron Leader Rick Phillips)

BELOW The view from the back seat of Squadron Leader Rick Phillips's Buccaneer as it takes on fuel from the Tristar while en route to Muharraq. (Squadron Leader Rick Phillips)

RIGHT After arriving in theatre, the Buccaneers underwent a short work-up period over the Saudi Arabian desert. Here, XX899/P was photographed at low level over the desert sand. *(Squadron Leader Rick Phillips)*

The Buccaneers flew with AIM-9L Sidewinder missiles on the number 3, port outer pylon. Supplies of the latest 'L' version had been flown in to Muharraq to supplement the AIM-9G version of the missile normally carried. Interestingly, flying as part of a package, against enemy radar, SAM sites and AAA batteries, a number of Buccaneer aircraft later reflected that this was the Red Flag scenario, but 'for real'!

Attacks carried on with Buccaneers continuing to spike for the Tornado GR.1s, but on 21 February, with air superiority established, agreement was given for the Buccaneers to dispense with the Sidewinder missiles and carry one or two 1,000lb Paveway II LGBs on the underwing stations – usually on the number 2 (starboard inner) and number 3 (port outer) pylons. It was the very first occasion an RAF Buccaneer had dropped a bomb in anger.

On 27 February, after two Buccaneer aircraft had successfully 'spiked' for Tornado GR.1 aircraft, the Buccaneers attacked a second target, the Iraqi airfield at Shaykh Mazhar. Each Buccaneer used its own Pave Spike to designate a target and the result was one An-12 destroyed and a captured Kuwait Air Force C-130 Hercules severely damaged.

It was the Buccaneer's final mission of the Gulf War. The 12 aircraft and 18 crews had flown 250 sorties without losing a single sortie to serviceability issues. As well as guiding 169 LGBs for Tornado GR.1 aircraft, the Buccaneers dropped 48 of their own. All this was accomplished without loss to either aircraft or crews.

The Gulf War was considerably different from many previous conflicts. In response to Iraq's invasion of Kuwait in August 1990, the United States and other countries launched military operations known as Operation Desert Shield and Operation Desert Storm, with the war being prosecuted on behalf of a 39-nation Coalition. On 25 August 1990, the United Nations passed a resolution to allow enforcement of the embargo by military means and on

ABOVE After the short work-up, the Buccaneers were soon put into action. XV352/U, named *Tamdhu*, was photographed while taxiing out ahead of a sortie. This image was taken during the earlier part of the Buccaneers' involvement as the aircraft has a defensive AIM-9L Sidewinder missile fitted to the port outer weapons pod. *(BAE SYSTEMS Image MoD G56-1)*

BELOW Early missions involved a pair of Buccaneers spiking for a group of four Tornado GR.1 aircraft. In this image, probably taken from the back seat of the second Buccaneer in the formation, Buccaneer S.2B, XW547/R, later named *The Macallan*, *Pauline* and *Guinness Girl* was photographed with four Tornado GR.1 aircraft. *(PRM Aviation)*

29 November passed a further resolution authorising the use of force from 15 January 1991. Consequently, transparency throughout the conflict was essential.

The media was provided with access to record much of the activities at the Allies' bases, while onboard weapons footage was often provided for broadcast. With the significant advances in technologies, many TV stations broadcast mission activities as they happened. It must have been akin to fighting a war in a goldfish bowl!

Why the Buccaneer was not initially deployed on Operation Granby . . . and other myths

There is a lot of controversy, at least in Buccaneer circles, as to why the RAF's only aircraft with an operational laser designation capability was not deployed at the start of Operation Desert Shield in August 1990, or once the build-up for Operation Granby had started in earnest. There can be no doubt there were those in authority – and perhaps industry – who didn't want the Tornado GR.1 to be upstaged by an ex-naval aeroplane nearing the end of its service life. However, there were also many practical reasons – although others might call them excuses.

The first was, quite simply, ramp space . . . or the lack of it. In theatre, there just wasn't enough for all the aircraft the Coalition air forces wanted to deploy; and the USAF had prior claim. Once the bed-down plan was settled, the Royal Engineers began pouring concrete in industrial quantities at the RAF bases such as Bahrain.

Back in the UK, the Buccaneer Force was part of 18 Group and now solely maritime in role. There was, however, still a cadre who were practised in overland laser designation, at low-level, in support of 2 ATAF. The Tornado was the RAF's primary bomber for attacking airfields (with JP233 which could only be dropped from 200ft, straight and level) and for Air Interdiction. The Tornado weapon system was extremely accurate, even with 'dumb' bombs, provided that the target and the radar fix points used to update the nav-attack system prior to attacking were surveyed beforehand to a high degree of accuracy. So there was no perceived requirement for the RAF to deploy a laser designation-capable aircraft.

Consequently, the build-up and the mission planning for the first 48 hours of the air campaign proceeded on this premise. Furthermore, there was a tacit agreement with the USAF that should there be a need to support the Tornado GR.1 with laser designation, then they would be able to meet it with their F-15 or F-16 aircraft.

After four nights of Coalition attacks on airfields, the Iraqi Air Force had effectively been neutralised; however, four Tornados were lost in low-level action during these attacks. As a result of these losses, it was decided to operate the Tornado GR.1 from medium altitude – around 20,000ft – where the rest of the Coalition was operating. This further enabled the Tornado GR.1s to operate within fighter cover and with US defence suppression support. However, all the US laser designation-capable aircraft potentially available to support the Tornados were now dedicated to the 'SCUD Hunt' – an unforeseen but essential task to keep Israel from intervening, and thus breaking up the Saudi-led Coalition as Saddam intended.

It had never been envisaged that, in the Central Region of NATO, the Tornado would drop unguided bombs from medium level and the ballistic data for that was not present within the aircraft's nav-attack system. The Tornados were able to attack area targets, such as oil refineries, and continued to do so, by day and night, throughout the conflict. However, the primary Coalition need was for precise attacks on specific Designated Mean Points of Impact (DMPIs) – and each target, be it an airfield, bridge or air-defence site, was considered in that way by the Coalition planners. So the RAF had to deploy a laser designation capability – and that capability could only be provided in the quantity required by the Buccaneer. Thus the statement by the Secretary of State that the Buccaneer had been deployed 'to improve the bombing accuracy' was true, but it was by no means the full story.

The other 'myth' about Buccaneer operations during Operation Granby was that once the Tornado got its own laser designation capability – with the TIALD pod – the Buccaneer was released to attack targets with its own LGBs. Only two TIALD pods were deployed, to Tabuk, where they were used for Tornado night LGB attacks. The Buccaneer continued to provide laser designation for the Tornado until the end of the conflict. However, at the start of the attacks on pontoon bridges (on 10 February 1991), it was accepted at all HQ levels that the Buccaneer could provide an additional attack capability using its own LGBs and clearance to do this was pursued as an urgent operational requirement. With its considerable endurance at high level, the Buccaneer was able to support a Tornado formation and then remain in the target area once the Tornados had departed to attack further specific DMPIs or targets of opportunity. This started on 21 February 1991 and continued until the 27th of the month.

Operating in the Gulf War

Group Captain Christopher Finn, MPhil, FRAeS, RAF (Retired) explains the role of the Buccaneer in Operation Granby:

On 26 January 1991 I was sent out to be the Buccaneer Staff Officer and UK LGB specialist in the RAF Air Headquarters (AHQ) in Riyadh, arriving just as the first Buccaneers were reaching Bahrain. While above ground in AHQ I worked for the RAF Air Commander (AVM Wratten) and was one of just two RAF Wing Commanders who were cleared to work below ground in the 'Black Hole'. Here, in the strategic targeting organisation, I worked for Brigadier General 'Buster' Glosson, USAF. Within a week, the Buccaneers and Tornado GR.1s had worked-up their tactics and had a few practice LGB drops on ranges in Saudi Arabia.

The Pave Spike pod was a late Vietnam-era piece of equipment and was designed to tie in to the F-4's IN (Inertial Navigation) system, such that the target markers on the Weapon System Officer's TV screen would be on the IN's target waypoint position. This tie-in was just one casualty of the 'austere' Buccaneer Avionics Update. So, to get the Pave Spike camera, and the navigator's eyes, on the target, the camera was manually harmonised with the pilot's bombing sight, on the runway before take-off. A pair of Buccaneers would fly in formation behind four Tornados who would

navigate to the target. The Buccaneer pilots would then acquire the target visually and put the sight onto the target, going into a dive to do so. Once the navigator called 'happy', the pilot would climb the aircraft back to the Tornado height (around 18,000–20,000ft), positioning the aircraft in a turn to keep the target in view of the pod. Once the Tornado pilot called 'store away' the Buccaneer navigator would start to 'lase' the target and maintain this for the 40 seconds' time-of-flight of the Paveway LGBs.

This was not as easy as it sounds! The TV screen was positioned between the navigator's knees, so he was head-down as the pilot pulled the aircraft around in what was sometimes a very tight turn. The pod controller was 9in to the left of, and level with, the navigator's left hip and he was using a 'thumb-ball' to keep the designator cross-hairs on the target. The

picture on the screen would be rotating as the aircraft turned and the cross-hairs rotating independently to show the amount the camera was depressed below the horizon by. Furthermore, the target was also often obscured by haze or smoke from other bombs, along with the contrast being affected by the sun. Finally, the pod had a well-known tendency to 'nod' as it approached its gimbal limits or under excessive 'G'.

While all this was going on, the pilot was giving a running commentary of time to impact, and of anything else that was going on: such as being shot at by anti-aircraft artillery or, occasionally, SAMs. The audio angle-of-attack warning would be going off as the pilot tightened the turn while the alarm tone from the Sky Guardian was going off as the aircraft was illuminated by gun- or missile-targeting radars. Finally there were the radio calls between the formations and in particular the supporting 'Wild Weasels' calling if they had launched an anti-radiation missile.

At the end of each day the video tapes of each attack designation were flown to Riyadh for immediate bomb-damage assessment. The first attack was on the As-Samawah Highway Bridge and was a complete success. I showed them to Brigadier General Glosson the next day. He was an ex-Vietnam F-4 pilot and on seeing the first clip said, 'Hell – these guys are doing this in rev (ie not inertially stabilised) mode!' I pointed out that the Buccaneer did not have an IN tie-in and

everything was 'thumb-stabilised'. He was mightily impressed and a great fan of the Buccaneer crews for the rest of the war.

The Buccaneer attacks were in three phases: firstly, against fixed major river bridges and then some pontoon ones; then against Hardened Aircraft Shelters (HAS); and lastly, against airfield surfaces and facilities, including a couple of aircraft.

On the later sorties, attacks were also carried out with the back-up LGBs carried by the designating Buccaneer. By the end of the conflict the Buccaneers had flown 148 operational sorties. The overall success rate of the 169 LGBs dropped by the Tornado and the Buccaneer was 45% of weapons carried to the release point hitting the designated target. This was due to a number of factors: technical failure, crew error and weather, but a lot were due to obscuration of the target to the second bomb in a 'stick' by smoke or dust from the first bomb. This might not seem high by today's standards, but the USAF F-111 LGB success rate was about 55%, the F-117's 75–80% and it was vastly better than the Tornado GR.1 accuracy from medium-level with unguided bombs.

A pilot's perspective of the Gulf War

Squadron Leader Rick Phillips, RAF (Retired) explains why the final operational role for the Buccaneer was somewhat unexpected and explains his own role in the conflict:

Following the unwarranted invasion of Kuwait by Saddam Hussein's forces in 1990, the hierarchy at RAF Lossiemouth decided to investigate viable options for the Buccaneer to be used in theatre, given that this was the only aeroplane in the RAF inventory at the time capable of laser-marking (spiking) targets for LGBs. The Buccaneer was, after all, a unique asset, fully capable of single-handedly destroying targets with great accuracy. A variety of sound ideas were put together by the weapons instructors across the station, and very soon we started to practise some medium-to-high-level overland LGB tactics. This was somewhat outside the normal training spectrum but, as ever, the

BELOW Tanker support was usually provided on sorties by Victor K.2 aircraft from 55 Squadron. Here, Buccaneer S.2B, XX901/N, named *Glen Elgin*, *Kathryn* and *The Flying Mermaid*, was photographed in company with Victor K.2 XL161 and an unidentified Tornado GR.1 coded 'N' from 'Snoopy Airways'. (Crown Copyright/Air Historical Branch Image GW-40)

Maritime Buccaneer Wing put its back into the challenge. The aircraft had continued to operate in a variety of overland roles, mainly at low level, and all crews took pleasure in maintaining this demanding capability.

Work got under way with a vigorous professional tempo to devise totally fresh tactics for the Buccaneer to spike and deliver precision guided weapons from a high dive profile. It was not long before a very senior officer from Command HQ visited Lossiemouth to talk to the aircrew. His message astounded us – we were to cease all such non-standard training forthwith and revert back to our standard maritime training with immediate effect. This was to include deploying imminently on pre-planned overseas detachments. This officer did, however, inform us that from a personal standpoint he fully understood, and furthermore supported, all we had done to date. He was very much in favour of sending the Buccaneer to war, but we were informed in no uncertain terms that the Buccaneer would never be going to support the British contribution in the Gulf. It had been decided that the Tornado would manage to do the task instead. All LGB planning stopped and within a couple of days 12 Squadron deployed to Gibraltar for a maritime exercise in the Mediterranean, while 208 Squadron deployed to RAF St Mawgan.

The Gulf War started soon afterwards, and I well recall watching live TV footage in a Gibraltar bar of the first low-level attacks against Iraqi airfields being made by Tornado squadrons, while enjoying a gin or two. Sadly, over this and the coming days, four Tornado aircraft were lost in action. We became rather bitter and angry that the Buccaneer had not been included in the war plan. All changed just a few days later, however, when it was decided that we were in fact needed after all, to laser-designate for the Tornado GR.1s that were now operating at medium level. Consequently, our station commander at Lossiemouth was informed that Buccaneers were to be deployed forthwith to the Gulf, and all detached squadrons were recalled immediately.

We returned to Lossiemouth and, over

ABOVE Buccaneer Wing groundcrew prepare Buccaneer S.2B, XX899/P, named *Linkwood*, *Laura* and *Laser Lips* for an early Operation Granby mission at Muharraq, which included the carriage of a single AIM-9L Sidewinder missile on the port outer pylon. *(Crown Copyright/Air Historical Branch Image GW-55-2-36)*

the next three days, some swift modifications were made, initially to six Buccaneers, which included the addition of the now-familiar desert paint scheme (ARTF – Alkali Removable Temporary Finish). Six of the most experienced crews were selected from across the Wing, given numerous briefings and what seemed like an equal number of anti-chemical and -biological injections!

And so, together with my navigator Harry, and accompanied by John and Mike on our wing, we left Lossiemouth in the dark early one morning and flew out with the paint still wet. We joined a Tristar tanker over the

BELOW Three CPU-123 Paveway II laser-guided bombs being loaded on to a Tornado GR.1 aircraft at Muharraq. The role of the Buccaneer was to designate these weapons on to their targets using the Westinghouse AVQ-23E Pave Spike laser-designator pods. *(Squadron Leader Rick Phillips)*

Channel, who refuelled us for the nine-hour flight direct to Muharraq in Bahrain. Included for personal survival, Harry and I ensured that two cases of local malt whisky were carefully stowed in the back of our aeroplane, along with our luggage. A further six aeroplanes and 14 crews joined us ten days later.

The Buccaneers were tasked to provide laser target-marking designation for the Tornado GR.1s, who had then replaced their standard iron bombs with LGBs. We could, of course, have carried our own LGBs and worked autonomously, but this was not to occur until later.

Initially, our targets were mainly bridges over the rivers Euphrates and Tigris, in order to maximise the disruption of enemy supply lines. Subsequently, we went on to bomb airfields, fuel installations and HASs. Most impressive of all were weapons storage facilities which would erupt and explode with spectacular effect once hit. In the latter days of this conflict, the Buccaneer was finally authorised to carry its own LGBs, and put its full capability to best use. Disappointingly, up to that stage, the success rate of the LGBs dropped by the Tornado force had been lower than expected, as we had recorded a number of LGBs falling short of the targets. None of these were due to any marking errors, and it seemed to me that the bombs were not always being released within the required parameters – or outside the 'basket' – as it was called. In simple terms, in order for an LGB to guide correctly and impact at the laser-marked target, it had to be released within a 45° cone rising up from the target. I was determined that any bombs dropped by myself or John, my wingman, would be guaranteed to be inside this essential basket parameter, so one evening I asked our resident staff officer weapons instructor to join us for a glass of whisky while we discussed the option of releasing our LGBs at a dive angle of around 60°. Both Harry and Mike were also very experienced weapons instructors, but we wanted to have our resident staff officer on side too as our intentions were unofficial. This had never been trialled, and so no release to service had been written or granted for this dive angle. Dropping bombs in a steeper dive would at least guarantee the basket parameter. Seeking official approval to do this would have taken months to get an answer, which would undoubtedly have been 'No'. We decided to apply the principle, as the saying goes, 'If you can't stand the answer, don't ask the question!'

We took off at first light. After some 'back-of-a-fag-packet' calculations and serious discussions aided by a few glasses of whisky, we granted ourselves a release clearance for 60° dive starting from high level. Neither I nor John ever missed the target with our LGBs. One slightly unpleasant side of this tactic was that one could see the flak coming up to meet us from the ground, and we had to dive down through it to release the bomb, and then pull out to climb back through it again on the way up! Dropping practice bombs on the range at RAF Tain once home, somehow never felt the same again after this experience.

It was with much relief that all aircraft and crews returned home to Lossiemouth at the end of the Gulf War. The Buccaneer had certainly proved beyond all doubt that it was a truly versatile multi-role aeroplane, and had made a significant contribution to the success of the war. It is essential to record here that an incredible 100% pre-sortie serviceability rate was achieved at Muharraq. Every tasked mission was launched: a direct result of a truly devoted and professional team of engineers supporting us on the ground. This applied to all those in theatre as well as behind the scenes back in the UK. The tireless hours of rectification, installing urgent operational modifications at short notice, often in the middle of the night, coupled with meticulous servicing, were directly attributable to our overall success.

Maintaining the Buccaneer fleet during the Gulf War

At the time of the first Gulf War, 208 Squadron were detached to RAF St Mawgan, while 12 Squadron were detached to Gibraltar. Peter Wright-Gardner recalls:

We all watched what was happening but had been informed that there was no requirement to send Buccaneers into theatre. Shortly afterwards, we were informed that the detachment was being cut short and that a bus was being sent to take us back to RAF Lossiemouth. However, when we arrived back at St Mawgan we were informed that a VC10 was being sent to collect us and fly us back to Lossiemouth. We realised there was an issue and knew we were being sent out to the Gulf; otherwise the bus would have

sufficed! Shortly afterwards, we were to be flown out to Bahrain in a Hercules.

After arriving back at Lossiemouth, we began preparing the jets, while gathering extra kit and getting the medical requirements sorted. The main party left Lossiemouth by Hercules on a Sunday afternoon, not really knowing what to expect. Once we arrived at Muharraq in Bahrain, a two-shift system was set up, the aim of the day shift being to support the flying programme while the night shift kept the aircraft repaired and ready for the day shift.

I was allocated to the night shift and, apart from carrying out some rectification work, my main focus was on checking that the armament system was serviceable. This took the form of connecting the Master Armament Safety Breaks (MASBs) in the wheel bay, then inserting the Weight on Ground key to override the circuit protection (to fool the aircraft into

LEFT At the conclusion of Operation Granby, all 12 of the Buccaneers that had deployed to Muharraq returned safely to Lossiemouth. Here, Squadron Leader Rick Phillips (dark glasses) and Squadron Leader Norman Browne received a welcoming committee upon their return in *Longmorn*. XX889/T was busy during the conflict, as the 14 mission symbols on the side of the aircraft can testify. *(Squadron Leader Rick Phillips)*

BELOW During the Buccaneer deployment for the First Gulf War, the main accommodation for the junior ranks was the Gulf Gate Hotel in Bahrain. With three people to a room there were facilities for obtaining food, drink and exercise; there was also an outdoor swimming pool. *(Peter Wright-Gardner)*

ABOVE Buccaneer S.2B, XV352/U named *Tamdhu*, was photographed carrying a CPU-123 Paveway II LGB under the port wing and while refuelling from 55 Squadron Victor K.2 XL164. The 'Sky Pirates' flag is prominent under the cockpit in this image. *(BAE SYSTEMS)*

LEFT All 12 Buccaneers deployed to Muharraq acquired nose artwork to some degree. All were named after malt whiskies local to Lossiemouth and all but one featured a 'Sky Pirates' skull-and-crossbones on the port side of the nose. Here, XW547/R *The Macallan*, *Pauline* and *Guinness Girl* is receiving the finishing touches to its *Pauline* artwork. *(PRM Aviation)*

BUCCANEERS DEPLOYED TO THE GULF FOR DESERT STORM

Serial	Code	Name (whisky brand)	Other names	Mission Symbols
XW533	A	*Glenfarclas*	*Miss Jolly Roger, Fiona*	11
XW530	E	*Glenmorangie*		12
XX895	G	*Glenfiddich*	*Lynn, Jaws*	5
XX892	I	*Glen Lossie*		8
XX885	L	*Famous Grouse*	*Caroline, Hello Sailor*	7*
XX901	N	*Glen Elgin*	*Kathryn, The Flying Mermaid*	9*
XX894	O	*Aberlour*		7
XX899	P	*Linkwood*	*Laura, Laser Lips*	–
XW547	R	*The Macallan*	*Pauline, Guinness Girl*	11
XV863	S	*Tamnavoulin*	*Debbie, Sea Witch*	6
XX889	T	*Longmorn*		14
XV352	U	*Tamdhu*		10

Note: * Also carries one Antonov An-12 symbol

Interestingly, the code letters of the first six aircraft arriving at Muharraq spelled 'PIRATE'. Two further aircraft – XV332 and XX893 – were prepared for deployment to the Gulf but remained at Lossiemouth.

ABOVE XX899/P, *Linkwood*, *Laura* and *Laser Lips*. *(PRM Aviation)*

ABOVE XV863/S, *Tamnavoulin*, *Debbie* and *Sea Witch*. *(PRM Aviation)*

ABOVE XX901/N, *Glen Elgin*, *Kathryn* and *The Flying Mermaid*. *(Lee Barton)*

ABOVE XW533/A, *Glenfarclas*, *Miss Jolly Roger* and *Fiona*. *(PRM Aviation)*

ABOVE XW547/R, *The Macallan*, *Pauline* and *Guinness Girl*. *(PRM Aviation)*

ABOVE XX885/L, *Famous Grouse*, *Caroline* and *Hello Sailor*. *(PRM Aviation)*

LEFT XX895/G, *Glenfiddich*, *Lynn* and *Jaws*. *(Crown Copyright/Air Historical Branch Image AHB-MIS-GranbyBuccaneer-2)*

RIGHT Buccaneer S.2B XX889/T named *Longmorn*. *(Peter Wright-Gardner)*

thinking it was flying) before selecting the correct settings on the Bomb Distributor in the rear cockpit and pressing the trigger. The test lamp was used to ensure that voltage was detected at the carts (the firing breeches, the 'holes' in the pylon where the cartridges would fire off the stores where fitted). Once all the tests had been completed, the aircraft could be handed back to the armourers to be 'bombed up' for the next sortie.

The Buccaneer had been sent to the Gulf to support the Tornado GR.1s and fill a significant gap in their capability. However, before the end of the conflict the Buccaneers even 'spiked' their own targets, claiming a couple of aircraft kills. It was somewhat ironic as the Tornado was supposed to be the Buccaneer's replacement.

In all, I spent 56 days in theatre. The only war previously in my lifetime was the Falklands Conflict, which had occurred before I had joined up; so war was never really discussed or even thought about. It came as a shock to many. The Sunday afternoon I flew out to Bahrain was something of a solemn occasion, especially when the RAF Regiment staff started carrying out respirator checks. Upon landing in Bahrain there were a number of compulsory briefings to be attended before we could go to the accommodation.

The main accommodation for the junior ranks was the Gulf Gate Hotel. With three people to a room there were facilities for obtaining food, drink and exercise. There was also an outdoor pool. Squadron Leader Tony Lunnon-Woodhead informed us in a briefing held before we departed that 'if you were going to have to go to war then Bahrain was the place to go'. Not only was the food good but there were also opportunities to get local delicacies as well as a KFC nearby. The only real difference to 'normal' work was that every so often the air raid siren would sound. When outside the camp, the air raid sirens were largely ignored. However, on camp it was a case of report to the nearest air raid shelter and don full NBC (nuclear, biological and chemical protective equipment, including respirator) and wait until the 'all clear' was sounded.

The Buccaneers arrived in theatre over the

period of 26–28 January and commenced missions on 2 February. Those missions took place daily with the last ones being on 27 February. The last missions were when the aircraft kills occurred. All Buccaneers returned to Lossiemouth on 17 March, with the groundcrew following shortly after. I flew back via Cyprus and then into RAF Lossiemouth.

From a serviceability perspective the Buccaneers performed exceptionally with only two missions being lost to technical issues. The only other reasons they failed to complete their missions were due to weather, smoke over the target area and one incident where the aircraft suffered a lightning strike.

ABOVE According to Peter Wright-Gardner, the only real difference to 'normal' work was that every so often the air raid siren would sound. Outside the camp, the air raid sirens were largely ignored. However, on camp it was a case of reporting to the nearest air raid shelter and donning full NBC gear. *(Peter Wright-Gardner)*

BELOW Shortly after returning to Lossiemouth, most of the Buccaneers had the 'desert-pink' colours removed. Instead they were painted in a low-vis all-over grey colour scheme, as seen here on 12 Squadron example XX885/L which continued to carry its Gulf War artwork as *Famous Grouse*, *Caroline* and *Hello Sailor* along with seven mission symbols. *(Crown Copyright/Air Historical Branch Image DPR-713-17)*

Chapter Seven

Flying and operating the Buccaneer

The Blackburn Buccaneer was originally designed for the Royal Navy as a carrier-borne tactical strike bomber to counter the threat of the Soviet *Sverdlov*-class cruisers. It served the Royal Navy well, initially as the Gyron Junior-powered S.1 and later as the Rolls-Royce Spey 101-powered S.2. Politics got in the way and a decision was taken to withdraw all Royal Navy aircraft carriers from service, while orders for the TSR-2 and F-111 meant the RAF needed a strike attack and maritime jet aircraft. Up stepped the Buccaneer and equipped a number of RAF squadrons, in a variety of roles.

OPPOSITE A spectacular view of a 208 Squadron Buccaneer S.2B, having just passed over the Tarbat Ness Lighthouse during the Buccaneer farewell media event at RAF Lossiemouth on 22 September 1993. Carried underneath the wings are, left to right: an AN/ALQ 101/10 pod, Carrier Bomb Light Store (CBLS), Pave Spike pod and another CBLS. *(Keith Wilson)*

105

During its time with the RAF, it was something of a 'Cinderella', but did undergo a number of (somewhat limited and cost-conscious) upgrades, now carrying a variety of new navigation equipment, weapons and defensive armaments. It finished its RAF career spiking for the Tornado GR.1 fleet during the Gulf War, before being allowed to carry and spike its own LGB weapons in theatre.

The Buccaneer was a truly versatile aircraft. The following are the weapons carried by the Buccaneer and the methods of attack used to deliver them:

Buccaneer weapons and attack modes

There were two ways of aiming at a target – either visually or by radar – and three basic modes of attack employed by the Buccaneer:

LAYDOWN was a level delivery usually at between 150 and 200ft above the target if aiming visually and 400ft if using radar.

DIVE attacks were at angles between 40°, from

RIGHT No 12 Squadron Buccaneer S.2B, XV332, on display at the Buccaneer farewell media event at RAF Lossiemouth on 22 September 1993.

1 Westinghouse AN/ALQ-101(V)-10 ECM pod
2 CBLS (Carrier Bomb Light Store)
3 Westinghouse AN/AVQ-23E Pave Spike laser-designator pod
4 CBLS
5 1,000lb (450kg) bomb (inert)
6 GBU-16 Paveway II Mk 83 1,000lb laser-guided bomb (LGB) (inert)
7 1,000lb (450kg) bomb (inert)
8 Raytheon AIM-9L Sidewinder AAR Missile
9 BAe Dynamics Sea Eagle missile (drill)
10 Anti-radiation Martel missile (inert)
11 4kg practice bombs
12 14kg practice bombs

20,000ft or so; and 5° or 8° if attacking a target from low level. All dive attacks were visual ones.

TOSS attacks involved the aircraft pulling up at 4G for either a set time (Vari-Toss) or until the Control and Release Computer released the weapon(s) (Long or Medium Toss). Timed attacks were visual ones overland and radar-based ones at sea (only with Paveway LGB). Medium Toss was the conventional (ie non-nuclear) weapon radar delivery against ships and Long Toss the nuclear one.

Attack speeds were between 500 knots (generally for training) and 550 knots (operationally). The choice of weapon and attack mode was determined by the target, its defences and the nature of the damage to be inflicted upon it.

The weapons can be broken down into the following categories:

GENERAL PURPOSE (GP) BOMBS

(predominantly a RN weapon): These were the 500/540lb and 1,000lb Medium Capacity Bombs, meaning the explosive charge and the case were about the same weight and they caused damage by both the blast of the explosive and the fragmentation of the case. They could have either ballistic tails for toss or high-angle dive attacks; or retard tails for low-level dive or laydown attacks – the retard tails prevented the bombs from exploding under the releasing aircraft. They could be fused to explode on contact or with a slight delay to allow them to penetrate the target before exploding (the usual setting), or with an extended delay, and could be used against any overland target, such as bridges or airfield targets, or against ships. Alternatively, they could be fitted with VT (radar) fuses which exploded 60ft above the target. These would be used, in Toss attacks, against ships or to suppress gun or SAM sites defending an overland target.

BL755 CLUSTER BOMB (RAF weapon

only): This had 147 bomblets with shaped charges designed to penetrate armour, but was equally effective against troops and soft-skinned vehicles. It was only used overland and delivered in visual laydown or dive attacks.

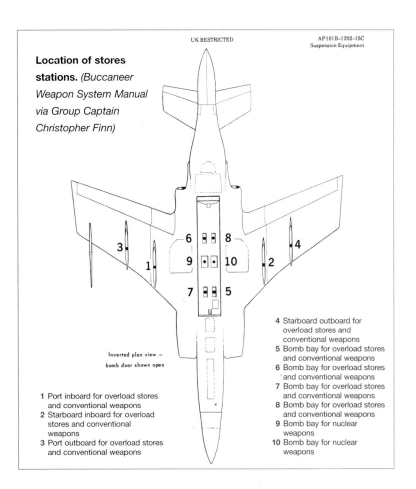

Location of stores stations. *(Buccaneer Weapon System Manual via Group Captain Christopher Finn)*

AP101B-1202-15C
Suspension Equipment

Inverted plan view – bomb door shown open

1 Port inboard for overload stores and conventional weapons
2 Starboard inboard for overload stores and conventional weapons
3 Port outboard for overload stores and conventional weapons
4 Starboard outboard for overload stores and conventional weapons
5 Bomb bay for overload stores and conventional weapons
6 Bomb bay for overload stores and conventional weapons
7 Bomb bay for overload stores and conventional weapons
8 Bomb bay for overload stores and conventional weapons
9 Bomb bay for nuclear weapons
10 Bomb bay for nuclear weapons

BELOW A posed image taken at Honington on 10 October 1972 with armourers preparing weapons for 12 Squadron Buccaneer S.2 XT288. On the left-hand trolley are four inert 1,000 lb (450kg) bombs: the furthest from the camera with a No 114 ballistic tail; the centre pair with No 952 VT (radar proximity) fuses; closest with a No 117 retard tail. On the right-hand trolley are a drill (inert) BL755 CBU (nearest the armourers) and a Drill Lepus flare. *(Crown Copyright/Air Historical Branch Image PRB-2-2576-9)*

ABOVE A 12 Squadron Buccaneer S.2, XT270, firing SNEB rockets in October 1972. *(Crown Copyright/Air Historical Branch Image TN-1-6685-1)*

ABOVE RIGHT A SNEB rocket pod being loaded on to a 12 Squadron Buccaneer S.2, XT288, at RAF Honington on 10 October 1972. *(Crown Copyright/Air Historical Branch Image PRB-2-2576-11)*

These were the only visual weapon deliveries conducted at night.

PAVEWAY LASER-GUIDED BOMB (RAF weapon only): This was a 1,000lb bomb fitted with a laser guidance kit which, unlike the GP bombs and the BL755, could not fit in the bomb bay and had to be carried on a wing station. This weapon was Vari-Tossed against ships and was used in high-angle dive attacks during the 1991 Gulf War.

BELOW Live firing on an AIM-9B Sidewinder missile from a 237 OCU Buccaneer S.2B, XZ432/HC, during a missile practice camp at RAF Valley in March 1987. *(Planefocus Image GHL871430-17a)*

LEPUS FLARE (predominantly a RN weapon): This was a 1 million candle-power parachute flare tossed over a ship target, such as a Fast Patrol Boat (FPB) or landing craft, to enable visual attacks with rockets and bombs.

ROCKET PROJECTILES (RP) (predominantly a RN weapon): The 2in and SNEB RP were aimed visually and used against small maritime and mobile overland targets, the latter in level or very shallow dive deliveries.

SIDEWINDER (AIM-9B/G/L) This could be fitted to either of the outer wing stations, but at the cost of another weapon.

ANTI-SHIPPING MISSILES The anti-radiation Martel missile was a defence suppression weapon which homed on selected Soviet ship radars; it was also a very good covert target detection system. The TV-guided version was data-linked to the firing aircraft and flown on to the target by the navigator using a joystick and the same TV screen as was used for the Pave Spike designator pod. Sea Eagle (RAF Buccaneer

ABOVE A drill TV-guided Martel missile being prepared in front of 12 Squadron Buccaneer S.2 XT288 at RAF Honington on 10 October 1972. *(Crown Copyright/Air Historical Branch Image PRB-2-2576-89)*

ABOVE A Buccaneer S.2B from 12 Squadron (XW527 – nearest the camera) and 208 Squadron – each loaded with four drill Sea Eagle missiles under the port wing. The image was taken near Helmsdale on 21 September 1993. *(Crown Copyright/Air Historical Branch Image DPR-747-22)*

only but also carried by Sea Harrier) was a long-range sea-skimming development of the Martel. All could only be carried on the wing stations.

WE177 One or two WE177 nuclear bombs could be carried in the bomb bay. It could be used in Long Toss against ship targets and in either Vari-Toss or laydown modes against land targets. Overland targets could be attacked visually by day and on radar by night and in bad weather.

Fuel and endurance

In simple terms the Buccaneer could carry about 12,000lb of fuel internally; 2,000lb in each of the two under-wing tanks; 3,500lb in the bomb-door tank; 3,400lb in the bomb bay tank; and 1,000lb in the refuelling pod. In practice this meant that an internal fuel-only aircraft could do a 1-hour sortie including 30 minutes on a bombing range. Underwing or bomb-door tank fuel extended this to 1 hour 30 minutes, and both to 2 hours. Flying some of the sortie at high level, such as a maritime attack profile, could add another 45 minutes or more. The bomb bay tank was used in the maritime role either in lieu of the underwing or bomb-door tanks; or with both in the 'maxi-tanker' fit. At high level a Buccaneer with 19,000lb of fuel, a standard transit fit, could go from Lossiemouth to Pisa, about 1,200nm, in under 3 hours and have 5,000–6,000lb of fuel remaining – depending on wind, weather and air traffic control.

Carriage stations

There were two carriage 'stations' on each wing. The inner pair could carry a mix of under-wing fuel tanks, a refuelling pod, a TV Martel data-link pod or a Pave Spike pod and any conventional weapon. The outer pair could carry any conventional weapon, the AIM-9 Sidewinder and the AN/ALQ 101-10 jamming pod. Any of the inner or outer stations could also carry two 500/540lb bombs or Lepus Flares on a Tandem Beam, a heavy and high-drag twin-store carrier. As part of the ASR 1012 upgrade programme, the AN/ALE-40 chaff dispensers were moved from under the jet-pipes to the inner face of both outboard pylons. The chaff dispensers remained on the underside

BELOW Although the Buccaneer had a conventional role, it also provided a considerable nuclear strike capability with which it would fly with up to two WE177A nuclear weapons. A drill (training) WE177A (of 600lb/272kg) is shown here. *(Crown Copyright/Air Historical Branch Image SLIDE-NUCLEAR-WE177-4)*

RIGHT Westinghouse AN/ALQ-101(V)-10 ECM pod fitted to a 16 Squadron Buccaneer at RAF Laarbruch. This was normally carried on the outboard pylon and provided protection across a wide band of frequencies. *(Crown Copyright/Air Historical Branch Image RAFG-DC-05)*

ABOVE The Westinghouse AVQ-23E Pave Spike laser-designation pod fitted under the port wing of Buccaneer S.2B, XW544, at Bruntingthorpe. *(Keith Wilson)*

RIGHT A chaff/flare dispenser carried aboard Buccaneer S.2B, XX894, at Bruntingthorpe. *(Keith Wilson)*

between the hook and airbrake, where the 'holdback fairing' used to be.

The bomb bay could carry up to four GP bombs or BL755s; one or two WE177s; or a fuel tank. It could also carry a photo-reconnaissance pod (occasionally used by the RN) or a baggage pod.

Port-side pilot's cockpit layout in Buccaneer S.2B, XW544, at Bruntingthorpe. *(Keith Wilson)*

1 Emergency braking system pressure gauge.
2 Tail plane blowing system pressure gauge.
3 Wheel brakes triple pressure gauge.
4 Cockpit lighting control panel incorporating
  Cockpit floodlighting selector switch
  Cockpit floodlighting port dimmer switch
  Cockpit floodlighting starboard dimmer switch
  IFIS (Integrated Flight Instrument System) lighting selector switch
  IFIS (Integrated Flight Instrument System) lighting dimmer switch
  Instrument panel lighting selector switch
  Instrument panel lighting dimmer switch
5 Telebrief indicator lamp
6 CASS (Central Audio Selection System) station box
7 UHF switch panel, incorporating Press-to-transmit emergency switch
  UHF homer switch
  UHF aerial switch
  Standby UHF selector switch
  UHF muting switch
8 Rudder and aileron trim control
9 TACAN (tactical air navigation) aerial selector switch
10 Sidewinder coolant selector switch
11 Standby tailplane trim switch
12 Radio altimeter control unit
13 Stores jettison selector switch
14 MRG (Master Reference Gyro) alignment and display unit
15 Attack selector switch

Pilot's cockpit, forward view of Buccaneer S.2B, XW544, at Bruntingthorpe. *(Keith Wilson)*

1 Deck landing airspeed indicator
2 Strike sight display unit
3 Pave Spike line of sight indicator
4 Radar altimeter
5 Normal accelerometer
6 Angle of attack indicator
7 Pave Spike range display unit
8 Wing blowing system pressure gauge port
9 Wing blowing system pressure gauge starboard
10 Blowing system indicators (port and starboard)
11 Tailplane flap position indicator
11a Flap aileron droop position indicator
12 Airspeed indicator and Mach meter
13 Standby artificial horizon
14 Standby airspeed indicator

15 Standby altimeter
16 V/UHF take command switch
17 Compass card locking switch
18 Altimeter
19 High-pressure shaft speed indicator port
20 High-pressure shaft speed indicator starboard
21 Autostabiliser selector panel, incorporating Autostabiliser channel selector
22 Switches (yaw, roll and pitch) Yaw damper selector switch
23 Oxygen flow indicators (pilot and navigator)
24 Vertical speed indicator
25 Attitude and slip indicator
26 Navigation display

27 Turbine gas temperature indicator port
28 Turbine gas temperature indicator starboard
29 Mainplane flaps selector control and aileron droop selector control
30 Control stick with weapons release trigger safety catch
31 Low-pressure shaft speed indicators port
32 Low-pressure shaft speed indicator starboard
33 Landing gear position indicators
34 Tailplane trim switch
35 Engine oil pressure indicators (port and starboard)
36 Windscreen emergency demisting control
37 Cabin altimeter

38 Tailplane position indicator
39 Rudder pedal and wheel brakes foot selector (port)
40 Rudder pedal and wheel brakes foot selector (starboard)
41 Fuel/no-air valve override switches (port and starboard)
42 Autopilot engage push-button
43 Bomb-door position indicator
44 Aileron trim indicator
45 Rudder trim indicator
46 Throttle lever damping control
47 Emergency wheel braking and parking handle
48 Combined throttle and HP fuel cock controls port
49 Combined throttle and HP fuel cock controls starboard

Pilot's cockpit, starboard side lower of Buccaneer S.2B, XW544, at Bruntingthorpe.
(Keith Wilson)

1 Autostabiliser selector panel, incorporating Autostabiliser channel selector
2 Switches – yaw, roll and pitch
   Yaw damper selector switch
3 Flying controls hydraulic integration valves and switches (port and starboard)
4 Bomb-door standby selector switch
5 Arrester hook standby selector switch
6 Landing gear emergency override switch
7 Mainplane flaps standby selector switch
8 Tailplane flap standby selector switch
9 Aileron droop standby selector switch
10 Blowing system switch
11 Fuel/no-air valve override switch port and starboard
12 Fuselage fuel tanks contents indicators
13 Fuel proportioner failure indicator (port)

14 Fuel proportioner failure indicator (starboard)
15 Fuel contents indicator supply changeover switch
16 Recuperator check push-button

17 Fuselage inter-tank transfer switch
18 Cross-feed fuel cock indicator
19 Cross-feed fuel cock selector switch

20 Fuel pump inlet pressure indicator (port)
21 Fuel pump inlet pressure indicator (starboard)
22 Fuel tanks pressure indicator

23 Flight refuelling intake selector switch
24 Main tank fuel jettison control

Navigator's cockpit, starboard lower of Buccaneer S.2B, XX894, at Bruntingthorpe.
(Keith Wilson)

1 Weapons system recorder controller
2 Multiple stores indicator lamps
3 AN/ALE-40 chaff and flare dispense button
4 Indicator bearing (radar warning receiver)
5 Control receiver (radar warning receiver)
6 Inertial navigation control and display unit
7 Canopy emergency unlock lever (red)

Pilot's cockpit, starboard side of Buccaneer S.2B, XX894, at Bruntingthorpe.

(Keith Wilson)

1 Windscreen emergency demisting control
2 Flying controls hydraulic systems pressure gauges (port)
3 Flying controls hydraulic systems pressure gauges (starboard)
4 DC supply test switch
5 AC supply bus-tie contractor position indicator
6 Windscreen heating switch
7 Ice detector control switch
8 Engine anti-icing valves selector switches (port and starboard)
9 Emergency wheel braking and parking handle
10 Hydraulic pump failure indicator (port)
11 General services hydraulic system indicator
12 Hydraulic pump failure indicator (starboard)
13 Main tank fuel jettison control
14 Standby warning panel, incorporating
   Aircraft power supply test push-button
   Muting push-button
   Cancel push-button
   External power supply test push-button
   Fire extinguisher push-

button – port engine
   Fire extinguisher push-button – starboard engine
   Servicing warning lamps
15 Bomb door tank fire extinguisher push-button
16 NBC role selector

17 NBC fan switch
18 Aileron gear change selector
19 ILS localiser/glide path receiver
20 V/UHF radio control unit
21 Downward identification lamp switch

22 Formation lamp switch
23 Upper strobe light selector switch
24 Lower strobe light selector switch
25 Navigation lamps dimmer switch

26 Navigation lamps selector switch
27 Oxygen regulator Mk.17F
28 Wings folding selector control lever
29 ILS marker

Navigator's cockpit, lower starboard side of Buccaneer S.2B, XX894, at Bruntingthorpe. *(Keith Wilson)*

1 TACAN offset computer
2 IFF/SSR control unit
3 Pressure error correction switch
4 Telebrief indicator light
5 RP station selector switch
6 Radio and communications selector box (CASS)
7 Cockpit lighting control panel, incorporating
   Cockpit floodlighting selector switch
   Cockpit floodlighting dimmer switch
   Radio, radar control and instrument panel lighting selector switches:
   ON/OFF
   NIGHT/OFF/DAY
   Lighting dimmer switch
   IFIS lighting selector switch
   IFIS lighting dimmer switch
8 Radar set control
9 HF radio control unit
10 Pre-release timer
11 Pivoted arm rest
12 Oxygen regulator (under arm rest)
13 Anti-G test switch

Navigator's cockpit, forward and port side of Buccaneer S.2B, XX894, at Bruntingthorpe. *(Keith Wilson)*

1 Sidewinder missile station and armed-unarmed selector switch
2 Latitude resolver unit
3 Bomb fuzing switch
4 Weapons system recorder auto/fast switch
5 V/UHF control box
6 Bomb bay/bomb-door fuel tank contents gauge selector switch
7 Bomb bay door tank fuel transfer switch
8 Bomb bay door tank fuel transfer switch
9 Azimuth range indicator (Blue Parrot Radar)
10 Radar altimeter limit lights
11 Stopwatch and clock
12 Control Indicator (weapon-aiming and radar offsets – pre-Avionic Update)
13 Fold-down chartboard
14 Indicator bearing (radar warning receiver)
15 Bomb distributor
16 Miscellaneous temperatures selector switch and gauge assembly
17 Wing fuel tanks contents gauge (port)
18 Overload fuel tanks fuel transfer switches
19 Wing fuel tanks contents gauge (starboard)
20 Radio bay cooling override switch
21 Reconnaissance flare height setting control panel
22 Press to transmit switch (mute switch on opposite side)
23 Air-to-air refuelling tanker role panel
24 Navigation display repeater
25 Combined speed indicator (IAS and TAS)
26 ECM control indicator (AN/ALQ 101-10 pod)
27 Vertical speed indicator
28 Altimeter

A pilot's view

Squadron Leader Rick Phillips
RAF (Retired)

My first sighting of a Buccaneer was as a schoolboy from a classroom window in 1961. It flew along the valley in bright sunshine, and made a lasting impression upon me. At the time I was fascinated by all aeroplanes, yet this machine was clearly something quite different. The overall colour scheme was white, and the image passed all too swiftly for me to fully take in the unique shape, but I was distinctly impressed with the purposeful progress along the Spey Valley. I scribbled a few notes, but the rest of the lesson was totally lost to me as I dwelt on what I had seen. I was determined

to find out more about this aeroplane, and described it in as much detail as I was able to a friend who always shared his *Flying Review* magazine with me, in exchange for my *Airfix* magazines. We built model aeroplanes in our free time and resolved to attempt a visit to Lossiemouth, in those days HMS *Fulmar*.

Years later I became fully aware that what I had witnessed was, in fact, a Buccaneer S.1, the direct descendant of the NA.39, and flown from nearby Holme-on-Spalding-Moor. Furthermore, that first Buccaneer I saw was most likely from 700Z Flight at Lossiemouth, and possibly flown by one Ted Anson, a most respected officer in the Fleet Air Arm, under whom I was later to serve when he was Captain of HMS *Ark Royal*.

It was a further 13 years before I was eventually to start my long association with this magnificent aeroplane. I had impatiently completed my schooldays, been accepted into the Royal Air Force as a pilot and completed the fast jet flying training process on the Chipmunk, Jet Provost T.3 and T.4, culminating in the diminutive but totally delightful Folland Gnat. As ever, there was a 'holding period' prior to going to an Operational Conversion Unit (OCU), but I was fortunate to spend that year flying the Vampire, Chipmunk, Meteor, Jet Provost and Beaver.

Following my training there were no postings to the Buccaneer, so I was to fly the Canberra. Having an ulterior motive, I managed to persuade the posting department to appoint me to No 360 (RN/RAF) Squadron. That was a brilliant tour, and I made best use of this 'stepping stone' to secure my main aim: a posting to the Buccaneer. By good fortune, mid-tour, the squadron commander changed to a naval officer from the Fleet Air Arm, who had been heavily involved in bringing the Buccaneer into naval service. I spent many an hour listening to our new Commanding Officer, as well as to other naval aircrew who had flown the Buccaneer, all of whom spoke with great passion and admiration about this aeroplane. I soon had a posting to the Buccaneer OCU at Honington, preceded by the full long course on the Hunter at Chivenor. The Hunter featured prominently in the Buccaneer world as a number of T.7 and T.8 aircraft were converted to carry the Buccaneer cockpit instrumentation.

First Buccaneer flight

I can clearly recall my first flight in a Buccaneer. It was the only flight I ever flew with another Buccaneer pilot in the back seat and I was most fortunate to be allocated a laid-back true gentleman of an instructor for this sortie, who could not have been bettered for the task. I use the word 'instructor' in title only as, on this occasion no instruction as such was given. There was just the occasional word of advice while Bob fiddled with the radar, a strictly 'back-seat' piece of equipment essential to the role of the aircraft. The first sortie for any new Buccaneer pilot followed a rigorous ground school and associated systems exams,

interspersed with numerous sorties in the flight simulator with one's navigator, or observer in naval parlance. Crew cooperation was key to the successful operation of the aeroplane and many crews remained together as a pair, sometimes for more than two tours on type. The simulator sorties were not what one would call enjoyable as much of the time was spent dealing with multiple emergencies, repeated until one was deemed sufficiently safe to fly the real thing. I was to spend a memorable 1 hour and 10 minutes flying my 'Familiarisation One' sortie from Honington, during which I carefully explored the unique flying qualities of this aeroplane. For me, the most striking aspect of this sortie was the smoothness and comforting solidity exuded by the Buccaneer – an enduring feature that we all came to respect and appreciate. In short, it was a delight to fly, particularly in its element at low level and high speed where it had simply brilliant flying qualities. Later, I described flying a Buccaneer as being akin to riding a ball bearing across a sheet of glass.

Low-speed handling

After some manoeuvring at medium and low level, it was time to experience the lower speed range. Once below 300 knots Buccaneer handling qualities became quite different. Utmost concentration and accuracy of flying was needed, or else the aeroplane would bite back in a most unforgiving manner. As per the briefing, Bob calmly talked me through all the normal flap and droop configurations one would subsequently become so familiar with. These are still firmly engrained in the mind: 15/10/10, 30/20/20, 45/25/25 and, lastly, 45/10/10, the latter being the 'unblown' approach configuration. To the layman this may all sound rather complex but, although unique to the Buccaneer, these flap, aileron and tailplane settings soon became very familiar.

The essential requirement, apart from ensuring one had the correct 'blow' pressures, was to ensure that the tailplane flap moved upwards at precisely the same rate as the ailerons drooped downwards. This was very closely monitored by way of small but highly visible gauges called 'cheeses', prominently displayed on the top left of the pilot's instrument panel. Any disparity observed had to be instantly acted upon by 'freezing' the tailplane flaps and aileron droop by way of a pair of standby spring-loaded switches on the starboard cockpit wall on the coaming. In addition to all of these settings, one also extended the most effective airbrakes at the tail of the aeroplane by way of a rocker switch on the inboard throttle lever, thereby permitting a higher power setting to provide the blow pressure while keeping the speed stable. All of this was to provide the aeroplane with an acceptably reduced landing speed to enable carrier landings to be made at a basic datum speed of 127 knots, adjusted for weight. It also meant that the engines were 'spooled up' on the approach and the 4,000lb psi hydraulic pressure meant that they could be closed fully in under 2 seconds, thus enabling the aircraft to overshoot safely even if on just one engine. This entire procedure was backed up further by an airflow direction detector (ADD) which was audible to both crew members.

On this first sortie, one only briefly covered flying in each configuration before returning to do four circuits back at Honington, three of them 'rollers' and finally a 'full stop' landing in the normal configuration. This was a lot to pack into a first trip, but what a satisfying experience it was. Thereafter, I only flew with an observer, a navigator, or, after a year in my first tour, occasional passengers, senior officers, groundcrew, press or aircrew from other types.

The Buccaneer was the perfect aeroplane to really impress anybody who had the privilege to fly in one. It would fly extremely well at 50ft

and 580 knots indicated, and passengers loved to experience this. (A clean aeroplane would easily exceed the speed limit, and continue to accelerate beyond 600 knots, but one was aware that directional control was on a knife edge at such speed.) Equally impressive was the effectiveness of the airbrakes – fully extended at the 580-knot limiting speed, with the throttles brought to idle, the deceleration was such that one was thrown forward with some force against the shoulder restraint harness, while the airspeed indicator unwound at an astonishing rate. On landing, the wheel brakes were equally impressive, as one could literally stand as hard as possible on them and come to a halt in a remarkably short distance. Years later I practised stopping in 1,200ft after landing, when asked to deliver a Buccaneer into Brough, where it was designed and built, but never flown. The runway was a mere 3,445ft long with a two-storey building across the far end!

First Buccaneer posting to XV Squadron

On completion of the OCU, my navigator and I were posted to join our front-line squadron – No XV Squadron – stationed at RAF Laarbruch in Germany. We flew together as a crew almost exclusively for three years. It is hard to describe here what a privilege it was to be crewed up with just a handful of totally dedicated, professional and perhaps I should add brave, back-seaters over all the years I flew the Buccaneer. Once one is well worked-up as a crew, remarkably little needed to be said between the seats – one had complete trust and faith in the other crew member doing his duty correctly and safely, as this was essential to effective operational flying.

First QRA

Having arrived on XV Squadron, Dick [navigator] and I were delighted at the pace with which we were programmed to fly in order to become fully strike combat-ready. There was a set series of sorties to be flown, all low-level, and including much weaponry practice on the bombing ranges. We flew twice per day and managed to achieve our bombing scores within the prescribed standard required. This we did in just over one month, and as a new crew, we felt really proud of ourselves in qualifying so swiftly.

BELOW Rick Phillips's first posting on to the Buccaneer was with XV Squadron at RAF Laarbruch. Here is XX891/E at Laarbruch in 1975. *(Squadron Leader Rick Phillips)*

Then we realised why: we were the junior crew on the squadron, and it was fast approaching the time of the summer ball in the officers' mess. None of the other crews wished to miss this lively and highly popular event, yet there still remained the requirement to stand duty in the Quick Reaction Alert (QRA) 'cage', where a number of crews were on permanent standby to scramble, armed with WE177 nuclear bombs. We stood this duty without fuss, the first of many such 24-hour periods, and thankfully were never called upon to scramble for real. Life in the cage could be tiresome and often frustrating, especially when the weather was fine for low-level flying.

Throughout this most enjoyable tour we became more operationally proficient as time went on. We all flew regularly, often exceeding our target minimum of 30 hours per month. If we flew just 20 hours, we were considered to be current, but not necessarily operational.

Therefore we all kept up a keen flying rate which was a pleasure, given an aeroplane that was such a joy to operate. In time we became formation leaders, initially as pairs lead, then fours. Most daily sorties were flown as four-aircraft formations, nearly all at low level, with lots of practice bombing on the ranges. The whole of West Germany and much of the rest of Europe was our low-level operating area, and we became very familiar with its landmarks and cities.

All too soon my Germany tour came to an end and I was so delighted to finally secure a posting to 809 Naval Air Squadron, just in time to join HMS *Ark Royal* for her final commission. This was the realisation of a lifelong wish, not only to fly from an aircraft carrier, but to fly the Buccaneer in the environment and roles for which it was specifically designed.

Getting my feet wet

I volunteered for secondment at the earliest opportunity, and soon had a posting back to the Buccaneer Operational Conversion Unit, No 237 OCU, to complete No 14 Pre-Carrier course at RAF Honington. After the obligatory check with a QFI in the Hunter T.8 (flying the Hunter was always a delight, even with an instructor!) the Pre-Carrier course consisted of 15 sorties, all of which were completed in three weeks.

Carrier flight deck operations were briefed

from the blackboard by the squadron QFI, followed by dummy deck landings practised on the airfield runway, where an area was painted to one side to resemble the carrier deck. These were known as Mirror-Assisted Dummy Deck Landings, or MADDL. A projector landing sight provided further realism, although this did not match the 4° approach slope required to be flown to the ship – this was 1° steeper than the normal runway approach. The 4° flight path at sea was to facilitate for the fact that the carrier was always under way during launch and recovery operations at speeds of up to 29 knots, consuming furnace fuel oil (FFO) at an alarming rate of 3ft per gallon. On board, the Landing Safety Officer (LSO) gave firm, clear landing directions to pilots, his instructions being obligatory. Although I had seen and indeed flown past aircraft carriers on many occasions, it was only now that I came to realise the full challenge of actually landing on one.

ABOVE An 809 NAS Buccaneer S.2, coded '026' (thought to be XN981), on the catapult and preparing for a launch aboard HMS *Ark Royal* in 1977. The Wessex on 'plane guard' duties is just visible in the background. *(Squadron Leader Rick Phillips)*

BELOW Buccaneers line up with the Sea King helicopters aboard HMS *Ark Royal*, just ahead of a harbour visit in November 1977. *(Squadron Leader Rick Phillips)*

Landing on a carrier

Initial approaches to the deck were carried out in the English Channel where the carrier (or 'Mother' as she was referred to over the r/t) was doing her pre-deployment work-up training. The pattern or circuit flown on arrival at the ship commenced with the 'slot'. Particular pride in one's airmanship as part of a crew started here, on the starboard side of the ship, abeam the island superstructure. The 'slot' was observed by those in Flyco on board, and was required to be achieved precisely 90 seconds prior to the 'Charlie' time of hook-on. One arrived here punctually, with hook down at circuit height of 800ft and 250 knots parallel with the ship's heading or the designated flying course (DFC) if she was still turning into wind. Once assured of correct spacing from any others in the circuit, one flew across the bow to track downwind where pre-land-on checks were completed, until abeam the stern.

From this point one flew with great accuracy, maintaining a precise angle of attack (AoA). The Buccaneer was fitted with a detector which displayed the actual AoA on a gauge, together with a precision deck landing airspeed indicator (ASI) on the front cockpit coaming, both being clearly visible to the observer in the rear seat. Additionally, the AoA sensor provided an audio tone, which the crew could hear. The aim was for the pilot to maintain the 'steady note' in the earphones, which permitted maximum concentration outside the cockpit waiting to pick up the landing sight or 'meatball'. So long as the steady note was maintained by power and pitch, then the correct 'datum' speed for the approach

was being flown. The observer remained very quiet at this stage, not from fear as I first thought, but to ensure he did not talk over the all-important information coming over the radio from the LSO. One hoped for the calm voice direction of 'steady' and 'roger', which meant that the LSO was happy with one's progress, and the correct flight path was being flown by reference to the sight and one was 'on the meatball' as it was called. Other commands might be 'slightly high', or if low, 'a little power'. On the rare occasion the LSO was not happy with the approach, his voice would become slightly raised, and finally, if the approach was a disaster, then he would issue the command of 'wave off', at which point one selected full power, airbrakes in and climbed away back into the pattern. Once close in on a good approach, the LSO would remain silent, or say 'hold that' if the deck was pitching, following which one arrived on deck, hopefully engaging the No 3 arrester wire, the target wire of four normally rigged.

For the first visit to the deck, all new pilots would make up to six passes, during which time the hook would remain up and the LSO would provide a short debrief of each approach to the crew while downwind after each roller landing. On such passes, full power was applied and simultaneously airbrakes selected 'in' as soon as one clattered on to the deck. The aircraft was literally flown into the deck with no 'cushioning', which for the Buccaneer was the normal way of landing ashore as well – so not a new technique as such. Eventually, once the ship was ready to accept aircraft on board, and those in command in Flyco (Commander Air or 'Wings' as he was called and his deputy, Lieutenant Commander Flying or 'Little F') were all happy, an r/t call of 'hook down' would be made. At this point, the pressure was really on, as one was then expected to 'trap' next pass. Failure to do so would mean a 'bolter', and being sent ashore to wait another day – not an option to be considered, as we were all keen to embark.

Arrested

As soon as one had arrested and come to a halt, the hook was immediately selected up, followed by folding the wings and applying power to taxi out of the wires. In the Buccaneer, the airbrakes remained fully extended, as this shortened the length of the aircraft, thus enabling very tight parking. This was an expeditious affair, as eventually when we were fully worked-up, the aim would be to land all aircraft on board at 35-second intervals maximum, and 'zip-lip' (ie with no r/t at all). The flight deck crew would direct you to the bow of the ship to a parking area known as 'Fly 1' or the 'graveyard'. This was to starboard and outside the wingtip safety line to permit the next a/c landing on to do a bolter in safety. Wingtip safety lines were a mere 6ft from other obstructions, people or aircraft – a real eye-opener to us RAF aircrew used to vast safety distances ashore by comparison!

My initial shock, when vacating the cockpit after my first landing, was the strength of the wind, despite having been warned, as the ship was doing the best part of 30 knots into wind. This brought home to me that the flight deck was a place to be treated with the utmost care and respect. Following a debrief and the customary mug of coffee in the aircrew buffet (ACRB), we were sitting in the briefing room to have a refresher brief from the Senior Pilot on launch procedures. This had, of course, been covered and examined ashore in depth, but after the excitement of one's first 'trap', there was no time to relax. As soon as the engineers had turned the aircraft around, the ship repositioned and switched from recovery to launch mode. Back on the flight deck, this time aware of the wind over the deck, we walked to our aircraft, by now repositioned at the stern of the ship in 'Fly 3', on the starboard side opposite the Phantoms of 892 NAS.

First carrier launch

Here was another difference – the usual pilot's walk-round checks of the aircraft were somewhat shorter than ashore, as the wings remained folded and the rear fuselage aft of the main wheels was over the side of the ship above the sea some 50ft below! A 'pipe' (broadcast) was made by 'Little F' warning the ship's company to 'stand clear of intakes, propellers and exhausts', and we started engines. With checks complete, one was then marshalled up the flight deck towards the 'Y director', who then allocated you either to the bow or waist catapult (cat). These differed

insofar as the bow was about two-thirds the length of the waist cat, and consequently was even more exciting for the launch. The end speed required was the same off either cat, so the acceleration off the bow was much greater. One was marshalled with great accuracy on to the cat track, initially with quite a jolt, as the nose wheel rolled over the shuttle, around which the launch towing bridle would be placed. One then ran up firm against the hydraulic-operated roller chocks in the deck, which precisely aligned the aircraft. These were spaced for each aircraft type operated by the ship. The parking brake was *never* applied on the cat, for obvious reasons.

At this stage the Flight Deck Officer directed wings to be spread, the seawater-cooled jet blast deflectors would be raised behind the jet and other checks completed. Once the flight deck crew (or 'badgers' as they were called owing to their black and white jackets) were happy with the aircraft configuration, a hold-back link at the rear of the fuselage was secured to the deck and the launch strop was attached round the shuttle and on to the take-off hooks, one either side of the aircraft. The whole aircraft was then tensioned back on to its tail skid by the catapult strop, raising the nose wheel well off the deck, thus placing the aircraft in a correct flying attitude, and the tailplane trim angle was checked by the FDO. Only then, the FDO would raise his green flag to indicate a wind-up signal to the pilot to advance throttles to full power. The crew then completed all pre-launch checks, and once happy, the pilot placed his right hand clearly in the starboard quarter light, indicating ready for launch. No pilot will ever forget his first launch – no briefing quite prepares you for the acceleration experienced.

In the Buccaneer, we made the launch 'hands-off' (ie the stick was not held at all), with the pilot placing his right hand on his knee, and the left hand firmly locked behind the throttles held at full power. With a final check, the FDO looked all round, checked green 'traffic lights' on Flyco and the cat team and smartly lowered his green flag to the deck, the signal for the catapult officer to fire the cat.

At once the aircraft hurtled down the track, achieving an airspeed of 135 knots in about 2 seconds. At first this adrenaline-filled experience seemed barely survivable, but as soon as the wheels left the deck the apparent massive deceleration signalled the time for the control column to be taken by the right hand and the aircraft cleaned up swiftly for normal flight.

Most sorties flown from the deck involved some formation flying, usually as a pair or four aircraft, often in association with the rest of the air group, with the Phantoms providing either escort or opposition, and the AEW Gannet giving fighter and strike direction. Maritime tactics profiles against ship targets were the order of the day, either against or in support of our own surface group, or often by finding targets of opportunity. A coordinated attack profile for either simulated TV Martel or conventional bombs would be flown, and if against our own ships, the obligatory 'flypast' would follow.

Royal Navy rules permitted us to fly our standard formation attack profiles at not below 50ft over the sea by day, which was quite demanding, particularly when also having to keep a sharp lookout astern for any opposition. It was, however, normal to climb to 100ft for hard turns. There was rarely a sortie flown that did not involve air-to-air refuelling, either from one of our own Buccaneers fitted out as a tanker, or any other available tanker fitted with a hose and drogue. Tanking would become an essential requirement for operating in hot climates with heavy weapons, when topping up to full post-launch weight was the norm. Later in the commission, when we had qualified for non-diversion flying, tanking was a skill that had to be second to none, as occasionally occurred when there was a problem on deck prior to recovery. On rare events such as this, the 'alert tanker' – a Buccaneer – would be launched to keep the air group aloft in the wait, pending the clearance of the emergency on deck.

Splash target

Finally, at the end of most sorties, the formation would 'attack' the carrier, followed by the firing of 2in rockets (RP) or practice bombs on to the splash target. This target was a device made by the ship's carpenters, similar to a pallet on a wire towed behind the ship. Metal scoops fitted to the rear of the target forced plumes of water up into the air, thus enabling the splash

to be more visible from some distance out. The carrier had a couple of army officers on board whose primary role was to provide forward air control (FAC) ashore, as well as ground liaison for ground attack operations. At sea, they would man the gun direction platform (GDP) up on the superstructure, and provide scores for the weaponry dropped or fired at the splash target. The splash would regularly be 'shot off', particularly by the 2in rockets, as these were very accurate, as well as being great fun to fire. After losing the splash, we would then be cleared to bomb in the wake of the ship, which on occasion became quite close to the stern, causing some anxiety among the non-air group members of the ship's company!

Night flying

Having become adequately accomplished at day flying from the ship, later in the commission I was somewhat shocked to be selected by the Senior Pilot to become night deck qualified. I had hoped that my lack of experience would naturally bar me from such demanding duties, but with 1,000 hours of Buccaneer flying under my belt, I was considered a suitable candidate to bolster the small, select and quite senior team who regularly flew at night. Up to this point, I had considered all the flying to have been great fun – night flying was never fun in my opinion! Again, there was no QFI to take you through this evolution, and as we always flew as set crews, my trusty observer, Ken, had to bravely endure this alarming training with me.

The first few launches and recoveries were called 'duskers', and these were flown as the sun was setting – quite tricky light conditions in any event, but thought to be a gentle lead in to the eventual full black of the real night. The night launch was even more exhilarating, and as one came off the end of the cat, the radar altimeter warning light was instantly in the red at its setting of 50ft, with no visible horizon, so quite an uncomfortable scenario. The night sorties themselves followed the same profiles as day, but with the tactics adapted for night. We flew as pairs, and the main weaponry event was to toss a Lepus flare as leader, under which the wingman would position to dive on the wake of the chosen target to simulate either a rocket or dive-bomb attack. The lead aircraft, meanwhile, having recovered from a 40° high nose-up unusual attitude, rushed round a tight low-level pattern at 300ft and 540 knots, with the intention of pulling up once more and achieving a similar attack with one's own weapons before the 9 million candle-power flare hit the sea!

At night, the recovery to the ship was always by way of a radar approach (CCA) rather than a visual circuit, and one was supposed to stay 'head in' until a range of 1 mile out on the approach, when the CCA controller would say 'look up for sight'. What a shock that was – just a few dim lights in a very small area. It seemed incomprehensible that there was a carrier of 54,000 tons doing the best part of 30 knots among this tiny collection of fairy lights. The mind was concentrated like never before, and the relief of being safely back on board our 'small' ship was overwhelming.

The final disembarkation launch took place after sailing from Gibraltar for the last time after an outstanding run ashore – having delivered all our aircraft to RAF St Athan, we repaired for the 809 Squadron disbandment function, followed by the HMS *Ark Royal* decommissioning ball.

Feet dry!

Following the sad but inevitable demise of conventional British carrier aviation, it was back to dry land for me, but still in a predominantly maritime role. I was posted to a series of tours on Nos 12, 216 and 208 Squadrons, initially returning to Honington, before the entire RAF Buccaneer force was gradually relocated back to Lossiemouth. The Buccaneer had gone full circle, though this time Lossiemouth had reverted (in 1972) to being an RAF station. Here the Maritime Buccaneer Wing was formed, assigned to Supreme Allied Commander Atlantic (SACLANT). The main weapons employed were a mix of anti-radar (AR) and TV Martel missiles, complimented by the Paveway laser-guided bomb (LGB). Most training sorties flown entailed tactics specific to Tactical Air Support of Maritime Operations (TASMO), with air-to-air refuelling (AAR), plus practice weaponry on the bombing ranges frequently included. The finest of low-level flying country was at our doorstep, and here the Buccaneer was really at home. Additionally, Tain, Rosehearty and Garvie bombing ranges were all within easy reach, and used daily.

LEFT Rick Phillips photographed at RAF Brize Norton after achieving the 6,000-hour fast-jet milestone on 4 September 1990. *(Crown Copyright RAF Brize Norton Image 288-1)*

BELOW No 12 Squadron Buccaneer S.2, XX895, going vertical on 10 March 1993. Rick Phillips flew the cameraship and photographer for this photoshoot. *(Crown Copyright via Squadron Leader Rick Phillips)*

So started the final years of the Buccaneer in RAF service. The Buccaneer was a particularly versatile aeroplane, and would often be used as a tanker enabling aircrew to maintain AAR currency in-house. The RAF tanker fleet was also used on a regular basis, with the Victor, VC10, Hercules C.1K, Vulcan and lastly the Tristar, all being used to extend the aircraft's already excellent range, especially for long transits to overseas detachments.

In 1987 I was on 208 Squadron when it was equipped with the Sea Eagle missile. This gave the Buccaneer a true all-weather day and night capability to destroy enemy shipping totally undetected. Soon after we were declared operational with Sea Eagle, I was tasked with forming, training and leading a constituted six-aircraft formation to carry out effective deep-water attacks against targets at night.

We had never flown six-aircraft night formations before and this was not particularly popular among the crews. Their attitude was understandable, given that such a sortie would involve over 2 hours of close formation in the dark, at 300ft above the sea, frequently in foul weather! Ably assisted by my excellent navigator of that period, Mike and I worked up a very soundly constituted team. Some of the work-up sortie debriefs were almost as lengthy and tiring as the sorties themselves, lasting well

into the early hours of the morning. We were determined to get it right.

The fruits of our labour came to a most satisfying conclusion during Exercise Teamwork in 1988. This culminated in a copybook night attack with all six aircraft being undetected until arriving over the target from different directions as we flew the missile profiles. To add to the satisfaction, the entire sortie of some 3 hours' duration from start to finish had been carried out in complete radio silence, also including the AAR. I doubt this was ever repeated again, and it was particularly satisfying to have achieved the aim.

Queen's birthday flypast

In 1993, the Buccaneer was selected to lead the annual Queen's birthday flypast over London and I was honoured to be asked by Group HQ to lead the event. Heavily assisted by Harry [navigator], we put together a team of crews from across the Wing, and started the exacting process of planning the entire event: flying a 'diamond sixteen' formation of Buccaneers over Buckingham Palace. At first I thought I was just leading the Lossiemouth contingent, but soon I was to discover that the entire formation was to be under my leadership – I was to plan for everyone, with the 16 Buccaneers at the front of a large number of other formations of different

BELOW Twenty Buccaneer and two Hunter aircraft lined up at Manston just ahead of the Queen's birthday flypast in June 1993. *(Squadron Leader Rick Phillips)*

aircraft types, totalling over 80 aircraft in all. Having been involved in these events before, I now had free rein to plan and execute the entire event my own way.

Following a few practice sorties at Lossiemouth, it was decided to mount the flypast from RAF Manston, as this would cut the transit times for the practices to a minimum. By this time Harry had been posted, and Nigel Maddox, my squadron commander, took his place as my navigator. Together we first flew the route in a helicopter right down the Mall, and I carefully memorised the salient features to ensure I would fly not just over the balcony on time, but straight at it. In the past I had been led over the palace at a few degrees angled off, and always felt it looked less than perfect. To ensure we had a built-in redundancy, I had an additional four Buccaneers in a 'spare' formation to cater for any unserviceable airframes, in addition to a couple of Hunter aircraft acting as overhead 'whips' to call us into the correct position should they stray slightly out of symmetry. In the event, none was needed,

but it was a great comfort to know they were there behind us. What a spectacle it was to look over my shoulder as we taxied on to the runway at Manston, to see 20 sets of folded wings being spread together on my call. All those spare aircraft departed once we reached 10 miles to run.

Thankfully, the weather was kind to us on the day, Nigel got the timing absolutely spot-on to the second and we left London and climbed out to Lossiemouth to overfly our home station with our immaculate 'diamond sixteen' formation one more time, in thanks for the station's support.

The fact that Buccaneer aircrew gather every December in London from all over the world, to dine and drink together, speaks volumes for the machine that brought us all together in the first place. I know of no other aeroplane where its aircrew are indeed part of such a really happy family. I have been very privileged to fly an excellent spread of mainly classic British military aeroplanes, but, without doubt, the very best of these was the last all-British bomber – the Buccaneer.

ABOVE All of the aircrew involved in the Queen's birthday flypast, photographed at Manston in June 1993 with Rick Phillips (right) and Nigel Maddox (left) in the front of the group. *(Squadron Leader Rick Phillips)*

A navigator's view

Group Captain Christopher Finn, MPhil, FRAeS, RAF (Retired)

Christopher Finn grew up in Cheshire and went to William Hulme's Grammar School in Manchester. His interest in flying was sparked by a flight from Blackpool in a Cessna Skylane when he was just 12 years old. He joined 1196 Bredbury, Romiley and Marple Squadron of the Air Training Corps in 1966, thus beginning an association with the RAF which lasts through to today as a guide at the Battle of Britain Memorial Flight. A couple of weeks after his 16th birthday, he gained the Gliding A and B Certificates on the open-cockpit Slingsby Cadet at RAF Spitalgate. Then, in the summer of 1971, he undertook a Flying Scholarship at Perth which gave him 30 hours' flying on the single-engine Cessna 150. Chris takes up his story:

In September 1972 I joined the RAF as a Direct Entrant Navigator on a Permanent Commission, my eyesight now precluding me from pilot training. At the Air Navigation School (which I later went on to command) at RAF Finningley, I discovered that I had a penchant for low-level visual navigation. Fortunately, the RAF agreed and having gained my Navigator's Brevet was posted to the Buccaneer, via a 20-hour low-level lead-in course on the Jet Provost T.4A, along with 25 hours in the Hastings T.5 'Flying Classroom', learning the art of low-level overland radar navigation.

The best of the best

The Buccaneer Force, and 237 Operational Conversion Unit (OCU) in particular, had a reputation as a very demanding and professional organisation where only the best was acceptable – this was both right and proper, and true. The Buccaneer could 'bite' if mishandled, particularly in the circuit, and both cockpits were often described as ergonomic slums. However, the Buccaneer S.2, with its Rolls-Royce Spey engines, was, at its operating speeds of 420 knots or higher, a superb, stable but manoeuvrable low-level platform, with a good weapon-carrying capacity and, after the F-111, the longest-ranged twin-engine bomber of its day in NATO service. The Buccaneer has the pilot's seat offset to the left with the navigator's raised and offset to the right, providing the navigator with a clear view forward. It was also extremely capable at high level and could cruise at 30,000ft-plus at Mach 0.8, burning only 10lb of fuel for every nautical mile (nm) flown. However, by the early 1970s, its navigation system was already showing its age.

About two-thirds of the way through the OCU course I found out there was a posting available on 809 Naval Air Squadron (NAS) and duly volunteered for it. At the conclusion of the OCU course I was posted to 208 Squadron! However, this oversight was quickly sorted out and I was then crewed-up with Brian Mahaffey for Number Eight Post-graduate Pre-carrier Course. By this stage, I had 90 hours' experience on the Buccaneer and the 30-hour course was designed to introduce us to some of the additional roles and weapons that we would come across on the carrier. The other objective was to introduce the pilot – in particular – to landing the Buccaneer on an aircraft carrier flight deck through repeated MADDL on the dummy-deck at Honington under the supervision of the squadron Landing Sight Officers, or LSOs.

One of the highlights of the course was the two shots off the static catapult at RAE Bedford. This could only be done when there was enough wind and from the right direction – RAE Bedford could not steam at 30 knots into wind and there was only about a 20ft drop off the Bedford catapult – as opposed to just over 60ft from the deck of HMS *Ark Royal*. Our first launches were with an experienced RN pilot or observer in the other seat and then we launched off together for a low-level photographic reconnaissance sortie into Wales, recovering to RAF Honington for even more MADDL. We were also introduced to the 2in rocket projectile and to live forward air control (FAC) on the Sennybridge Range in Wales. No 809 NAS returned from sea at the end of July and I was crewed-up with Lieutenant Julian Bond, RN, who was returning for his second tour on the squadron having just completed a tour as a QFI on Bulldogs.

Over the next 18 months I was to gain

another 350 hours on the Buccaneer, complete 125 catapult launches and deck landings (cats and traps) and fly over 80% of those sorties with Julian. Our first deck landing together was on 22 September 1975, when we joined HMS *Ark Royal* in the Channel for 'wire pulling'. This was primarily to work-up the flight-deck crews but also to give us some deck landing practice before we deployed as a full squadron.

Anti-shipping role

One of the great things about carrier flying was its variety. No 809 NAS, with its Buccaneer S.2A and S.2B aircraft, had three different roles. Its primary role was that of anti-shipping, which is what the Buccaneer was originally designed to do. The weapons and attacks we could use in this role ranged from a single aircraft tossing a WE177 nuclear weapon against a Soviet capital ship, to formation attacks using bombs and rockets against fast patrol boats, at night, by the light of Lepus flares. However, the standard conventional (*ie* non-nuclear) attack profiles involved four-aircraft formations, always referred to as a four-ships, using various combinations of the Martel anti-radiation and TV-guided missile, as well as 1,000lb bombs tossed at the target from 3 nautical miles. These were practised by flying the attack profiles (without releasing any weapons) against naval or unsuspecting merchant shipping. Weapons deliveries were practised on most sorties, using small practice bombs, often against a 'splash target' towed behind the carrier or another warship.

Non-stick coating

But the squadron also had an overland role and my first squadron deployment afloat was in the late autumn of 1975 to the north Norwegian Sea for Exercise Northern Wedding. The Royal Navy very proudly told us that the ship now had a new non-slip coating to the flight deck. This was so until it was coated with salt water and aviation fuel, when it resembled a well-oiled frying pan! On one day, when the sea-state was particularly high, only one aircraft at a time was going to be released from the lashings holding it down to the deck and towed by heavy flight-deck tractors to the catapult. The first Buccaneer was unlashed and we all watched

fascinated as the whole combo started slipping across the deck as the ship rolled from one side to the other. Fortunately the engineers got the lashings back on it and the whole launch was – much to everyone's relief – scrubbed. From then on the exercise was known as Northern Deck-slide! A lot of the sorties were flown as four-ships against land targets in Norway, including FAC in support of the Royal Marines in the Narvik area.

The final role of the squadron was that of air-to-air refuelling. This was to extend the range of the Buccaneers (which did not have the bomb bay door fuel tank that the RAF aircraft later had) and of the Phantom aircraft of 892 NAS, whose primary role was to defend the carrier.

Carrier flying excitement

But carrier flying had its own unique excitements. While being loaded on to the catapult you had to check the pilot had the correct elevator trim setting for the hands-off launch and that the compass had been correctly aligned to the ship's master gyro. The launch got you from 0 to about 135 knots in less than 2 seconds but, provided the Flight Deck Officer launched you when the bow was pitching up, was generally uneventful. The next bit was – for the navigator – the most challenging. In the maritime role you often didn't know where the target was – but when flying from a carrier (particularly in those days) you often didn't know where you were starting from either. It was not uncommon to climb up to transit to an overland entry point, take a radar fix and find yourself 30nm or more from where you should have been. You then had to be careful to correct the ship's position on your chart for when you recovered. This was particularly important on exercises when you were not allowed to use your radar within 100nm of the carrier to avoid giving its position away. In bad weather, or at night, you then had to navigate yourself by old-fashioned DR (dead reckoning) to a pre-briefed bearing and distance from where the ship would be at your designated recovery time.

For the landing you were in the hands of your pilot and, to a lesser extent, the LSO. If the stern was pitching down as you landed it would be a relatively gentle arrival; if it was pitching up, however, the landing gear was stressed to 6G in the vertical plane, and you felt it. I also had my first night sortie from the carrier with the Squadron QFI, who proceeded to demonstrate to me how not to do a night recovery and what a night 'bolter' (missing the wires) was like!

All change into the RAF

In January 1977 I was again posted to my choice of squadron, this time XV Squadron at RAF Laarbruch in Germany. RAF Germany (RAFG) was as operationally and culturally as different from the Fleet Air Arm as chalk from cheese. Although on the Dutch–German border, RAF Laarbruch was less than 30 minutes' flying-time from the Inner-German Border and East Germany. Here was the greatest concentration of Soviet and non-Soviet Warsaw Pact air and land forces, which were also their best equipped and trained forces.

The role of the NATO forces opposing them was that of deterrence with – in the Laarbruch Buccaneer Wing (XV and 16 Squadrons) – both nuclear and conventional weapons. On arrival at XV Squadron I was crewed up with Tony Schimmel, who had been on the same OCU course as myself, and the first priority (as with all new crews) was to get me Strike qualified – *ie* doing my share of QRA. This meant spending 24 hours 'on state' with a nuclear-armed aircraft and came around about three times a month. This was a relatively quick process as I only had to get back up to speed on night, low-level, overland, navigation and bombing. This was – for me anyway – the most challenging task for a Buccaneer navigator. The radar was optimised for finding ships at long range and, consequently, was far from ideal for picking out single overland radar returns from the background 'clutter'. The 'Blue Jacket' Doppler navigation system was linked into the radar display, so you could manually position the radar 'markers' on a target or waypoint position. But 'Blue Jacket' was not consistently accurate and had to be updated, or 'fixed' every 10 minutes or so. To do this we used Continuous Mosaic Radar Predictions (CMRPs), which showed what the radar picture should look like 10nm ahead of you on the planned track. It was based on identifying distinctive shadows caused by higher terrain ahead of you, and there wasn't

much of this on the North German Plain. So, if you were on track, it was fairly easy to fix your position; if you weren't, it wasn't! Later on, a digital waypoint computer was added which made this process a lot easier.

This was all done while flying at 500ft above the highest ground or obstacle within 10nm of track on night low-level routes in what was known as the 'Charlie System'. Each trip comprised a dummy attack on a Radar Bomb Scoring Unit (which tracked your position and gave an assessment of how accurately you had 'attacked' a target), and a live radar laydown attack at 400ft against the radar target on the Nordhorn bombing range, located on the Dutch border around 50nm south of Emden. We also had a 35mm camera fitted to the radar visor and took photos of fix-points and targets for subsequent debrief. The 'Charlie 7' route was a short one so you went round it twice – the sortie lasting over 2 hours. The Nordhorn radar target never 'showed' on the radar until the last couple of miles to go, although the power lines beforehand did, so you had to have confidence in your navigation, especially on the qualifying sortie when the target lights were switched off. The saving grace was that you always approached Nordhorn from the north and so could get a good radar fix from a coastal feature on Emden Bay about 7 minutes from the target. While the basic techniques for visual overland navigation were the same as on 809 NAS, the conditions in which we did it in Germany were not. Over the sea the visibility is generally either outstanding or awful; however, over Germany it was often poor to marginal. The minimum visibility for military low-flying was 3½nm – *ie* 30 seconds' visibility ahead of the aircraft at the usual transit speed of 420 knots – and we always flew down to the limits. It was part of the RAFG ethos of being the best force in the Central Region and, although we didn't discuss this in the crew room, an essential part of conventional deterrence.

Exercise Red Flag

In August 1977 the United States Air Force opened up Exercise Red Flag to foreign participants and the RAF Honington and Laarbruch Wings each sent a squadron-sized detachment, in our case made up equally of

crews from both XV and 16 Squadrons. Tony and I were one of those selected crews.

The Exercise Red Flag area was about the size of Wales and all the flying in it was at 100ft above the ground – one had to pull up a bit for weapon release because of the time it took the weapons to fuse. Each sortie was about an hour long against targets representative of those in the Central Region defended by Soviet SAM and Gun systems (with recording devices for the subsequent mass debrief) and F-5 fighter aircraft (known as the 'Aggressors') employing Soviet tactics. The Buccaneers were painted in desert camouflage for this Red Flag exercise only. They were all from RAF Honington, had air-to-air refuelling probes and were ferried over and back by the UK crews.

One of the early trips was as single aircraft simulating a Strike sortie – you felt very vulnerable in the clear desert air and appreciated the value of grotty weather in Germany to keep you hidden from fighters. But the other missions were all in formations, being built together into bigger packages, or 'Gorillas', with integral fighter protection against the Aggressors. We were also able to drop live weapons, including on one occasion the BL755 cluster bomb, on some sorties. One sortie involved a medium-level transit to and from a separate range area in Utah and the whole formation got off track a bit on the way back, sightseeing the Grand Canyon!

At one level Red Flag was a professional, highly satisfying opportunity to operate in as close to a real environment as was possible – and the USAF expected to lose aircraft doing so, but in the expectation then of fewer losses

in combat. On a personal level it was FUN – flying with a pilot you trusted, at 100ft and 500 knots plus, while you looked behind for the fighters and controlled the formation; and still hitting the target on time was what being a Buccaneer navigator was all about.

A year later I did Red Flag again, this time with Rip Kirby, as the operational phase of our Qualified Weapon Instructor (QWI) course. The targets were now almost all direct replicas of East German airfields and the packages a bit more complex.

Fatigue

My time flying Buccaneers on XV Squadron came to a sad and unexpected end on 7 February 1980 when Ken Tait and Rusty Ruston (also on XV Squadron) were killed when their Buccaneer XV345 broke up in flight during a Red Flag sortie. The cause was major fatigue failure in a wing-root and the entire fleet was grounded.

237 OCU

As a QWI with over a thousand hours on the Buccaneer I was, unsurprisingly, posted as an instructor on 237 OCU back at RAF Honington, joining the unit on 7 July 1980. The Buccaneer was finally cleared for flight again, although the fleet size had reduced as some aircraft were fatigue-damaged beyond economic repair and, on 7 August, I flew a Buccaneer sortie to Holbeach Range with the CFI, Pete Atkins. The role of the OCU differed little from six years previously. Having no flying controls or instruments in the rear cockpit, all student pilot/staff sorties (except for the first one) were

ABOVE All of the RAF Germany aircrew involved in Red Flag 9-2 at Nellis AFB, Nevada, in 1977. Chris Finn is on wing, far right; Rip Kirby on wing fifth from right; and Tony Schimmel sitting on wing tank. (*Group Captain Christopher Finn*)

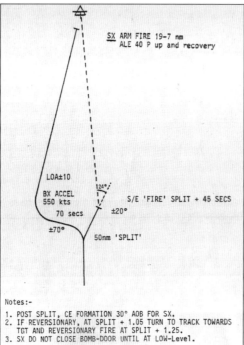

SX ARM FIRE 19·7 nm
ALE 40 P up and recovery

LOA±10

BX ACCEL
550 kts

70 secs

±70°

124°

S/E 'FIRE' SPLIT + 45 SECS

±20°

50nm 'SPLIT'

Notes:-

1. POST SPLIT, CE FORMATION 30° AOB FOR SX.

2. IF REVERSIONARY, AT SPLIT + 1.05 TURN TO TRACK TOWARDS
   TGT AND REVERSIONARY FIRE AT SPLIT + 1.25.

3. SX DO NOT CLOSE BOMB-DOOR UNTIL AT LOW-Level.

SIERRA 1 - SNOWCAT

flown with a navigator in the back seat and vice
versa. Consequently, I spent most of my time
teaching weaponry and tactics (including basic
fighter evasion) on the ground, to full courses,
and in the air to pilots. This had its challenges,
particularly going down the Wainfleet Range
at 400ft and 500 knots on a pilot's first night
weaponry sortie. At least the QWI course
enabled me to have some more relaxed sorties
with experienced student and staff pilots. One
change, however, was that the OCU now
decamped to RAF Akrotiri in Cyprus twice each
winter, to escape the UK weather during the
familiarisation and high-level navigation phases
of the OCU course.

208 Squadron

At the end of November 1983 I was posted
to HQ 18 Group at RAF Northwood but the
following July I was suddenly posted to 208
Squadron at RAF Lossiemouth, on promotion to

Squadron Leader, as the Weapons Leader. No 208 Squadron was one of the two remaining Buccaneer squadrons (along with 237 OCU) that formed the Maritime Buccaneer Wing. Being a SACLANT-declared squadron we did not do QRA, but participating, usually as Opposition Forces, in major NATO maritime exercises was a fundamental part of our lives. Routine squadron training comprised practice bombing, mostly on Tain and Rosehearty ranges, and practising maritime formation attack profiles, known as 'Tactics', against whatever shipping was around. We also did this at night, in close formations of two or three aircraft. No 12 Squadron had the TV-guided Martel missile with a stand-off range of about 12nm which kept the aircraft out of the range of the worst of the Soviet defensive systems. But 208 Squadron had the Paveway laser-guided 1,000lb bomb as its primary weapon, which was 'tossed' at the target from 3½nm. These were guided on to the target by a Pave Spike designator in another. However, being electro-optical systems, TV Martel and Paveway/Pave Spike were day-only options, so tossing sticks of unguided 1,000lb bombs from 3nm at a modern Soviet warship was retained as a night-only option. We also retained a nuclear option, tossing the WE177 at the target. However, unlike overland Strike missions, which were always by single aircraft, to give the Strike aircraft a chance of surviving to weapons release it was screened by a conventional attack using Martel and 1,000lb bombs, and later Sea Eagle missiles, as the 'Sierra 1' Tactic (see the illustration on page 128) shows.

'Delta One' tactic

The 'Delta One' tactic (see the illustration above) shows how the day option was orchestrated between the bombers and the spikers. The logic was that, with four bombers pulling-up at 4G, at pretty much the same time and on two separate axes of attack, most would get to weapon-release point and the spikers would be at low level further away, and heading away, from the target.

But all our primary conventional weapons were wing-carried so we couldn't generally use the underwing fuel tanks. About half the squadron's aircraft were fitted with the bomb

bay fuel tank, bringing us back to 19,000lb of useable fuel which could give us up to an additional hour of flying time, if we flew a hi-lo-hi profile to a target in the Atlantic or Norwegian Sea, which was a standard exercise task.

We had to keep some bomb bays clear for the WE177 and night 1,000lb options and so, just like on 809 NAS, we still had some aircraft with underwing tanks and kept one or two aircraft in the tanker fit, both for exercises and for maintaining pilot tanking currency. However, on major exercises a lot of tanking was done by either the VC10 or Victor aircraft.

'Echo One' and Sea Eagle

By the late 1980s, the Soviet Navy was re-equipping with modern, and much better-defended, ships such as the *Kirov*, *Sovremenny* and *Udaloy*-classes, against which attacks with short-range weapons would be pretty much suicidal. The RAF's response was Sea Eagle, a

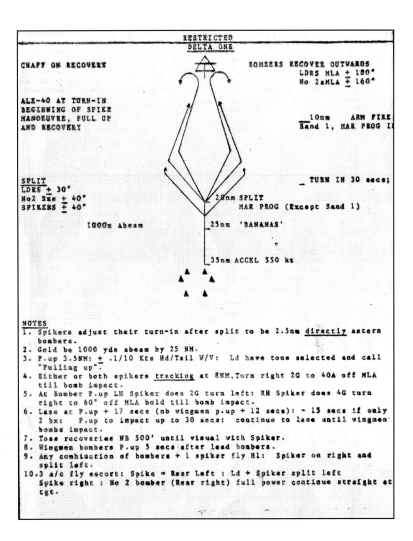

ABOVE The 'Delta One' tactic. *(208 Squadron Aircrew Tactics Manual via Group Captain Christopher Finn)*

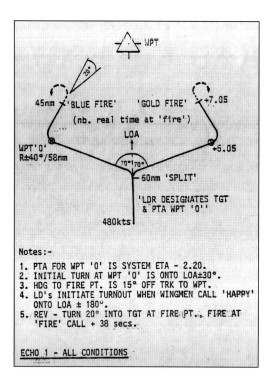

development of the Martel missile. Sea Eagle had three great advantages over the earlier weapons: it had a long range, over 60nm; it was a sea-skimmer that only became visible to the target when, at about 12nm from its target position, it 'popped-up' and turned its radar on to find the target; and its homing-head was very sophisticated for the time. Its one weakness was its small warhead. 'Echo One' tactics were therefore designed to cater for up to six aircraft, each carrying four Sea Eagles.

This would put 24 missiles into the air at once and give the target the additional problem of dealing with two different threat axes simultaneously. Firing at 45nm provided a bit of flexibility for the missile if the target was not quite where anticipated, and some residual fuel in the missile at impact. This would form a fireball and cause as much damage as the warhead explosion – a lesson learned from the Falklands Conflict.

Avionics upgrade

In 1987, the Buccaneer received its long-awaited but much-curtailed (for financial reasons) avionics update. At the heart of it was the Ferranti FIN 1063 Inertial Navigation (IN) system which replaced Blue Jacket; plus a new software-based Radar Warning Receiver (Sky Guardian); and an update to

the Westinghouse 101-10 jamming pod. Once the overheating problems – caused by an inadequate cool air flow in the radio bay – were solved, the IN proved to be just what was needed. While it could not be 'fixed' regularly and its errors compensated for (as was possible in the Tornado overland), a position error that varied by up to 4nm or so was sheer luxury for a Buccaneer navigator brought up on Blue Jacket and was perfectly adequate for the role. It also meant we could fly with two three-ship formations in 10nm trail and conduct a coordinated six-aircraft attack at night or in bad weather – finally giving the Buccaneer the maritime attack capability the aircraft deserved.

SURPIC

An essential aid to our finding a target in the open ocean was the Nimrod maritime patrol aircraft. They would shadow a target group using radar and staying well outside the enemies' defences – this was fine if outside shore-based enemy fighter cover and while they did not possess a carrier-based fighter capability. The Nimrod would broadcast a Surface Picture (SURPIC) on HF radio providing the target group's position, track and disposition. With an HF receiver in the squadron operations room we could get the latest target information just as we 'walked' – vital information for a successful attack on major exercises such as the regular Joint Maritime Courses (JMCs), run by a joint RN and RAF staff at Edinburgh and involving aircraft and ships from all of the NATO nations. The Nimrod would then provide bearings and distances to the target (VASTAC), but this tied the Nimrod to closing with the target to a position where it could see both the target and our IFF transponders.

Empirical evidence gained on exercises and training sorties with the Nimrods soon showed that our navigation systems were sufficiently accurate for us to fire our missiles on the SURPIC alone, without even being detected by the target group's radars. However, to allow us to assess how accurate our attack would have been, and to give the ships practice at missile defence, we would, after the nominal firing point, fly at 100ft and 550 knots, pulling up at

12nm and switching our radars on to simulate the missile profile. Needless to say this also gave us the opportunity for a high-speed and low fly-by of the target! Of course, the ships always then claimed that all the Buccaneers had been shot down before they reached them until the exercise umpires stepped in and pointed out the errors of their ways.

CTTO

For the next 21 months I was the Buccaneer specialist on the Central Tactics and Trials Organization (CTTO). During this tour I ran the first in-service Sea Eagle firing, of a telemetered round on the Hebrides Range, off Benbecula. At the same time I was able to run a trial to assess the accuracy of targeting Sea Eagle missiles on Nimrod SURPIC alone, which enabled us to dispense with VASTAC. This was also one of those rare organisations where staff officers were obliged to maintain currency on their operational type and I flew 35 hours on the Buccaneer, with both squadrons, on TACEVAL, on exercises and on a detachment to Gibraltar.

My last Buccaneer sortie was on 24 August 1989 with Terry Yarrow, who was taking over from me at CTTO, conducting a chaff and flares trial on the Larkhill Ranges, from Boscombe Down. It gave me a grand total of 2,254 hours on the Buccaneer.

Cinderella

Looking back, the Buccaneer was a fine aircraft, particularly in terms of its weapons capacity, range and performance at both high and low level. But it was always a bit of a Cinderella to the RAF and never had the timely and complete updates to its navigation attack systems and weapons it required. That said, its other strength was that it was a two-man aircraft and working as a crew was what made it possible to deliver the results it did in the 1991 Gulf War. For me, carrier operations had their own particular challenges and excitements, and being a QWI on a RAFG squadron at the height of the Cold War had its own special 'edge'. But as a navigator I found dealing with the complexities and challenges of leading Buccaneer formations in the maritime environment of the late 1980s the most satisfying of all.

Driving the TBAG Buccaneers

Flt Lt Ollie Suckling

Ollie Suckling joined the RAF in 2007 after leaving university. Following officer training at Cranwell he completed Elementary Flying Training (EFT) on the Grob Tutor where he was lucky enough to be streamed on to fast jets. The normal fast-jet training route followed on the Tucano and Hawk T.1 before he was role-disposed to the Tornado. After training on XV Squadron – the Tornado OCU – he was posted to 31 Squadron, which is where he spent his first tour. During this time, he went to hot places, sandy places, and hot and sandy places! With the drawdown of Tornado, Ollie volunteered to move to RAF Valley and is now on 4 Squadron flying the Hawk T.2, currently training to be a QFI.

Ollie started flying civilian jets in 2014 after a good friend – Oliver Wheeldon – persuaded him to sell his motorbike and buy a share in a Jet Provost T.3. Since then he has obtained his Display Authorisation (DA) and has completed many displays both as a pairs team, as well as a singleton in the Jet Provost T.3, T.5 and Strikemaster.

Ollie continues the story:

I have always been interested in historic aviation. Since I was 15, I volunteered at (and still get to visit occasionally) the Yorkshire Air Museum at Elvington, firstly on the museum aircraft as a whole but later to work on Andre

BELOW Ollie Suckling on board one of the TBAG Buccaneers – XW544 – during a successful 'anti-det' run at Bruntingthorpe, 23 July 2016. *(Keith Wilson)*

Tempest's wonderful Handley Page Victor K.2. I was never shy of a bit of spannering, and in 2010 saw an article written by TBAG's own Francis Wallace about the Buccaneers at Bruntingthorpe. I sent him an email and that was it! I joined the group when XW544 was just coming back to life – which was great to see – and it was an awesome privilege for me to take her for her first taxi run in 28 years, back in 2011. Since then, I have been a regular visitor to Bruntingthorpe where I have been fortunate enough to 'exercise' the Buccaneers on numerous occasions.

Starting the Buccaneer

I begin each Buccaneer engine start by checking everything is switched off. We have a lot of visitors and it wouldn't do to injure one of the groundcrew during an engine start because the bomb-door switch had been left 'open' or something similar! I then run through the full 'left to rights' as per the FRCs (Flight Reference Cards) to set everything up for starting the jet, and check that the 'crackers' are working in both engines.

Once everything is checked and I'm satisfied we can proceed, the STAD (external air starting supply) is fired up and connected to the aircraft by a hose. We usually start the port engine first. I signal for the STAD to be run at 'max-chat' and then request 'air on'. Then a check that I have a flashing rotation green light located between the two HP rpm gauges (this means the low-pressure compressor is spinning the right way) and with 12% indicated on the HP rpm gauge I advance the throttles from 'shut' to 'ground start'.

The engine will then light up rapidly and I monitor the TGT (Turbine Gas Temperature) to make sure it doesn't exceed 535°F, which is the starting limit. (It rarely does but you can never be too careful!) At 35% I call for 'air off' and, at this point, the engine is self-sustaining and runs itself up to 53%. The STAD can be put back to idle and the hose moved underneath the jet to the starboard engine. Generator 'On', captions 'Out' and a quick check of the General Services and Flying Control pressures on the port side, then I follow the start procedure for the starboard side.

Once both engines are running, I carry out the 'DC Bus Tie' test to make sure all is well with the electrics, then put both generators 'On'. Next, I check all hydraulics are where they should be and all captions are out on the CWP (Centre Warning Panel). We then commence functional checks on all the flying controls and services (flaps, bomb door, etc.) before I run through the pre-take-off checks as per the FRCs. I don't actually read them as I have spent a great deal of time in the cockpit memorising them; just like the current types of aircraft I operate. After the groundcrew has been cleared away I do a quick figure-of-eight to check the nose wheel steering and brakes are functioning correctly, before lining up on the end of the runway.

Smoke and noise!

With the canopy closed and locked (with the light out) and the pressurisation 'On' – which makes it nice and quiet in the cockpit before the aircon comes on. With brakes 'On', I slowly move both throttles forward and take them up to 90% HP rpm. I do this slowly because the engines have IGVs (Inlet Guide Vanes) that move between 80 and 86% and if the jet has been standing still for a while these can sometimes

stick, which could cause an engine surge, so I go through the IGV range carefully. I've never had any problem with them on XW544 though.

In the cockpit you can hear when the IGVs move and the bleed valve closes, as the sound of the engines changes to become very high pitched and the nose wheel hunkers down. You really do get a sense of the power at this point. One final check of everything and I release the brakes and advance the throttles to the stops. The acceleration is brisk for an aircraft of the Buccaneer's size and at the weights we operate at it would definitely catch you by surprise if you were without previous experience. As I go down the runway I make sure the engines are stable (97.5% and 585° TGT with 'blow' off are the figures I am looking for) and then keep an eye on the rapidly increasing speed.

I have a great deal of trust in XW544 and I usually aim for 110 knots, which usually ends up with a peak of around 120 knots. At 110 knots indicated, I move both throttles back to idle, airbrake out and flap and droop fully down before moving the control stick fully back – slowly and carefully – to obtain the maximum drag and

get the weight on the main wheels for when the braking starts. The brakes on the Buccaneer are brilliant and if applied correctly will barely be warm after a fast taxi run. I try to leave it until about three-quarters of the way down the runway before making one smooth application of the brakes to slow the aircraft down. By this time the aircraft has been off the power for a while and the speed has already reduced to 80 knots or so.

After a fast taxi run we carry out a brake and tyre check at the far end of the runway and then it's a slow plod back to the line and the waiting audience.

The aeroplane really is very, very serviceable. All the systems work as they should do, right down to all the flight instruments. If I let her, she would get off the ground with no problem at all!

It is a real privilege to be able to taxi these aircraft. I know it is not flying, but the chance for future generations to hear the sights, sounds and smells of these old aircraft close up is something awesome. Having flown the Tornado GR.4 – which is fairly 'old school' – it's not a massive step to drive a Buccaneer. However, flying one would be a completely different matter!

BELOW Smoke and noise! Ollie Suckling accelerates away swiftly in the TBAG Buccaneer S.2B, XW544, during the Cold War Jet Day at Bruntingthorpe, 28 May 2017. *(Keith Wilson)*

Chapter Eight

Maintaining the Buccaneer

The Blackburn Buccaneer goes back to the 1950s and made its first flight at Bedford on 30 April 1958. Initially underpowered by the de Havilland Gyron Junior, it later received the Rolls-Royce Spey 101 engine and was able to achieve its full potential, and in some cases exceed it. However, it was clearly 1950s technology and despite a number of effective upgrades to its systems (primarily weapons and avionics), it would always remain 1950s technology.

OPPOSITE A clever composite image created to demonstrate the wing-folding mechanism on TBAG Buccaneer S.2B, XW544, at Bruntingthorpe. This was shot during one of the regular 'anti-det' runs performed on the aircraft. *(Matt Wellington)*

Despite this (and maybe even because of this) the Buccaneer was held in fond regard by the aircrews who flew her and especially by the groundcrew who worked on her. The Buccaneer was not always the easiest of aircraft to work on; she had a few foibles all of her own, but she was an honest aircraft. At least four skill sets were always required on the Buccaneer – Rigger, Electrical, Sumpy and Armourer – on the flight line, as well as in the hangars. Consequently, teamwork was paramount in keeping her in the air. Perhaps that teamwork and camaraderie was yet another of her attractions?

After having been withdrawn from RAF service in 1994, the fondness for the Buccaneer has continued and today has a new-found following among a number of preservation groups and enthusiasts who continue to maintain the venerable old Buccaneer in a 'live' ground-running condition.

Before we consider the efforts required by the preservation groups to keep the Buccaneer running, let us take a look back with those people who spent many years keeping her airworthy while in RAF service:

Reminiscences of a rigger

Pete 'Ossie' Osborn joined the RAF in 1966 as an airframe mechanic; initially on Victors, as well as the Station Flight at RAF Wittering. Next up was a role as a line mechanic and 'flying spanner' on 46 Squadron Andover C.1 aircraft at Abingdon before his next move saw him

transferred to Singapore where he continued his line mechanic career on the Lightning F.6s of 74 Squadron at RAF Tengah. A Fitters' Course was followed by a posting to undertake structural repairs with the Belfast Major Team at RAF Abingdon. Pete continues his story:

I first came across the Buccaneer in October 1973 when I attended the Buccaneer Engineering Course at RAF Honington. It was quite a challenging course; my, what a complex aircraft the Buccaneer was! Blow, tailplane flap, aileron droop and a rotating bomb door.

A posting to XV Squadron at RAF Laarbruch in Germany followed that December. Almost immediately I was introduced – by a Klaxon – to War Games in the guise of a Minival (a small tactical evaluation) at 5am; into nuclear preparation with the fitting of 'special weapons' fairings into the bomb bay. Once generated in the war role, the aircraft were towed to the dispersed revetments (long before Laarbruch had Hardened Aircraft Shelters) in our sector of the airfield loaded with 'small live practice bombs'. We then split into our two shifts and played 'techie-turned-soldier' for the following two or three days. Often Luftwaffe F-104 Starfighters and other NATO aircraft would carry out mock air raids on the airfield.

365 days a year, aircraft from each resident squadron (16 Squadron was the other Buccaneer unit) at Laarbruch were fitted with live Special Weapons and on Quick Reaction Alert. For two weeks the groundcrew were locked in – 24 hours on, 24 hours off. Along with the aircrew, we had our own chefs (hence the food was amazing), a volleyball pitch, Uckers and other entertainment, so it wasn't too tedious. Nuclear fairings were fitted as the 'special weapons' required a smooth airflow when released.

My stint as XV Line Ramrod in 1974

During my three-year tour with XV Squadron, we received many Mk.2B aircraft straight from the factory at Brough, along with some reworked former Royal Navy S.2As. In general, the serviceability with the Buccaneer was good, although hydraulic leaks due to failed bonded seals were a constant pain; often, I got home

BELOW The young and enthusiastic XV Squadron 'linies' pose in front of the XV Squadron hangar at RAF Laarbruch in 1975. Pete 'Ossie' Osborn is the skinny corporal to the far left of the picture. *(Peter 'Ossie' Osborn)*

in the early hours of the morning stinking of OM15. Wheel changes were quite an art too as the very heavy wheel/brake slotted into a fork which had to be perfectly lined up to fit correctly; in the early days many an axle bolt had to be ground out. We often cursed the aircraft and its complexities, but in general we thought highly of it. As a rigger I cannot think of any easy jobs on it!

Charging the liquid oxygen tank in the radio bay was full of hazards but generally it was removed and a filled one fitted. Nose steering actuators often required replacement; being short was an advantage for this task. The main oleo was heavy and awkward to replace, while powered flying control units – especially the rudder – required special 'Houdini' skills. I suppose the most challenging job was replacing a hydraulic pipe for the aileron in the outer wing. Muggins (me that is!) worked out the only way was to remove the outer wing; a job for 2nd Line, I thought! Well, it took me seven days to do it on the squadron. . . .

Often we were required to be 'rolled', to adjust micro switches, etc, in the bomb bay. It was a little dangerous and a bit scary. The best thing to do was defuel the bomb bay, hand crank it and position a strut in place!

The Buccaneer was totally reliant on ground equipment as it had no APU or internal start capabilities. The Palouse – a petrol-driven hydraulic rig – was quite a challenge to start, with many a sore thumb resulting; how we never burned a hangar down, I'll never know, especially as we often used rags in the

carburettor to act as a choke. Much later, diesel- and electric-powered rigs made life much easier.

Armament practice camps

Each spring we would deploy to an armament practice camp (APC) in Sardinia (Decimomannu) where live bombs would be dropped on the range at Capo Frasca. A number of us were lucky enough to get a 'trip' in the back seat of a Buccaneer – something that was not permitted while in Germany – while visits to Smokey Joe's restaurant and Poetto beach were a must when off duty.

Operation Knightsbridge

Towards the end of my three-year tour I spent four months detached to Eglin AFB in Florida for Operation Knightsbridge; there were just 12 groundcrew from XV and 16 Squadrons with, initially, two aircraft and in the final month, four aircraft.

LEFT The ground servicing hydraulic trolley – in this case a Mk.3 powered by a Coventry Victor 4-cylinder, 4-stroke, air-cooled petrol engine. These particular servicing trolleys are started by means of a crank handle located at the front and are capable of generating significant colourful language when they don't start or kick back! The hydraulic pump on this model produces 3,000psi of pressure. The pump itself is mounted to the engine via a gearbox and clutch assembly. *(Keith Wilson)*

LEFT All of the aircrew, groundcrew, RAF Laarbruch Station Commander, Boscombe Down staff and representatives from Westinghouse (including the Westinghouse representative in the (then) trendy trousers) involved in Operation Knightsbridge at Eglin AFB, Florida. Involving crews from both XV and 16 Squadron, the purpose of the operation was to evaluate the Westinghouse ECM pod against 'threat' radar and SAMs that were in place on the ranges around Eglin AFB. *(via Peter 'Ossie' Osborn)*

The aircraft were incredibly reliable with just one 'crew-in snag'; a starter motor which Arfur (Geordie) Thompson (our only Sumpy) replaced in time for the cabs to meet the very expensive range slots. The purpose of Operation Knightsbridge was to evaluate the Westinghouse ECM pod against 'threat' radar and SAMs that were in place on the ranges around Eglin AFB. The four aircraft were able to try differing formations and develop the optimum tactics for the ECM.

Honington MCSF

In December 1976, I was posted to RAF Honington's Mechanical Component Servicing Flight (MCSF), overhauling Buccaneer hydraulic components. Shortly afterwards, I was promoted to sergeant and took over the wheel and brake bay. Occasional detachments supporting both 12 and 208 Squadron followed, including Red Flag, which was a real bonus for a 'Clingon' (the term given to non-squadron personnel).

On reflection, the aircraft were significantly over-serviced. Serviceable components were removed for overhaul, requiring a significant number of personnel to be employed at 2nd Line.

In early 1980, 12 Squadron was relocated to RAF Lossiemouth. I didn't actually volunteer but moved with them anyway, managing the overhaul of both Buccaneer and Hunter flight controls, hydraulic selectors, actuators and filters, and environmental system components, such as water extractors and cold air units. By this time we knew most of the Buccaneer mechanical components in depth, but I did have to learn a lot about the Hunter aircraft as the spar failure problems later resulted in all of the Buccaneers being grounded, while aircrews maintained their flying currency on Hunter T.7 and F.6 aircraft.

Structural problems

An explanation of the structural problems suffered by the Buccaneer fleet is required here. In 1979 and '80, two aircraft were lost due to separation of the wing in flight. The first was due to a fatigue failure of the wing-fold latch pin mechanism, but examination of the aircraft lost in Nevada revealed fatigue cracks in the steel main spar and a fleet-wide grounding followed. During subsequent inspections, a significant number of aircraft were found to have cracks. This situation was not expected as the fatigue test specimen hadn't revealed any critical fatigue failures.

Subsequent flights with stress gauges fitted to critical areas of the airframe and the subsequent collection of data revealed that the loadings on the test rig at Brough was not actually representative of RAF operation of the aircraft. The test rig was restarted with asymmetric loading applied. A recalculation by Farnborough and British Aerospace was then required as the rig was well behind the fleet leaders in terms of recalculated Fatigue Index (FI). FI is a measure of aircraft life usually to a maximum of 100FI. Consumption of the FI depends on a number of factors including the role fit (ie long-range fuel tanks, weapons, pods, etc) and the type of sortie and G pulled as recorded on the fatigue meter installed in the aircraft.

My final post at the Buccaneer Engineering Authority was to see me well immersed in the

BELOW Diagram of the Buccaneer inner wing highlighting the area of fatigue cracking. *(via Peter 'Ossie' Osborn)*

BOTTOM Diagram of the Buccaneer rear spar indicating areas of cracking. *(via Peter 'Ossie' Osborn)*

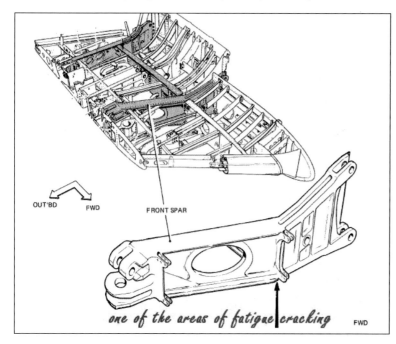

OUT'BD   FWD   FRONT SPAR

one of the areas of fatigue cracking   FWD

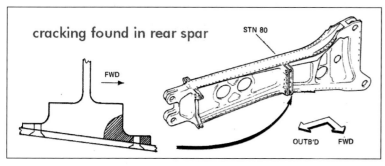

cracking found in rear spar   STN 80

FWD

OUTB'D   FWD

problems and solutions as further failures on the test rig were revealed, especially as it caught up with the fleet.

One of the tasks (at '1FI' – every time one unit of FI was consumed) was to remove alternate fasteners from the lower flange of the front and rear spar for magnetic flux NDT (non-destructive testing) to be conducted while the aircraft was stress jacked. If a defect was found, the offending hole was re-reamed until the defect was cleared. The hole was then 'cold worked' by passing a mandrel through the hole, pre-stressing the area surrounding the fastener hole in compression and an oversize fastener fitted. During flight the lower spar is bent in tension; in effect the area around the fastener experiences reductions in local stress which has been found to significantly lessen the likelihood of fatigue cracking.

Escape from the bays

It was a great relief to escape the bays (everyone wanted to be at the sharp end – *ie* on a first-line squadron) when I was posted to 208 Squadron when they moved up from RAF Honington to RAF Lossiemouth in 1983. Shortly afterwards, I was promoted to chief technician.

In-depth inspections saw a reduced fleet of Buccaneers back in the air. Ten years on and the serviceability had reduced across the entire fleet – especially the number of defects found during use and inspection – and the night shift meant just that, starting at 16:30 and often working through until the day shift started.

From September 1983 six Buccaneers were deployed to Cyprus in Operation Pulasator – equipped with Paveway and Pave Spike LGB capability – to provide support for the British Peacekeeping Force in Beirut. This deployment was a joint 12 and 208 Squadrons deployment, and generally the aircraft were reliable (well, the weather was warm). We returned to RAF Lossiemouth in early spring of 1984. I was still in Cyprus at the end of the deployment, although the most exciting thing (for us engineers, anyway) was a lightning strike on the pan lighting! That said, the low-level passes at street level in Beirut by the Buccaneers were apparently spectacular; there were no hits on our aircraft, although I do believe SAMs were fired at them.

Strike Command

In August 1985, I was posted to HQ Strike Command as Mechanical Systems Advisor at the Buccaneer Engineer Authority. We were essentially the engineering management for the entire Buccaneer fleet.

In conjunction with the manufacturers at Brough, I wrote the necessary inspection schedules to keep the fleet flying. There were two chiefs, two squadron leaders and a wing commander in post. We made regular visits to Lossiemouth, St Athan and Abingdon in order to stay up to date with the hardware and implementation of modifications and inspections; as well as regularly visiting the manufacturer at Brough and then to Woodford to visit Dowty for undercarriages and hydraulics and Boulton Paul for flight controls and filters. I was later awarded a C-in-C Commendation for my work on Buccaneer structural integrity.

Life after the RAF

I left the RAF in late 1989 to take up a post as lecturer in Aero Systems at Brunel Tech College. I survived this for ten years until headhunted to be technical instructor at Bahamasair, then training manager at Cayman Airways. More recently, I have been part-time trainer for various airlines while also teaching aircraft structural integrity for REME aircraft technicians. The Buccaneer structural integrity experience came in very handy for this.

I thoroughly enjoyed my 13 years on the Buccaneer fleet, joining as a junior technician and leaving as a chief technician. Clearly, the highlights were the many detachments when I was on both XV and 208 Squadrons, locations ranging from the Mediterranean to Canada.

I was fortunate enough to get a 'trip' in the back seat in Sardinia; passing over a ridge upside down at 500 knots did my brain and stomach a world of good, but I kept all my breakfast in the supplied bag, honest! Operation of the airbrake over the sea at 500-plus knots was impressive and the subsequent repairs to the airbrake strake were straightforward.

It was a sad day when the Buccaneer was withdrawn from service. I attended the disbandment event up at RAF Lossiemouth, where it was great to see so many of my old colleagues.

Electrical maintenance on the Buccaneer

Peter Wright-Gardner arrived on 208 Squadron in April 1984 and as a JT (junior technician) spent most of his early time on the line carrying out flight line servicing. He recalls his first impressions: 'When I first walked into the 208 Squadron hangar, the first thing that struck me was the size of the aircraft. It looked so much bigger than the Royal Navy variant guarding the gate at RAF Lossiemouth.'

Peter's primary trade was aircraft technician electrical; although after a while, time on the line was shared with carrying out rectification work. Promotion to corporal followed three years later and then the focus shifted to being IC (in charge) of an HAS (Hardened Aircraft Shelter) team or trade work. He also covered Line Control, Rects (Rectifications) Control, Line training and Eng Ops. He received notice of promotion to sergeant on the last day of the squadron.

During his time with 208 Squadron, he completed many training courses including Buccaneer Electrical, Systems, and Mk.20B IFR (in flight refuelling) pod to name just a few.

He took part in many overseas deployments as well as a number of aircraft recoveries. 'In those days, aircraft were often sent abroad for training purposes and luckily for me, sometimes they went unserviceable!', he recalls. Peter also served in the First Gulf War before eventually leaving 208 Squadron in 1994 when the Buccaneer was finally withdrawn from service.

After 208 he was posted into the Air Electrical Bay at RAF Kinloss, working on Nimrod equipment, then 56(R) Squadron on Tornado F.3s at RAF Leuchars before joining 3(F) Squadron at RAF Coningsby with their Typhoon aircraft. Peter is still in the RAF today, working as a requirements manager at MoD Abbey Wood, where he is responsible for bringing new capabilities into service.

Peter fondly recalls his time working on the Buccaneer:

Flight line

Flight line servicing on the Buccaneer was relatively easy; the only tools required would be a GS screwdriver, touch, bottle key and an adjustable spanner. The GS or General Service screwdriver was about 12in long with the shaft passing through the handle. It was a multi-faceted tool – not only could you use it as a screwdriver but also as a crowbar or chisel. Because of its construction it was also able to be bounced off the floor and caught, which became a popular distraction at times on the line.

On the line, both seats had to be tidied and visual inspections carried out on the top of the aircraft to ensure there were no missing vortex generators or panels, or any hydraulic leaks from the tailplane area. On the underside of the aircraft, all of the pressures were checked: GS (General Service) hydraulics 20–30psi; Flying Controls 2,000psi; brake accumulator 1,100–1,300psi; arrester hook dependent on position lowered 500–540psi or raised 760–800psi; main tyres dependent on all-up-weight 240–270psi and nose wheel 300–305psi.

The LOX (liquid oxygen) was contained in

BELOW Peter Wright-Gardner during his detachment to Muharraq during Operation Granby, posing alongside Buccaneer S.2B, XW533/A. She is painted with Gulf War artwork of *Glenfarclas*, *Miss Jolly Roger* and *Fiona*. *(Peter Wright-Gardner)*

a LOX pot fitted in the radio bay; acceptable contents were three-eighths for daytime flying, five-eighths for night-time flying, and six-eighths if they were air-to-air tanking. Next it was the turn of the engine oils which were checked twice. Firstly, the engine oils were checked between 0 and 5 minutes after shutdown while the contents of the CSDU (Constant Speed Drive Unit – with one per engine each driving a generator) were checked, and again between 5 and 20 minutes after shutdown. Two air-cooled, self-exciting, brushless generators provided the initial 200V 3-phase, and because frequency relies on the generator rotational feed, this must remain constant. To achieve this, a CSDU is fitted between the engine and generator. Between engine speeds of ground idle to max rpm, the CSDU output/generator input will remain at 8,000 revs which equates to 400Hz. The CSDU fitted is purely mechanical with no electrical control.

Finally, the hydraulic fluid levels were checked. There were two panels identified as 'forward' and 'rear accessories panel', just in front of the bomb door where both contents and pressures were checked.

Fuel was added with fuel states being selected on the fuelling panel; when the lights went out, that particular tank was full. The refuelling process was that fuel requirements would be passed by the aircrew to Rects Control who would then inform the Line Team. If there were no external tanks on the aircraft it was normal practice to fill everything up, which would normally provide a sortie time of around 90 minutes. On the flight line the refuelling bowser would turn up and be connected straight to the aircraft; however, when working in a HAS environment, the bowser was parked in an annex to the HAS and would connect into underground pipework. The aircraft would connect into a similar system inside the HAS.

Undercarriage locks not removed

Sometimes the 'remove before flight' flags on the undercarriage locks would become damaged and then – very occasionally – could be missed by the pilot and groundcrew during the pre-flight walk-around checks. Because the aircrew used to retract the undercarriage almost

as soon as 'weight off wheel' was achieved, it was rare to see an aircraft just after take-off with the wheels down; you just knew that the aircraft would RTB (return to base) and the main cause of the problem would usually be forgetting to remove the lock!

Crash strips

The aircraft had five pairs of crash strip elements on the under surface – forward of the nose wheel, on each wingtip fairing, aft of the bomb bay and on the under surface of the bomb door. These were basically two strips of metal encased in rubber which would operate when pushed together. Once two had operated, the five fire extinguishers would be fired. The crash strips were inspected visually during the flight servicing but could also be checked electrically by depressing two test lights contained in the radio bay. Many times, especially while on detachment to places exposed to the cold, moisture or ice would get into the crash strips and give the indication that one had operated. Half of the crash strips would illuminate one test light, while the remainder would operate the other, so you could narrow the fault-finding down to one of five crash strips utilising these lights. Depending upon what light had actually illuminated, this would narrow the fault down to just 50% of the crash switches and then it would be a case of visual inspections before the defective crash strip would then be replaced. It was not a particularly difficult task as the wiring was connected with quick-release 'jiffy connectors',

ABOVE Most of the cockpit electrical wiring drops down on the port side into two nose bays. The forward bay hosts the majority of the electrical terminals, as can be seen here. Almost all other wiring enters the cockpit directly via connectors known as cockpit breaks. As the cockpit was pressurised, so all electrical breaks had to be fully sealed.
(Keith Wilson)

although the crash strips did not come from stores with the mounting holes pre-drilled, so the removed crash strip was used as a template for drilling the new holes.

Fire bottles on first wash

During the first few months of my time on 208 Squadron I was instructed to take an aircraft to the wash pan. However, nobody told me that the battery had to be disconnected prior to washing as the pressure from the hoses, or moisture getting into the crash strips could operate the fire bottles. Just seconds into my first wash there were a series of bangs from the fire bottle cartridges and white fire extinguisher 'gunk' dripped from the aircraft. It was a salutary lesson learned!

Fault investigation

For the electrical tradesman, the Buccaneer was an easy jet to fault-find on. There were numerous terminal blocks where voltages could be checked, so wiring faults were easily traceable. The pitot static system could, however, prove a bit more difficult to trace faults on, mainly due to the age of the aircraft. However, located in the wheel bays were isolation switches so at least you could ascertain if the fault was inboard or outboard of the wheel bay. Typical problems were pitot static unions (the interconnections between the pipes) coming loose. Because pitot pressure is dynamic, any leaks could usually be found with the application of 'Snoop' (a washing-up liquid-type substance that when applied to a suspected area would bubble up if there was a leak).

Typically, component replacement was relatively easy; however, the replacement of the standby artificial horizon could be a protracted affair as the main electrical connector was located behind the main instrument panel and had to be located and fitted completely blind – by touch alone.

All electricians carried a test lamp; this was basically an aircraft press-to-test lamp with cables and crocodile clips attached to it. It was used for fault investigation and even on conventional weapons testing to ensure that the voltage was reaching the firing breeches, the 'holes' in the pylon where the cartridges that would fire off the store were fitted.

I do remember one particular incident that occurred while I was involved in the fitting and testing of the underwing tanks (UWT). It was the electricians' job to ensure that the fuel and tank jettison circuits were serviceable. This meant that one person connected their test lead into each of the two electrical connectors, while another person operated the switch in the cockpit. I was in the cockpit and was switching to 'on' and 'off' and listening for the person at the UWT to shout 'on' or 'off'. Once completed, we signed the aircraft up and passed it over to the armourers to connect the fuel jettison plug. When they did connect the plug, the fuel jettison operated and the contents of the fuel tank ended up on the floor of the HAS. The aircraft had just been returned from Major Servicing and the switch had been wired up incorrectly – with 'off' being 'on' and vice versa!

The cockpit instrument lighting consisted of pillar lamps, which at times proved to be temperamental. They could quite easily become detached and become a loose article in the cockpit – definitely not something you want to happen! When carrying out work on the main instrument panel it would be easy for the lighting cables behind the panels to become trapped and blow the fuse when power was applied. Unfortunately, when the panel was removed to allow access behind it, the electrical short was removed, so it was difficult to find the fault. One technique used was to refit the panel, use an AVO meter in place of the fuse, then apply electrical power while having one person upside-down with his head under the instrument panel and another person standing close with a fire extinguisher. Then, apply power and watch for the faintest wisp of smoke that identified where the problem was. Maybe not necessarily an authorised procedure, but used effectively many times.

During a two-aircraft deployment to RAF Mildenhall to display the Buccaneer, the aircrew connected a big Houchin (power set) to the aircraft and were amazed when nothing worked. The debrief from the aircrew was reported back to the squadron and passed on to myself (as it was a weekend I was working from home). Electrical power faults were usually fairly easy to trace due to the fact that the ECHO (a special piece of electrical wizardry that allowed the frequency, output voltages and phase rotation to be monitored) test set could be connected into the system at a number of places to see if the required outputs were being obtained. My initial thought was that the debrief from the aircrew had been incorrect and that the most likely cause was that one of the two CPUs (Control Protection Units[1]) had failed. This could easily be proved by swapping the two CPUs over and seeing if the fault moved to the other side of the system. This was done, but I was surprised to see that actually nothing was working – which was confusing to say the least! After a bit of head-scratching and looking over the wiring diagrams, I decided to go back to basics and checked the main 50-amp fuses; to my surprise a number of these had blown. The aircraft was due to fly the following day and no 50-amp fuses had been carried by the maintenance crew (I had never heard of them blowing before or since the incident) so the decision was made to 'borrow' them from the 12 Squadron jet that was on static display at the show. Even though it may have been an easier option, I would not let the 12 Squadron jet do the display. It took most of that night to remove, replace and functionally test the aircraft but the 208 Squadron jet made the flying display the following day.

Miscellaneous electrical maintenance activities

Primary servicing was carried out on the squadron. These were fairly routine (for the electrical trade, anyway) and just required an adjustable spanner, ratchet screwdriver, torch and wire locking pliers. The anti-skid generators on the wheels were replaced and tested, the ADD (airstream direction detector) which was located on the starboard side of the nose and consisted of a movable probe with holes cut into it and, depending on the aircraft's angle of attack, would move and indicate to the pilot both visually and audibly, was tested for torque and alignment, a check of the LOX connector was carried out, plus a check of the fire protection system.

The worst job, however, was the removal of the lid to JB RG (Junction Box Radio Bay G is the panel location[2]), a JB that contained relays and TBs (terminal blocks) for airbrake control and indication circuitry that was located at the rear of the airbrakes. We had to check for the presence of moisture and mechanical/electrical serviceability. You could always tell when somebody had carried out this job as their arms were thickly caked in sticky grease and dirt.

Sometimes when the pilot reported a 'hang up' – where a practice bomb would not release – testing showed that the trigger would work sometimes depending on how much pressure was applied. The trigger could be adjusted using a 1.5mm Allen key. Sometimes this solved weapons 'hang ups' and was far easier than changing the whole control. If it reoccurred, the stick top would need to be replaced, which was a time-consuming task.

SEM Bucc 22 (Service Equipment Modification for the Buccaneer number 22) introduced a TB located on the underside of the instrument cowling. This was required as the connector to the camera would frequently need replacing and the addition of this TB close to the camera made the task quicker and easier.

A Phimat Chaff Dispenser Pod was fitted under STF/Bucc/127 (Special Trials Fit for the Buccaneer number 127); however, one of the issues with this fit was that it didn't go through the MASBs (Master Armament Safety Break) or circuit protection, so could be inadvertently operated on the ground. This happened a few times and posed serious health risks. MASBs were basically connectors with shorting links to complete certain circuits and would be fitted by the aircrew during their walk-around and removed by the groundcrew when the aircraft returned after a sortie. Circuit protection relays would only operate when the aircraft was in an 'off the ground' configuration. Therefore, armament circuits would be inoperative on the ground. The Phimat pod, however, did not have the same protection. For whatever reason, the Phimat pod was not adopted as Buccaneer role equipment, so was only on the squadron for a limited amount of time.

---

1 The CPUs allow the generator to come online once correct generator output is detected and when the ground power lead is disconnected. The CPU would also take the generator offline if it detected any under/ over voltage, over/under frequency or negative phase sequence faults. Some of these could be reset up to a maximum of four times; the under frequency would automatically reset once the fault had cleared, while the negative phase sequence would 'lock' the generator offline.

2 On the Buccaneer, all components are identified by their position, and in this case R stands for Radio Bay including Air Brake Assembly, while G is the panel location.

Maintaining the TBAG Buccaneers

Maintaining two Buccaneer aircraft in a 'live' condition at Bruntingthorpe takes a great deal of time, dedication and enthusiasm – not to mention money. Leading the engineering aspect of the TBAG team at Bruntingthorpe is Francis Wallace, an electrical and mechanical engineer with a love of Cold War jets and, in particular, the Buccaneer.

Enter Francis Wallace

My love of aviation was forged at an early age when my parents took me to a couple of the Greenham Common airshows in the late 1970s. I recall watching in awe as various aircraft raced into the sky and I was hooked from then on!

Growing up I always felt that I would become a pilot or do something aircraft-related. However, that was not to be and I pursued a career in electrical and mechanical engineering instead. After years spent visiting as many airshows and museums as possible, I finally decided that I wanted to get on the other side of the fence and mix my acquired electrical and mechanical skills with something aviation-related. Perhaps being too long in the tooth to consider it as a career move, it dawned on me that something in the way of aircraft restoration would be far more suitable as a pastime.

My particular interest in aviation has always been British vintage jets and so something along those lines was what I was looking for. Cockpit sections would have presented me with something to work on, but I was actually looking for something more complete that could be restored back to some form of limited operation. While discussing this with a friend back in early 2003, he mentioned to me that he knew Guy Hulme – the then owner of Buccaneer XX894 – which had just relocated from Farnborough to Bruntingthorpe. Guy was not only looking for someone electrically minded to put the myriad severed wires back together, but was actually wanting to get the aircraft ground running. The prospect of getting involved with electrical work on a British jet aircraft with a view to making it taxiable was

too mouth-watering an opportunity to pass up and I arranged to meet Guy at Bruntingthorpe the following weekend. That, for me, was how it all started!

Going to airshows during the 1980s and early 1990s I was fortunate enough to see Buccaneer aircraft fly while still in RAF service. For whatever reason the Buccaneer rarely appeared in the flying programmes, but could often been seen among other aircraft in the static parks. I don't know why the Buccaneer never displayed that frequently, so it was a real treat for me when one did. It would always grab my attention as being something of a rarity. Nowadays, I'm kind of grateful for those rare displays as it meant that I was making an extra effort to watch something flying around the sky that I would unknowingly get to work on some 10 to 15 years later!

Having previously been to Bruntingthorpe in the 1990s to watch various aircraft fly or perform high-speed taxi runs on the 'Big Thunder' days, I already knew what the airfield had to offer, along with its resident collection of classic British jets. Joining the 'Buccaneer XX894' team right at the start of the restoration, in an environment surrounded by like-minded individuals and vintage jets was simply inspiring and it was agreed that I would take the lead role in restoring XX894's electrical systems. This was exactly the opportunity I had been looking for and I began reading up on the Buccaneer electrical systems in earnest. Twelve months later would see most of the electrical systems repaired, rewired and fully functional. Next, I was to put my mechanical engineering skill set to good use and start work on the hydraulics and fuel system, before lastly working on the engines.

A little over a year after XX894 had arrived at Bruntingthorpe for her restoration, Buccaneer XW544 was delivered on the back of a low-loader with another restoration team in tow. Although the two teams actively assisted with each other's projects, it would be some years before the two finally merged to become what is now The Buccaneer Aviation Group!

Francis Wallace describes the maintenance regime required to keep the TBAG Buccaneers in a 'live' running condition:

'Anti-det' run

Every 28 to 42 days both TBAG Buccaneers are readied for an anti-deterioration exercise known simply as an 'anti-det' run. The purpose of the 'anti-det' run is to exercise all electrical, mechanical, hydraulic and pneumatic systems on the aircraft, wherever possible.

There are many reasons why we need carry out the 'anti-det' runs. Firstly and perhaps most importantly is that we get to start, run and watch the Buccaneers being exercised close-up. After all, this is the main reason TBAG exists! Keeping the aircraft alive is what we work so hard for. All the blood, sweat and tears are rewarded by seeing and hearing the two Spey 101 engines spool into life. The many hours spent out on a freezing cold, windy airfield are forgotten when we see the pilots take them out on to the runway for a drive. Granted they will never fly again, but that's not what it is all about: it is about preserving something for future generations to enjoy, bringing them one step closer to imagining what it must have been like to see Buccaneer aircraft operate in their heyday.

Secondly, the Spey engines *need* to be kept exercised. It's not so much the engines perhaps but more the fuel system. Fuel doesn't keep well over time and its deterioration can cause all manner of problems, particularly if it goes off in the fuel nozzles, located towards the rear of the engines within the burner cans. We treat our fuel with chemical additives to help prevent

LEFT Refuelling panels open showing the ground refuelling coupling (left) and the refuel/defuel control panel (right). Both panels are located on the starboard side just aft of the folding nose on XX894 at Bruntingthorpe, 26 November 2016. *(Keith Wilson)*

ABOVE The refuel/defuel control panel showing master switch, tank selector switches, refuelling indicator and density selector. The Buccaneer could be fuelled or defuelled by selecting the required switches. *(Keith Wilson)*

BELOW The hinged cover for the refuel/defuel control panel is fitted with two guard brackets which prevent it from being closed if any of the tank selector switches are inadvertently left in an incorrect position. *(Keith Wilson)*

LEFT A sprung airspeed switch override is fitted to simulate 'weight on ground' in order that undercarriage retraction tests can be carried out when the aircraft is on the ground. During the tests, the aircraft would of course be up on jacks and the switch manually held in the 'up' position in order to enable the circuit protection relays to function. *(Keith Wilson)*

deterioration, but the best way to completely avoid fuel issues is to burn it. What better way to do this than to fire the engines up!

Finally, the hydraulic system has very many rubber sealing washers and O-rings within it. If left inactive, these can dry out and perish in the harsh environment of an airfield. In time, if the hydraulic fluid starts to seep past a seal, it becomes sticky – just like treacle – when in contact with the surrounding air. When the hydraulic parts do move the various rams and shuttles within the system, they should move freely and be well lubricated. However, if the fluid has become sticky, the seals can drag, causing further wear and eventual failure. Frequent exercising can avoid scenarios such as these and keeps the hydraulic components well oiled and free to move.

Maintenance and preparation ahead of the 'anti-det' run

The Buccaneers are serviced ahead of each 'anti-det' run and additional checks are made to any specific areas that may have received any remedial works; for example, a change of parts or fuel line repair.

Before commencing with an 'anti-det' run there are certain activities that have to take place in preparation. These include removing all protective covers over the canopy, wheels and pitot tubes. A fully charged battery is installed into the rear radio bay of the aircraft and the canopy opened using electrical power. A customary glance at the cockpit volt meter usually confirms that 24V DC is available.

Engines, fluids and pressure levels

The morning of an 'anti-det' run usually starts by checking all fluid and pressure levels on the jet. Firstly, the engine oil levels are checked. The Rolls-Royce Spey 101 engines fitted to the Buccaneer have a partial-loss oil system, which means some of the oil is expelled out of the jet pipes along with the hot exhaust gases. The quantity of oil lost during normal operation is relatively small, so if the oil tank is down by some considerable measure, say half a pint or more, then an investigation would begin for any signs of leakage. Leaks, if found, are usually quite obvious due to the bright yellow nature of the OX38-type oil used. Ordinarily, the oil is only ever topped up in quantity as a result of works that have been carried out on the system necessitating oil removal or loss. A simple window with a measurement gauge (measured in pints) is located on the side of the engine oil tank and is used to visually check the correct oil level.

Next, the CSDU (constant speed drive unit) oil levels are checked. The CSDU is a device connected to the engine gearbox at one end and to a 30kVA electrical generator at the other. The purpose of the CSDU is to provide a constant output of 8,000rpm to the generator throughout the entire speed range of the engine. The generator in turn provides the required 200V 3-phase 400Hz electrical supply to the aircraft electrical systems. The CSDU is of the swash plate type and so a lack of oil simply means that the generator will not turn in order to provide any electrical power. Once again, there is a simple window with a measurement gauge (in pints) located on the side of the CSDU oil tank. This is used to check that the oil is at the correct level.

Once the oil levels are checked, a visual inspection is then performed to the airframe to ensure that all is in order; all fixtures and fittings, both mechanical and electrical, are secure and wire locked where required, while no fuel or hydraulic leaks are present.

Hydraulics and pneumatics

The Buccaneer has two main hydraulic systems which provide pressure to General Services and the Flying Controls. The General Services

system operates at a pressure of 4,000psi and provides motive force for the following services:

- Undercarriage retraction/extension
- Wing fold
- Tail skid
- Bomb door
- Airbrakes
- Arresting hook
- Mainplane flaps
- Wheel brakes (although the pressure is reduced at the brake relay valve to 1,700psi at the wheels)
- Nose wheel steering

The General Service hydraulics is driven from a pump mounted on each engine gearbox. They are fed with hydraulic oil type OM15 from a main general service reservoir located in the forward lower accessory bay. The main reservoir is a cylinder with a piston mounted within it; one side of the piston contains the OM15 and the other side air. As any of the hydraulic services listed above operate, the piston moves backwards and forwards, effectively maintaining system pressure as and when any valves are opened or closed. It essentially acts like a buffer, smoothing out pulsations as the fluid is pumped around the system while helping to maintain a constant pressure.

The first thing to check is to ensure that there is plenty of OM15 in the main reservoir. There is a printed note on the side of the main reservoir which indicates how much oil to add dependent upon the aircraft's current configuration (ie wings folded or spread, airbrakes open or

ABOVE LEFT Replenishing the General Services hydraulic reservoir with OM15 hydraulic oil. A Risbridger is used to hand pump the oil into the reservoir via the Avery coupling located on the lower starboard fuselage side, as seen on XX894. *(Keith Wilson)*

ABOVE CENTRE Francis Wallace operates the Risbridger hand pump to transfer OM15 hydraulic oil from the 1-gallon tin to the General Services reservoir during maintenance on XX894 at Bruntingthorpe, 26 November 2016. *(Keith Wilson)*

ABOVE RIGHT Francis carefully monitors the level of the hydraulic oil in the General Services reservoir while replenishing OM15 hydraulic oil into XX894. *(Keith Wilson)*

closed etc). Typically, the volume of OM15 required almost always equates to the main reservoir being approximately filled halfway.

If OM15 is to be added, it is done with the use of a hand-held pump typically known by its manufacturer name of 'Risbridger'. The suction end of the 'Risbridger' is screwed into a 1-gallon can of OM15 and the supply end is connected to the aircraft hydraulic supply coupling located on the starboard side of the airframe. A bleed screw on the side of the Risbridger's hydraulic coupling is released to ensure an air-free flow of OM15 into the main reservoir.

The air side of the main reservoir needs to be maintained at 20–32psi and is usually kept within this range by taking bleed air from the running engines. If the engines are not to be run, but hydraulic checks made with a ground servicing trolley only, the air side will be topped up to the correct pressure with dry nitrogen.

The Flying Controls operate at a pressure of

3,300psi and provide the motive force for the following services:

- Ailerons
- Rudder
- Tailplane

The Flying Control hydraulics are also driven from a pump mounted on each engine gearbox. They are also fed with hydraulic oil type OM15 from two reservoirs located in the forward lower accessory bay. The reservoirs are large cylinders with one large and one small piston connected together within. Unlike the General Services main reservoir, both outer sides of the piston contain the OM15 with the inner side being free of any fluid. The larger piston face is connected to Flying Control services, whereas the small piston face is connected to a steel accumulator. Similar to the main General Service reservoir, the accumulator is a cylinder with a piston mounted within with one side of the piston containing the OM15 and the other

side air or dry nitrogen. Unlike the 20–32psi required for the General Services, the Flying Control accumulators need to be charged up to 2,000psi with dry nitrogen as they are not supported at all by engine bleed air.

The Flying Control reservoirs have a large printed line around their circumference indicating where the correct fill level should be. The process of filling them with OM15 is as described for the General Services, except that the coupling connection is located on the port side lower aft of the cockpit.

Charging the nitrogen side of the accumulators is done by connecting a nitrogen trolley or bottle to the adjacent Schrader connection via a regulator, high-pressure hose and Turner adaptor. The Turner adaptor is a small device that depresses the Schrader valve, thus allowing the one-way flow of nitrogen into the accumulator. Once fully charged to 2,000psi the regulator can be shut off, the hose vented and the Turner adaptor removed.

Ordinarily, when carrying out an 'anti-det'

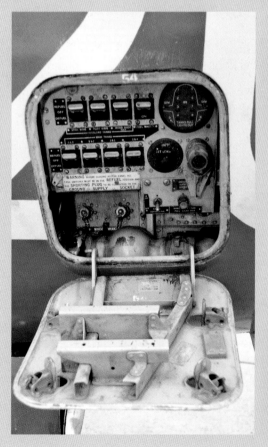

RIGHT The refuel/ defuel panel also contains the Schrader valves used to replenish oxygen-free nitrogen (OFN) into the handbrake and footbrake accumulators. The two Schrader valves complete with dust caps can be seen to the lower left of the refuel/defuel control panel on XX894. (Keith Wilson)

ABOVE The refuel/defuel hinged panel door is accessed by means of four quick-release panel fasteners, as seen on XX894 at Bruntingthorpe. (Keith Wilson)

BELOW The OFN charging line connected to the handbrake accumulator Schrader valve on XX894. (Keith Wilson)

run, it is unlikely the aircraft is to move under its own power, so the wheel chocks always remain firmly in place. Even so, it is common to run the engines up to at least 90% in order to exercise the inlet guide vanes. Although the Buccaneer is unlikely to ever climb over the wheel chocks at this power, it is an absolute must that the brakes work effectively, should the pilot ever be required to use them!

Wheel brakes

The wheel brakes are operated by pressing the rudder pedals which have a small hydraulic foot motor mounted on the back of them. When the Buccaneer isn't run for a period of time, it is usual for the pressure to dissipate from the foot motors, leaving the rudder pedals feeling spongy or flat. When recharging the foot motors it is customary to start with the port side first.

A small bung has to be removed from the top of the foot motor and can prove to be quite fiddly due to the limited room provided to remove it. Access has to be gained to the charging ports by first opening the folding nose and locating them on the lower left-hand side adjacent to the windscreen washer bottle. Using a tin of OM15 and the 'Risbridger' connected to the port charging point, the OM15 is pumped into the foot motors until an air-free flow of oil is seen at the opening where the bung was removed. The same process is repeated for the starboard side.

The wheel brakes themselves are fed from the General Services hydraulic system but the pressure is reduced from 4,000psi down to 1,700psi in the brake relay valve.

Accumulators filled with OM15 on one side of a piston with dry nitrogen in the other are used within the system, in order to help provide smooth, progressive braking. The accumulators also have a very important secondary function, that should the main hydraulics fail for any reason, there will be enough residual pressure held to allow for several full applications of the brakes.

The method for bleeding the wheel brakes is much the same as is done on a car; a bottle with a rubber hose is connected to the

ABOVE Francis Wallace charging OFN into the handbrake accumulator while monitoring the pressure on one of the two pressure gauges which can be seen in the upper part of the large number '0' on the side of the fuselage of XX894. *(Keith Wilson)*

ABOVE The OFN is charged from the cylinder via a regulator pre-set to the desired pressure. In service the OFN would have been supplied from a bottle trolley (which is also used by the TBAG team at Bruntingthorpe). In this instance, a small portable bottle is quicker and easier to use on XX894. *(Keith Wilson)*

ABOVE The two brake accumulator pressure gauges are conveniently mounted on the outside of the aircraft, just above and to the right of where the Schrader valves are located: 'Normal' – footbrake pressure; 'Hand' – parking brake pressure. Inflation pressure is also conveniently displayed. When the engines are running both gauges should read 4,000psi (*ie* with the needles on the '40'). The pressure gauges allow the 'see-off crew' to check the brake pressures prior to releasing the aircraft, a clever safety feature from the Buccaneer's aircraft carrier heritage! *(Keith Wilson)*

ABOVE The port side main wheel brake on XW544 being bled. Brake bleeding is carried out in much the same way as on many road vehicles, by connecting a transparent rubber hose to the main wheel bleed valve with the other end going into a transparent container. With the bleed valve opened, the foot pedal is depressed until a clear non-aerated flow of fluid (OM15) can be seen in the transparent rubber hose and container. *(Keith Wilson)*

ABOVE The brake bleeding process is a team effort! Instructions on when to apply and release the brake pedal is carefully coordinated, along with when to open and close the main wheel bleed valve. 'Brakes on' is indicated with clenched fists and 'brakes off' by open hands, as is the case here with TBAG's Andrew Webber, orchestrating events at Bruntingthorpe, 26 May 2017. *(Keith Wilson)*

ABOVE With 'brakes on/bleed valve open' being signalled by Andrew Webber, the fluid will now flow from the main wheel bleed valve into the transparent container. This procedure will be repeated until all air is expelled from the system. *(Keith Wilson)*

ABOVE The starboard main wheel brakes on XW544 being bled at Bruntingthorpe on 26 May 2017. When bleeding the brakes, the accumulators can become extinguished or 'flat' in just three or four applications of the pedal or parking brake. A hydraulic servicing trolley is used to maintain system pressure, and coordination through hand signals is essential at times when it is too noisy to hear each other speak. *(Keith Wilson)*

ABOVE The hydraulic servicing trolley is connected to the aircraft via flow and return self-sealing Avery couplings. The small hose is the high-pressure supply into the aircraft and the larger hose is the low-pressure return back to the servicing trolley. *(Keith Wilson)*

ABOVE RIGHT The brake pedals have small hydraulically operated foot motors operating at reduced pressures to the final working pressure in the main wheel brake packs. All hydraulic components or gauge lines that enter the cockpit are reduced in pressure for safety reasons. As a result, the foot motors require bleeding separately from the main wheel brakes, which can often require considerable dexterity to reach the foot motor filler caps! TBAG member Kay 'Red' Bennett was photographed bleeding the brake pedal foot motors on XW544 at Bruntingthorpe on 26 May 2017. *(Keith Wilson)*

wheel brake bleed valve. The bleed valve is repeatedly opened and closed as the brake pedal is depressed until a clear non-aerated flow of OM15 can be seen. In the process of doing this, it can sometimes happen that the accumulators are fully exhausted to their minimum operating pressure of 1,300psi. This is not a problem as once the engines are running the General Services will restore the pressure back to 4,000psi. Should the accumulator pressures ever fall below 1,300psi, they must be replenished using dry nitrogen, using the same process as used for inflating the Flying Control accumulators, the Schrader connections this time being found on the port side below the refuel/defuel panel.

The hand (or parking) brake operates from the wheel brake hydraulic system but also has its own accumulator that can be discharged in order to bring the aircraft to a standstill. The only real difference between the two systems is that the rudder pedals provide differential braking, whereas the handbrake applies equal pressure simultaneously to both wheels.

Final engine checks

Before the 'anti-det' run actually takes place, the engine blanks are removed. The intake and blades of the engines are checked for any obvious signs of damage and are spun by hand to check freedom of movement. The jet pipes are then inspected to ensure that no foreign objects are present that could pass through the engines and get blown out the back when the engines are running.

'Anti-det' run pre-briefing

The 'anti-det' run is typically briefed and led by TBAG members Andrew Webber or Andrew King, as they both have the most experience in the group at conducting the lead.

During the 'anti-det' run, the back seat can be occupied by another team member and we try to rotate this privilege through the group. Occasionally, it is offered to a guest, providing the exercise is just a routine run. However, if maintenance has been carried out on such things as brakes, cockpit instrumentation or engines, etc ahead of the run, then an engineering member will always occupy the rear seat, in a monitoring or testing capacity.

The run itself is a well-rehearsed drill with group members being given their assignments just after the servicing has been completed. This will comprise of who is responsible for operating the Stad (the low-pressure engine air starter); who is moving the Stad hose from engine to engine; and who is manning the fire bottles. The pilot is briefed as to which engine will be started first (usually it is the port engine) and as to what functions will be carried out; all along with any specific checks relating to any recent rectification or service works done. On completion of the briefing everyone takes up their assigned positions.

The 'anti-det' run

The aircraft is towed to the pan using the tow bar and a tug. The aircraft is positioned as far as possible away from the concrete floor expansion joints of the pan, as these can harbour all manner of hidden detritus, stones and other loose articles. As far as is possible the aircraft is always parked facing into the direction of the wind and a thorough FOD (foreign object damage) inspection made of the surrounding area. A sweep of the ground area around the intakes is made with a broom for good measure.

The 'anti-det' run itself is usually performed in the same manner every time and typically in the following order:

1   Stad on – the operator signals to the pilot that air is ready.

    The Stad is a low-pressure air starter

BELOW Two pilots, one cockpit! In addition to being a regular 'anti-det' run on XW544/O at Bruntingthorpe on 27 May 2017, this was a pilot familiarisation run to allow the newer pilot chance to observe the start-up procedure prior to carrying out a later run himself. The ground equipment in the foreground is a low-pressure air start trolley or Stad. The hose from the Stad is connected via a quick-release coupling to the air starter mounted on the auxiliary gearbox of the port Spey engine of the Buccaneer. *(Keith Wilson)*

ABOVE With the second pilot observing the action from the rear cockpit, the pilot in command calls for 'Air On' and the Stad operator signals 'Air On to Engine Number 1' (which is always the port-side engine). The pilot cannot see which engine the air start hose is connected to, so the indication from the Stad operator is very important. *(Keith Wilson)*

ABOVE With air on to engine number 2 (starboard), the personnel in the foreground will be responsible for disconnecting the hose after the engine has stabilised at idle following the start routine. *(Keith Wilson)*

RIGHT Although not a frequent occurrence, this image shows the effect of a 'wet start' where ignition has taken place after a small quantity of atomised fuel has already escaped the jet pipe prior to combustion. The escaped fuel has then ignited behind the jet pipe. *(Keith Wilson)*

trolley used to provide low-pressure high-volume air to the Buccaneer's Spey engines in order to rotate them to a speed at which they can ignite and run. The Stad has a battery-started gas turbine engine mounted on a towable trolley, complete with fuel tank and operator control panel. The Stad is also equipped with several metres of 4–5in-diameter flexible hose that connects from the gas turbine – via a quick-release coupling – to the air pressure starter mounted on the gearbox of the Spey 101.

2 Pilot opens the port LP (low-pressure) fuel cock and calls for air on.

The port and starboard LP (low-pressure – relates to the LP turbine) fuel cocks are located to the rear, left of the pilot's ejection seat. They are connected via mechanical linkages to shut-off valves found within the bomb bay. The LP fuel cocks when closed isolate the fuel supply from all of the fuel tanks into the fuel inlet pipes mounted towards the back of the engines.

3 The Stad operator checks everyone is clear from around the aircraft and signals 'Air Supply On'.

4 The Stad hose connected to the port engine inflates and the engine fan blades begin to rotate.

5   At approximately 12% HP rpm (high-pressure revs per minute, which relates to the HP turbine speed, which can be read on the instrument labelled 'HP rpm' – port or starboard) the pilot opens the throttle to 'Ground Start' while simultaneously pressing the igniters.

6   As fuel and compressed air ignite, the engine rapidly starts to spool up.

7   At approximately 35% HP rpm the pilot signals for 'Air Off'. The Stad operator turns off the air supply and the hose goes flat.

8   The engine continues to accelerate up to 50% whereby the pilot pushes the throttle through the gate to 'Ground Idle'.

9   The pilot checks the TGT instruments which should reveal that the engine has sustained a healthy 400°C. Then he checks the LP rpm which should indicate '25%' and the oil pressure gauges are reading 'cross hatched/high'.

10 The port generator is switched on by the pilot and power to the cockpit and the aircraft instruments and systems come online.

11 Hydraulic pressure gauges for General Services should now indicate 4,000psi and for the Flying Controls 3,300psi.

ABOVE With both engines successfully started and running, electrical generators and hydraulic systems online, the pilot then exercises all of the aircraft systems. He starts by unfolding the wings. The comms lead to the groundcrew can be seen along the ground, running up into the main wheel bay where it is connected into the comms socket. This allows the aircrew to communicate with the groundcrew. *(Keith Wilson)*

ABOVE The wings continue to unfold until . . . *(Keith Wilson)*

LEFT . . . they are fully unfolded and locked down. *(Keith Wilson)*

LEFT With the wings fully lowered, the mainplane flaps are selected down and the ailerons drooped. The mainplane flap is the larger (inboard) one of the two. *(Keith Wilson)*

Providing all is well from both inside and outside the cockpit, the Stad hose is moved to the starboard engine and the process repeated.

With both engines running, both generators online and no warnings present on the CWS (combined warning system), all hydraulic and electrical services such as internal and external lights can be tested and this is performed as a well-rehearsed and choreographed process.

Normally the Buccaneers are stowed with their wings folded to save space, so the first service to be enabled is the wing spread. With wings down and locked, the mainplane flaps and ailerons are then drooped. This selection also enables the tailplane flap to raise, but it's purely an electrical motor-driven function linked to the hydraulic one. With the ailerons drooped, the BLC system will activate, which bleeds hot air from the seventh stage of the engine HP compressor out over the wings and under the tailplane. Depending upon whether there has been much rain since the last 'anti-det' run took place, this can result in quite a spectacular water spray!

With the mainplane flaps and ailerons raised, the airbrakes, bomb door, arrester hook, tailplane and rudder can all be cycled in turn as well as brake pressures tested.

With all hydraulic services testing successfully completed, the engines will then be progressively taken up through the speed range in turn until the inlet guide vanes (IGVs) are heard to operate. When this happens there is a very noticeable audible tone change in the running of the engines, along with an increase in air noise upon deceleration. The engine note becomes higher-pitched with acceleration, whereas the sound of the air flow becomes less noticeable until the IGVs cease to operate. The noise change is clearly noticeable both

ABOVE With the ailerons drooped, the BLC system is automatically activated. The BLC takes air from the seventh stage of the HP compressor, which is located approximately halfway along each Rolls-Royce Spey engine. The bleed air is directed out over the wings and under the tailplane. If there has been any significant rainfall since the last run, water can collect in the ductwork of the BLC system. With the engines running it is quickly expelled, as can be seen here. *(Keith Wilson)*

LEFT With the mainplane flaps and ailerons retracted, the BLC is automatically switched off. *(Keith Wilson)*

RIGHT Demonstrating its carrier heritage, the Buccaneer was fitted with a fairly sizeable tailhook, seen here in the lowered position. This is always exercised as part of the 'anti-det' run. *(Keith Wilson)*

BELOW The Buccaneer had an all-moving tailplane which can be seen here being exercised in the nose pitch down position . . . *(Keith Wilson)*

BELOW RIGHT . . . and also right through the pitch range to the nose pitch up position. *(Keith Wilson)*

LEFT Out on the runway! Prior to any show or event day, the Buccaneers are given a shakedown run to ensure that there are no last-minute unserviceable snags that will need addressing. Usually a high-speed run will be carried out along the Bruntingthorpe runway as part of these shakedown runs. *(Keith Wilson)*

career, the Buccaneer suffered from numerous fuel leak issues and post-career there's no exception! This particular fuel leak was known about ahead and was, in fact, no more than a continuous drip which proceeded to fill the inside of the bomb door. The main fuel gallery runs all over the roof of the bomb bay and a leak on a clamp over time resulted in this rather spectacular show when the bomb door was opened to release the trapped fuel. The laborious task of completely defuelling the aircraft had to be conducted before repairing the leak.
(Keith Wilson)

inside and outside the cockpit. From inside the cockpit it is loud and violent, and you can feel the jet wanting to break free. From the outside it is observed as screaming raw power wanting to be unleashed!

The IGVs are required to control the total air flow into the engines for the benefit of proper combustion across the full speed range. All engine instruments are monitored to ensure everything is within limits at this time.

Providing everything operates satisfactorily, the engines are allowed to run at idle prior to shutting down. During the idling time the wings are raised back to their folded position and the airbrakes are left open.

To shut down the engines, both throttles are pulled from 'Ground Idle' back through the gate, all the way to 'closed'. This starves the engines of fuel and so they begin to wind down. The wind-down time of both engines is carefully checked to ensure that they do not stop too quickly, indicating a possible tight bearing. Ideal wind-down run time is between 40 and 60 seconds.

All switches – such as the generators and lights – are then returned to their 'Off' positions before the pilot climbs down from the cockpit, when he joins the thorough debrief and any snags are reported and discussed.

Open day or event

If either of the Buccaneers is to participate in an event where it is required to be on the move, the 'anti-det' run usually forms part of a full shakedown test. This is almost always carried

out the day ahead of the planned run, allowing sufficient time for any snags to be fixed. In addition to the static 'anti-det' run, the following checks and tests are also carried out:

Tyres: The Buccaneers spend all of their time outside in the elements. Although we do our best to preserve the tyres with the correct covers, when not in use we prefer to remove at the very least the nose wheel and tyre and change them out for an old, worn unit; thereby retaining the good ones in our storage container. Nose wheel tyres are in very short supply so we have to look after what we have!

The tyres are checked for any signs of obvious damage and are inflated to the correct pressures. The tyres are inflated using dry nitrogen in either a 'walk-around kit' (a self-contained tyre inflation kit complete with a built-in nitrogen cylinder) or by using a separate inflation kit with an external, remote nitrogen cylinder. Tyre pressure checks do not often form part of the monthly 'anti-det' run unless there is an obvious sign of under-inflation, at which point the entire wheel will normally be removed for investigation and repair.

Maxaret anti-skid devices: The Buccaneer is equipped with Maxaret anti-skid devices, each consisting of two generators mounted to each wheel. If and when the wheels spin, so do the generators, which in turn charge up capacitors. If a wheel suddenly locks, the generator stops turning, allowing the capacitor to discharge and open a solenoid valve in the brake line. The release in brake pressure allows the wheel to turn again, regardless of pilot input.

To test the anti-skid, the aircraft will be jacked up so that the wheels are free to turn. The Maxaret is removed and spun by hand while another team member simultaneously rotates the wheel. The pilot pushes down on the associated rudder pedal to lock the wheel and just as soon as the Maxaret is stopped from spinning, the brake will release and be free to rotate even though the pilot still has his foot on the pedal. The process is repeated for both sides of the aircraft.

Undercarriage: The undercarriage fitted to the Buccaneer is strictly heavy duty, due mainly to the aircraft's Royal Navy shipboard heritage. The shock absorbers are of the spring type and are charged with oil type OX16, the nose being charged to 2,800psi and the mains to 3,600psi. Typically we check and charge the undercarriage springs annually as they are not subjected to the constant weight and compression changes that would have been seen when in operational service.

Nose wheel steering and brakes: With the tyres and anti-skid operations having all been confirmed as 'satisfactory', we now return to the 'anti-det' run procedure, just prior to shutting down the engines.

While the engines are at idle and all systems have been confirmed as 'satisfactory', the chocks are removed from around all three wheels. When all personnel and ground equipment is confirmed as 'clear', the signal is given by the lead for the pilot to move the aircraft forward. The nose wheel steering is engaged and power gradually applied until the aircraft rolls forward, whereupon a smooth but decisive application of the brakes is carried out. All being well, the Buccaneer pulls up square and is held against the brakes until being cleared to taxi to the runway.

Communications: Until recently, the comms have not been operational on either aircraft. I have been working through the comms issues and can report that they now work on both jets! My next aim is to get both the UHF and VHF radios working. I have secured all of the parts and the relevant manuals. All that is now required is to fit the parts to both of them and then to try to get the system working. If successful, both aircraft will be able to communicate with each other on the ground, along with the lead groundcrew, on hand-held radios.

Shakedown run or demonstration run: Whenever possible, it is our aim to run both jets together at an event or open day. Sadly, due to serviceability issues, sometimes this is not possible. The open days provide a means of demonstrating what we have achieved with the restoration and maintenance of these jets; the chance for a younger generation to

see an aircraft type they would only ordinarily see static in a museum; while also providing an opportunity to raise funds so that we can continue to fuel the aircraft.

The Buccaneer(s) will taxi out on to the runway and carry out a couple of handling checks with both the nose wheel steering and brake operation. This is usually done by driving around in a series of figure-of-eight patterns. As part of a display routine the figure-of-eight patterns would be done with a couple of pauses, allowing the demonstration of the wing fold and bomb-door operation to the public.

With the hydraulic demonstration completed, the Buccaneer is lined up on the runway centreline, where the flaps and ailerons are set. The airbrake and bomb door are 'closed', with the wings 'down' and 'locked'. The lead groundcrew member then carries out one last walk-around check to ensure that nothing is loose or leaking (both hydraulic fluids and fuel), that the brakes are cool (they shouldn't be radiating an excessive heat) and the tyres haven't picked up any debris or damage.

With all of the groundcrew clear of the aircraft, both throttles are simultaneously pushed to 90% against the brakes while a final sweep of the cockpit confirms all is reading. Finally, the throttles are pushed to the stops topping out at around 97% HP rpm. The nose undercarriage compresses under the strain until the brakes are released, allowing the Buccaneer to sprint forward. Typically, the throttles are pulled to 'Ground Idle' at the end of the crowd line as by that point there's no reason to keep the power on as no one really benefits from the speed or noise. Most fast taxi runs see speeds of between 110 and 130 knots reached by the Buccaneers, dependent upon the weather conditions on the day; quite fast enough to put on a great show!

The Buccaneers run all the way to the end of the runway before completing a 180° turn and taxi back towards the start point. Half-way down the runway, the groundcrew have repositioned and meet the aircraft for a walk-around check to be conducted. Once satisfied that all is OK, the jets are cleared to taxi back to the start of the runway, where they are shut down in front of the very large crowd – usually to rapturous applause.

Chapter Nine

Buccaneer survivors

Of the 209 Buccaneer aircraft produced at Holme-on-Spalding-Moor between January 1962 and October 1977, a healthy number have been preserved in the UK, the Republic of Ireland and South Africa, with some of them maintained by enthusiasts in a 'live' ground-running condition.

OPPOSITE The Buccaneer Aviation Group's S.2B, XW544/O, is preserved in 16 Squadron colours at Bruntingthorpe and is maintained in a 'live' taxiable condition. It was photographed at Bruntingthorpe on 11 February 2017 while undergoing one of its regular 'anti-det' runs with two members of the ground team paying particular attention to the aircraft. The flames on engine start-up were caused by unburned fuel detonating just behind the engine. The effect disappears within a few seconds. *(Keith Wilson)*

At the time of writing, the airworthiness of the three 'flyable' aircraft kept at Thunder City, near Cape Town, is unclear, as the licence to operate them was withdrawn by the South African authorities back in 2011. As a consequence, all three aircraft were put up for sale, although their current airworthiness status is difficult to ascertain.

However, it is wonderful to report that there is one Buccaneer aircraft in the UK that *may* just fly again. Buccaneer S.2B XX885 was registered as G-HHAA to Hawker Hunter Aviation Limited back in December 2002 and following an extensive rebuild at their Scampton base now undergoes regular maintenance and custodial ground runs – anti-deterioration exercises known simply as 'anti-det' runs. According to the Hawker Hunter Aviation website: 'The aircraft, its systems and spares are maintained in such a condition that it can be readily be activated to flight status should a contractual tasking arise which requires the performance and flight envelope of the Buccaneer platform.'

Buccaneer S.1 XN923

The oldest 'live' ground-running Buccaneer is S.1 XN923, which is preserved with the Gatwick Aviation Museum at Charlwood.

XN923 made its first flight at Holme-on-Spalding-Moor on 11 March 1962 and was then delivered to 700Z Flight, Fleet Air Arm as '685' on 8 May. On 20 July, XN923 was transferred to the A&AEE at Boscombe Down for Tropical Trials and Deck Clearance Trials of production aircraft. The Tropical Trials were conducted at RAF Idris, Tripoli, Libya, from 7 to 21 September 1962.

By December of the same year, XN923 became the first Buccaneer to conduct air-to-air refuelling behind a Sea Vixen and by February of the following year was busy undergoing Carrier Trials aboard HMS *Ark Royal* in the English Channel. XN923 continued in service with the A&AEE on a variety of trials work until it was returned to Holme-on-Spalding-Moor in September 1965 before being withdrawn from service in August of the following year.

In August 1967, XN923 was made airworthy again and joined the RAE at Farnborough for various ground and weapons trials before being moved to West Freugh from September 1970 to June 1973.

In May 1974, it returned to the A&AEE at Farnborough to undertake Electromagnetic Compatibility Trials but was struck off charge in 1977 and later remained at Boscombe Down, by then in a derelict condition, until July 1986.

After being put up for sale, it was purchased by Peter Vallance and moved by road to the Gatwick Aviation Museum where it arrived on 23 March 1990. It was painstakingly reassembled to static display in its former RAE colour scheme.

Following extensive work that started in 2011, the port Gyron Junior engine was spun over for the first time in early March 2012. The second time it was blown over 'wet' to ensure that no major problems were present in the fuel system. Finally, the 'crackers' were fired and the engine lit and ran smoothly. XN923 is now capable of running both Gyron Junior engines.

In March 2018, XN923 was dismantled and moved inside the museum workshops where a major restoration programme began. It is expected to take between two and three years to complete.

Buccaneer S.2 XN974

Originally ordered by the Ministry of Supply as a Buccaneer S.1, XN974 was reordered as an S.2 and made its first flight at Holme-on-Spalding-Moor on 5 June 1964. Within a month it had been transferred to the Ministry of Aviation for use on Controller (Air) Release trials.

It went straight to the RAE at Bedford for minimum launch and catapult trials before joining HMS *Eagle* for sea trials.

In July 1965, accompanied by XK527

and XN976, it was utilised on Tropical Trials and Carrier-compatibility Trials aboard USS *Lexington*. While in the USA, it appeared at displays at Edwards AFB and NAS Patuxent River before setting a non-stop crossing record of the Atlantic when it flew from Goose Bay, Labrador, to RAF Lossiemouth – a journey of 1,950 miles in 4 hours and 16 minutes – and became the first Fleet Air Arm aircraft to fly transatlantic non-stop without refuelling.

Later in 1965, XN974 continued in trails work with the A&AEE at Boscombe Down, the RAE at Bedford and Hawker Siddeley at Holme-on-Spalding-Moor. In 1971, it rejoined the RAF but its military career was relatively short-lived as it once again ended up on trials work with BAe at Warton.

After a long and successful career as a trials aircraft, Buccaneer S.2 XN974 was flown into retirement at Elvington in 1991. Here, it is maintained in a 'live' ground-operational condition by enthusiastic volunteers from the Yorkshire Air Museum.

In late 2016 and early 2017, XN974 underwent significant engineering and restoration work which included repainting the airframe into her original Royal Navy colour scheme, which she proudly displays today. Both the Buccaneer Air Crew Association and the Air Crew Association Archive Trust made significant contributions towards the cost of the restoration work.

Buccaneer S.2B XW544/O

XW544 was part of a 26-aircraft batch of Buccaneer S.2B aircraft built for the RAF by Hawker Siddeley at Brough. All were initially test flown at Holme-on-Spalding-Moor and XW544 was accepted by the RAF on 23 June 1972, before being delivered to XV Squadron, RAF Germany, at Laarbruch three days later.

ABOVE **XN974 is a Buccaneer S.2 preserved with the Yorkshire Air Museum at Elvington in a taxiable condition and regularly performs high-speed taxi runs for the visiting public. For many years it retained its former RAF camouflage but was recently repainted into its former grey and white Royal Navy colours. It was photographed here undergoing a fast taxi run at Elvington on 27 August 2017.** *(Lee Barton)*

By 1977, it was still with XV Squadron but now carried the code 'H'. In October 1979, XW544 was transferred to 16 Squadron and adopted the code 'O'. In February 1980, XW544 was – like all of the Buccaneer fleet – grounded, following the crash of XV345 at Nellis AFB, Nevada.

After the Buccaneer was released back into service, XV544 continued with 16 Squadron but in May 1982, it returned to XV Squadron with the code 'O'. Its stay with XV Squadron was short-lived as, in July 1983, XW544 was placed into storage with 27 MU at Shawbury and in October was allocated the maintenance serial 8557M. In February 1984, XW544 was transferred to No 2 SoTT at RAF Cosford as a ground instructional airframe before finally being withdrawn from service on 21 May 1985.

The airframe was acquired by Robert Goldstone and stored at RAF Shawbury before being transferred to Bruntingthorpe in October 2004. Later, the ownership was transferred to The Buccaneer Aviation Group (TBAG), which now maintains the aircraft in a 'live' ground-running condition. The aircraft is a regular performer at the Cold War Jet Days at Bruntingthorpe where it continues to entertain the visiting public with its display of 'smoke and noise', not to mention its spectacular acceleration up and down Bruntingthorpe's long runway during the fast runs.

ABOVE The TBAG's second 'live' Buccaneer at Bruntingthorpe is S.2B, XX894, which was delivered to the RAF in December 1975. Although it never served with the Royal Navy, it was painted in 809 NAS colours as '020', as part of the seven-aircraft farewell formation flown from Lossiemouth on 17 March 1994. This image was taken just ahead of an 'anti-det' run at Bruntingthorpe in June 2016. *(Keith Wilson)*

Buccaneer S.2B XX894/020

Buccaneer S.2B XX894 was part of a batch of 16 aircraft procured for the RAF and built at Brough. Another (XX901) was later added to the batch. All were initially test flown at Holme-on-Spalding-Moor and XX894 was initially accepted by the RAF on 4 December 1975 before being delivered to 16 Squadron, RAF Germany, at Laarbruch the following day.

It didn't remain with 16 Squadron for long as by February 1976 it was operating with XV Squadron with the code 'M'. XX894 was one of six RAF Germany aircraft flown to Nellis AFB, Nevada, for the ill-fated Exercise Red Flag 1980 when XV345 lost a wing and crashed, effectively grounding the entire Buccaneer fleet. XX894 spent a large part of early 1980 stranded at Nellis AFB until eventually being allowed to fly back to the UK. The following year XX894 was delivered to the A&AEE at Boscombe Down as a trials aircraft before being placed into storage with 19 MU at St Athan.

On 2 September 1981, XX894 was delivered to 12 Squadron where it adopted the code '894'. In April 1983, XX894 was one of ten Buccaneer S.2 aircraft (with XN976, XN983, XV164, XV168, XV333, XW530, XW542, XW547 and XX900) that flew to NAS Key West, Florida, to participate in Operation Western Fox – a live firing exercise of both TV-guided and anti-radiation Martel missiles against redundant US naval vessels.

In July 1983, XX894 was transferred to 208 Squadron and over the next few years the aircraft served with all three Lossiemouth-based Buccaneer units – 12 and 208 Squadrons, along with 237 OCU.

In February 1990, XX894 was chosen to receive a special 75th anniversary colour scheme (see image on page 12) with a green flash edged in black along the fuselage and tail.

In January 1991, XX894 was prepared for Operation Granby and received its ARTF desert-pink paintwork with the code 'O'. On 7 February, it joined XX863/S, XX885/L, XX895/G, XV352/U and XX901/N in the second batch of Buccaneer aircraft flown non-stop to Bahrain with in-flight refuelling. No nose art was added during the campaign but was later named *Aberlour* and seven mission symbols were added to the starboard nose below the cockpit canopy. XX894 returned to Lossiemouth on 17 March 1991 where it rejoined 12 Squadron.

In February 1994, XX894 was painted to represent '020/R' of 809 NAS, HMS *Ark Royal*, Royal Navy 1978 – the last Naval Air Squadron to operate the Buccaneer. It joined six further aircraft which were carrying the markings of all previous RAF squadrons who operated the Buccaneer for a final photo-call to mark the Buccaneer's retirement from operational flying on 31 March 1994.

After being withdrawn from service, XX894 was flown to St Athan for storage with 19 MU and its subsequent disposal. In 1995, it was acquired by a private owner who moved the airframe to Bruntingthorpe. It later spent a period of time at Kemble and Farnborough before being moved back to Bruntingthorpe in September 2003, where it has remained to this day.

XX894 is now operated by The Buccaneer Aviation Group (TBAG) and retains its Royal Navy colours as '020/R'. It is maintained in a 'live' ground-running condition and often performs alongside the TBAG's other aircraft, XW544/O, making smoke and noise at the Cold War Jet Days at Bruntingthorpe.

Buccaneer S.2B (Mod) XX897

Buccaneer S.2B XX897 was part of the same production batch as XX894. It made its first flight at Holme-on-Spalding-Moor on 19 March 1976 and was delivered to the Royal Signals and Radar Establishment (RSRE) at Pershore on 21 April 1976.

On 1 May 1977, XX897 was sold to the MoD(PE) and in December it was flown to the Radar Research Squadron (RRS) at the RAE/

DRA facility at Bedford for the installation of the Marconi AI 24 Foxhunter radar and associated avionics to undergo testing for the radar's suitability for the forthcoming Tornado ADV (later F.2 and F.3). Consequently, XX897 was fitted with a Tornado nose cone. The bomb-door fuel tank was removed and refitted with a standard weapons bay door. Interestingly, while Marshall's of Cambridge were given the Engineering Authority for this work to be carried out and supervised, all the work was undertaken at Bedford. Once the work had been completed, XX897 was flown back to Holme-on-Spalding-Moor on 15 August 1978 for the flight trials to be conducted. These were all completed by 15 September and crew familiarisation flights began.

On 16 January 1980, XX897 made its first radar shakedown flight, landing at RAF Valley. The majority of subsequent radar flight trials were conducted in the Aberporth Danger Area. Radar trials work continued until 31 January 1992, when XX897 made its final trials flight. It was finally withdrawn from service on 7 October 1992.

On 8 July 1993, XX897 was sold for just £17,000 at the Phillips London Auction and flown to Bournemouth on 19 August for its new owner Source Classic Jet Flight. In September 1998, XX897 was acquired by Nigel McKnight and during the spring of 2001 was repainted in European Aviation colours before being placed on display in the Bournemouth Aviation Museum, where the aircraft was maintained by the Bournemouth Engineering Support Team (BEST).

XX897 departed Bournemouth by road on 17 August 2012, en route to Atlantic Air Adventures at the Shannon Aviation Museum, where it arrived on 26 August. It was soon placed on static display at the museum but the owners were keen to have the aircraft in a 'live' condition and while it was not possible to run the engines in such a tight environment, it would be possible to activate the electrics and hydraulics. In stepped the 'T-Baggers' (The Buccaneer Aviation Group) who visited Shannon on two occasions – in January and April 2016 – and reactivated both systems successfully. XX897 is once again able to activate its electrics allowing the use of the cockpit lighting, navigation and anti-collision lights and strobes to function. With its new-found hydraulic system

now also functioning, XX897 is able to fold its wings, operate all control surfaces and flaps, rotate the bomb bay, lower and raise the hook and open and close the airbrakes.

Buccaneer S.2B XX900/900

Buccaneer S.2B XX900 was part of the same production batch as both XX894 and XX897. It was delivered to the RAF on 24 November 1976 and shortly afterwards issued to 208 Squadron at Honington.

XX900 was flown to Nellis AFB, Nevada, to participate in Exercise Red Flag 77 and acquired a temporary dark-earth and light-stone wrap-around colour scheme for the exercise, although these colours were removed once the aircraft returned to the UK. In July 1979, XX900 was transferred to 216 Squadron at Honington although this squadron was to be short-lived. In February 1980, like all Buccaneers in the fleet, XX900 was grounded following the crash of XV345. When the fleet was cleared to resume flying, it had been decided not to continue with 216 Squadron owing to a lack of sufficient airframes and XX900 was transferred to 12 Squadron before the squadron relocated to RAF Lossiemouth in November 1980.

Like XX894, XX900 participated in Exercise Western Fox at NAS Key West, Florida, in April 1983. In November of the same year, XX900 was used in trials of the ALE-40 Chaff/Flare Dispenser in support of Operation Pulsator, including flights made over the centre of Beirut. In 1986, XX900 underwent modifications 1724 to 1727, including the new Sea Eagle anti-ship missile capabilities, before receiving the Avionics Upgrade Programme (AUP) at Woodford.

ABOVE Buccaneer S.2B (Mod) XX897 is preserved with Atlantic Air Adventures at the Shannon Aviation Museum, Clare, Republic of Ireland, where it was photographed in April 2017. XX897 had been operated by the RRE and later by the RAE, where in 1976 it had been modified to carry a Marconi Foxhunter radar, as used by the Tornado F.2 and F.3 aircraft. *(Mike Overs)*

ABOVE The third Buccaneer preserved in a 'live' condition at Bruntingthorpe is the Cold War Jets Collection S.2B, XX900/900, which still retains its former 237 OCU colours. It too is a regular and welcome participant at the Cold War Jet Days, where it was photographed in May 2016.
(Keith Wilson)

In 1987, XX900 was reissued to 208 Squadron and continued to serve with all three Lossiemouth-based Buccaneer squadrons until being transferred to 19 MU at St Athan on 6 April 1994, for disposal.

It arrived at Bruntingthorpe on 17 October 1994 as part of the Cold War Jets Collection and is maintained by a small group of enthusiasts. Here, it is maintained in a 'live' ground-running condition and regularly delights visitors to the Cold War Jet Days with its noisy high-speed runs.

Status of the 'airworthy' Thunder City Buccaneers

Four Buccaneer S.2 aircraft were ordered from Hawker Siddeley Aviation Ltd for trials use by the RAE at Farnborough and West Freugh. They were allocated the serial numbers XW986 to XW989 but the last aircraft was subsequently cancelled. The remaining three aircraft were built at Brough and test flown at Holme-on-Spalding-Moor.

The first aircraft – XW986 – was delivered to MoD(PE) on 25 January 1974, painted in a non-standard, high-visibility, yellow, extra dark green and white colour scheme to ease tracking by camera and kinetheodolite operators. Aside from operating at West Freugh, it also saw service at Farnborough and Boscombe Down.

On 15 August 1983, XW986 arrived at East Midlands Airport for repainting in the new RAE raspberry ripple colour scheme of gloss signal red, white and Oxford blue. The work was completed in September 1983 and it returned to West Freugh. It continued with its service trials work until September 1994 when it was withdrawn from use.

The aircraft was acquired by Delta Jets and stored with 5 MU at RAF Kemble. In 2001, it was sold to Ian Pringle and flown to Cape Town, South Africa – departing Exeter on 4 August 2002 and arriving in Cape Town on 7 August. It was registered ZU-NIP and retained its RAE raspberry ripple colour scheme and continued to fly up until 2009.

The second aircraft – XW987 – was delivered to MoD(PE) on 15 March 1974, once again in a non-standard, high-visibility, yellow, extra dark green and white colour scheme. It soon took up its trial duties at West Freugh and was also operated at Farnborough. On 13 May 1982, XW987 was flown to 19 MU at St Athan to be

LEFT XW986 was the third former RAE Farnborough Buccaneer S.2B that was sold to Ian Pringle at Cape Town, South Africa, and became ZU-NIP, where it retained its former 'raspberry ripple' red, white and blue colour scheme. It was photographed at Cape Town in December 2005 and is believed to have made its last flight in South Africa during 2009. At the time of writing, ZU-NIP is thought to be in an 'airworthy' condition but is up for sale. *(PRM Aviation)*

Fly Supersonic Jets
www.thundercity.com

painted in the now-standard RAE raspberry ripple colour scheme, after which it continued to operate from West Freugh, Farnborough and Boscombe Down. XW987 was withdrawn from service in February 1995 and sold to Mike 'Beachy' Head the following year. On 1 April 1997, XW987 was flown to St Mawgan and departed for Cape Town on 30 April, arriving at its destination on 2 May. It was later painted in an all-over gloss black colour scheme and registered as ZU-BCR. For many years, back-seat rides were available for those with deep pockets and ZU-BCR was reported as having made its last flight as recently as late 2016.

The third aircraft – XW988 – was delivered to MoD(PE) on 16 May 1974, in the same high-visibility colour scheme as the other two aircraft. Shortly afterwards, it commenced its trials work at West Freugh.

When the Buccaneer fleet was grounded following the incident at Nellis AFB, XW988 was flown to Holme-on-Spalding-Moor and had strain gauges fitted to the inner wings. It remained here for ten months undergoing trials,

ABOVE The second RAE Buccaneer S.2B that became surplus to requirements was XW987, which was withdrawn from service in February 1995. It was sold and flown out to South Africa, arriving in Cape Town in May 1997, when it was registered ZU-BCR. It provided high-speed low-level jet rides for a number of years with Mike 'Beachy' Head's Thunder City operation and was photographed immediately after flying at Cape Town in November 2012. Reports indicate it made its very last flight in late 2016 but following the sad passing of Mike Head, is unlikely to fly again in South Africa. At the time of writing, ZU-BCR is thought to be in an 'airworthy condition' but is up for sale. *(Francis Wallace)*

until the fleet was returned to service. On 21 February 1981, XW988 was returned to the RAE at West Freugh for weapons trials, which were continued at Boscombe Down. Unlike both other aircraft in this batch, XW988 did not undergo a repaint into the new RAE raspberry ripple colours; instead it remained in the delivered colour scheme. It made its last flight in February 1995 and was withdrawn from service.

Like XW987, it was sold to Mike 'Beachy' Head in November 1995, before being flown to Exeter on 19 April 1996 to be made ready for

LEFT After becoming surplus to requirements with the RAE at Farnborough in the autumn of 1994, XW988 was sold to a civilian operator and flown out to Cape Town where it now resides in this black colour scheme as ZU-AVI. It was photographed flying at Cape Town in September 2008 and is believed to have made its final flight in South Africa during 2009. At the time of writing, the aircraft is thought to be in an 'airworthy condition' but is up for sale. *(PRM Aviation)*

its ferry flight. It departed on 2 May and arrived in Cape Town just three days later.

After arriving, it was registered as ZU-AVI and painted in a high-gloss black colour scheme before joining ZU-BCR providing back-seat rides at Thunder City. It was reported as having made its last flight in 2015 when displayed by Mike 'Beachy' Head himself at Windhoek.

The demise of Thunder City and the Buccaneers

Thunder City was an aircraft-operating company based at Cape Town and gained a reputation for owning the largest civilian collection of former military fast jets anywhere in the world. At one time, they operated three Lightnings, three Buccaneers and seven Hawker Hunters, although only four of the latter were probably airworthy. Supersonic flights up to the edge of space were available in the two-seat Lightning T.5 aircraft while the Buccaneer S.2Bs offered high-speed, low-level experiences.

On 14 November 2009, a Lightning T.5, ZU-BEX (formerly XS451), crashed while carrying out a display at the biennial South African Air Force Overberg Airshow held at Overberg AFB near Bredasdorp. The aircraft suffered hydraulic failure after a fire started in the rear of the fuselage. Sadly, the pilot was killed when his ejection seat failed to operate. The accident investigation found major shortcomings in the maintenance programme of the aircraft and as a consequence the South African Civil Aviation Authority suspended the company's Operating Certificate in March 2010.

On 9 September 2010, it was reported that the Thunder City fleet would no longer carry fare-paying passengers.

On 22 August 2011 a pair of single-seat Lightning F.6s, along with a single two-seat Lightning T.5, three Buccaneer S.2Bs and four Hawker Hunter aircraft (an F.6, GA.11, F.58 and T.68) were all listed 'for sale by private treaty' with Go Industry – an online asset-disposal company. The closing date for bids was 27 April 2012.

On 21 April 2012, Thunder City participated in an airshow for the first time since the 2009 crash, appearing at the Overberg AFB event. Since then, Buccaneer ZU-BCR is reported to have flown in November 2012 and was later displayed by Mike 'Beachy' Head at Windhoek in 2015, on the same day he displayed Hunter F.6A ZU-AUJ.

Sadly, on 21 May 2017, Mike 'Beachy' Head passed away, at almost 60 years of age. The fate of the Thunder City fleet, including the three airworthy Buccaneer aircraft is unclear, although at the time of writing it is believed that the aircraft *may* go to a new owner in Switzerland.

Complete Buccaneer aircraft

Aside from the six aircraft maintained in a 'live' ground-running condition in the UK, a further 21 complete Buccaneer airframes remain in the UK. Most are on display in museums or as gate guardians, although one or two are stored by private collectors. The condition of these aircraft varies enormously. Some are held and displayed in a first-class condition – Buccaneer S.2B XV865 at the IWM Duxford certainly qualifies in this category; while others – like Buccaneer S.2 XV864 held at the Defence Fire Training and Development Centre (DFTDC) at Manston, is in a very poor condition.

Interestingly, the oldest surviving NA.39 – XK488, the third pre-production aircraft that made its first flight on 2 June 1955 – is held in storage at the Fleet Air Arm Museum. It is awaiting a restoration programme, having spent many years out in the elements, just in front of the museum entrance.

Thankfully, many of these preserved aircraft are accessible in museums; most are stored under cover while some are displayed outside – often in cramped conditions that make photography difficult. Most of the airframes held in private hands require permission in advance before visiting.

BELOW The oldest complete Buccaneer currently preserved is NA.39, XK488, currently held in storage at Yeovilton where it was photographed in October 2017, surrounded by other stored airframes and memorabilia. XK488 was the third prototype NA.39 in the pre-production batch of 20 aircraft ordered and spent much of its test career on engine trials at Filton or Hatfield. XK488 was previously on display outside the Fleet Air Arm Museum before being brought inside.
(Keith Wilson)

LEFT For many years Buccaneer S.1, XK532, was displayed in 736 NAS colours as 'LM-632' as a gate guard at RAF Lossiemouth. It was transferred to the Highland Aviation Museum at Inverness in December 2002 where it is currently on display.
(Francis Wallace)

CENTRE Preserved with the Fleet Air Arm Museum at Yeovilton is Buccaneer S.1, XN957, where it is displayed in its former 736 NAS colours as '630'. It is exhibited within the Aircraft Carrier Experience in Hall 3, where it was photographed in October 2017. XN957 was withdrawn from service with 736 NAS in February 1971 with just over 900 hours recorded on the airframe. It was later flown into Yeovilton for preservation by the FAA Museum.
(Keith Wilson)

LEFT The final Buccaneer S.1 airframe preserved is XN964, which is on display at the Newark Air Museum in its former 801 NAS colours as '118' where it was photographed in April 2014.
(Keith Wilson)

LEFT Former 208 Squadron Buccaneer S.2B, XV361, made its last flight on 18 April 1994 and is now with the Ulster Aviation Collection and on display at the Maze/Long Kesh Regeneration Site in Northern Ireland, where it was photographed in October 2016. On the opposite side of the airframe it carries XV Squadron marks with the code '361'. *(Mike Overs)*

RIGHT Buccaneer S.2B, XT288, is displayed in its former 12 Squadron colours at the National Museum of Flight, East Fortune, where it was photographed in August 2002. *(Keith Wilson)*

RIGHT Buccaneer S.2B, XV168, is displayed at the Yorkshire Air Museum, Elvington, where it is painted as 'AF' of 208 Squadron. It was photographed there on 27 August 2017. *(Lee Barton)*

LEFT Former 809 NAS, Fleet Air Arm Buccaneer S.2D is displayed in the Aircraft Carrier Experience in Hall 3 of the Fleet Air Arm Museum, Yeovilton. Next to it is a dummy WE177A nuclear bomb. After being withdrawn from service with 208 Squadron, XV333 was flown from Lossiemouth into Yeovilton on 23 March 1994. Here, it was returned to its former 809 NAS colours as '234' and was photographed in October 2017. *(Keith Wilson)*

LEFT Buccaneer S.2B, XV863/S, is preserved at Weston near Dublin where it carries 'National Flight Centre' titling on the starboard engine. XV863/S retains its Gulf War RTF 'desert-pink' colours with the artwork of *Tamnavoulin*, *Debbie* and *Sea Witch* prominent on the nose and was photographed at Weston in October 2016. *(Mike Overs)*

LEFT Former RAE Buccaneer S.2B, XV350, is preserved at the East Midlands Aeropark where it was photographed in July 2011. *(Francis Wallace)*

LEFT Former 208 Squadron Buccaneer S.2B, XV865, was withdrawn from service in 1994 and allocated the maintenance serial number '9226M'. After being stored at Coningsby, it was moved to the Imperial War Museum at Duxford, where it is now displayed in its former RAF colours. *(Francis Wallace)*

LEFT Buccaneer S.2B, XW530, is prominently displayed on the forecourt of the Buccaneer Service Station on the A941 south of Lossiemouth and north of Elgin. Owner Ian Aitkenhead acquired XW530 shortly after it was withdrawn from service in February 1994 and maintains the aircraft in excellent condition. *(Francis Wallace)*

RIGHT Buccaneer S.2B, XW547, returned to Lossiemouth after its participation in the Gulf War on 17 March 1991 and rejoined 12 Squadron. It was withdrawn from service in 1993 and allocated the maintenance serial '9169M' before being moved to RAF Cosford where it became the first Gulf War aircraft to be preserved. It was displayed at RAF Cosford's Air Day in June 1999 before being moved by road to Hendon for display in the RAF Museum's Bomber Hall, where it retains its Gulf War colours as *Guinness Girl/Pauline/The Macallan*. *(Francis Wallace)*

LEFT Owned by Gary Spoors of GJD Aviation, Buccaneer S.2B, XX889/T, is preserved at Bruntingthorpe where it was photographed in July 2016. It still retains its Gulf War RTF 'desert-pink' colours with the artwork of the 'Sky Pirates' on the nose. *(Keith Wilson)*

Buccaneer Air Crew Association and XX901

Thankfully, the Buccaneer aircraft has its own – very active – Air Crew Association. When former Gulf War veteran Buccaneer S.2B XX901 was threatened with the scrap man, the association stepped in and purchased the airframe before placing her in the care of the Yorkshire Air Museum at Elvington. On display here, XX901 retains her Gulf War colours with the 'Sky Pirates' artwork on the port side and *The Flying Mermaid*, *Kathryn* and *Glen Elgin* retained below the cockpit on the starboard side, along with nine mission symbols below the cockpit canopy.

XX901 had been delivered to the RAF on 4 January 1977 and joined 208 Squadron. It was a veteran of Exercise Red Flag 77, when it acquired a temporary dark earth and light stone wrap-around colour scheme. In April 1979, XX901/K was deployed to Cold Lake AFB, Canada, for Exercise Maple Flag III and in September 1983 was one of six Buccaneer aircraft deployed to RAF Akrotiri for Operation Pulsator.

In February 1994, at the twilight of the Buccaneer's career, XX901 was painted in 216 Squadron markings for the now-famous seven-aircraft photoshoot to mark the Buccaneer's retirement on 17 March 1994 (see image on page 91).

On 5 April 1994, XX901 was flown to 19 MU at St Athan and entered its retirement before being acquired by the association.

ABOVE In 1979, Buccaneer S.2C, XV344, was transferred from the Royal Navy to the RAF and shortly afterwards was allocated to the MoD(PE). In 1982, it was issued to the RAE at Farnborough who used the aircraft in the TICM II (Thermal Imager Common Module) trials, fitted with forward-looking infra-red in a chisel nose and other equipment for low-level night flying. During this period, it earned itself the nickname 'Nightbird'. It was later transferred to A&AEE at Boscombe Down and used on laser technology trials from which the TIALD Laser/FLIR targeting pod subsequently fitted to the Tornado GR.1 was developed. XV344 was withdrawn from service at Boscombe Down in 1994 and in January 1998 was placed on display at Farnborough. On 1 July 2001, XV344 was repainted and put on display outside the QinetiQ headquarters at Farnborough. (*Francis Wallace*)

BELOW Buccaneer S.2B, XX901, is preserved by the Buccaneer Aircrew Association and is on display at the Yorkshire Air Museum at Elvington in its Gulf War colour scheme, complete with 'Sky Pirates' logo on the nose. (*Lee Barton*)

South African Air Force S.50 aircraft on display

The South African Air Force (SAAF) was the only export customer for the Buccaneer, purchasing 16 aircraft (although only 15 were delivered to South Africa), where they were all operated by 24 Squadron. The Buccaneers led a tough life and were flown hard, often in very difficult conditions. Due to political wrangling with the UK Government, spare parts were difficult to come by, and along with the tough operational career of the type, the attrition rate was high. No 24 Squadron, SAAF, flew their last operational Buccaneer sortie on 28 March 1991. At the time, only five Buccaneer aircraft remained with the squadron.

However, the Buccaneer was a much-revered aircraft and earned the nickname 'Easy Rider' among its crews. In a fitting tribute to an exceptional aircraft, all five aircraft were preserved, as follows:

412	Displayed as gate guardian, AFB Waterkloof (Pretoria)
414	On display at the SAAF Museum, AFB Swartkop (Pretoria)
416	On display at the SAAF Museum, AFB Ysterplaat (Cape Town)
421	On display at the SAAF Museum, AFB Swartkop (Pretoria)
422	On display at the South African National Museum of Military History (Johannesburg).

LEFT Former SAAF Buccaneer S.50, serial number 416, undergoing a major restoration programme at the SAAF Museum at Ysterplaat AFB in 2016. *(Johan Conradie)*

LEFT Former SAAF Buccaneer S.50, serial number 421, was photographed at the SAAF Museum facility at Swartkop AFB ahead of its restoration in 2013. *(Johan Conradie)*

LEFT Former SAAF Buccaneer S.50, serial number 422, is preserved at the South African National Museum of Military History where it was photographed in 2012. *(Johan Conradie)*

ABOVE The cockpit section of Buccaneer S.1, XN962, is displayed at the RAF Museum, Cosford, but for some inexplicable reason is marked as 'XN972' on the starboard engine.

(Francis Wallace)

Fuselage and cockpit sections

When the Buccaneer was finally withdrawn from RAF service at the end of March 1994, most airframes were destined for the scrap man's axe. Thankfully a good number of complete airframes were saved for preservation. However, a large number did end up being processed at a variety of locations throughout the UK – although that is not the end of the story for many of the airframes.

Scrap men are canny individuals, if nothing else, and as a result a large number of Buccaneer cockpit sections were cut from the aircraft and sold on to private collectors, of whom there are a large number. A visit to the annual 'CockpitFest' staged at the Newark Air Museum is testament to the following enjoyed by restored military aircraft cockpits. At the 2012 event, 28 cockpit sections were on display while 25 were present at next year's event.

In the UK at present, there are around 21 cockpit sections held in museums or within private collections, in addition to another four held by European collectors. As with the complete airframes, the condition of these cockpit sections varies widely.

On display and accessible to the public at the RAF Museum, Cosford, is the Buccaneer S.1 forward fuselage section of XN962, but for some inexplicable reason it is marked as 'XN972'. Meanwhile, inside the Fenland and West Norfolk Aviation Museum located on the outskirts of Wisbech, Cambridgeshire, is the cockpit section of Buccaneer S.2B XN983. This is in excellent condition with steps up to it, allowing a close inspection of the well-preserved cockpit interior.

The cockpit section from Buccaneer S.2B XW550, which was stored in a private garage in Essex for many years, was extricated from the premises in May 2016, although parts of the garage had to be dismantled to allow the cockpit to be removed. Now jointly owned by The Buccaneer Aviation Group and Francis Wallace, the cockpit section was taken by road to Bruntingthorpe where it is being placed on to a trailer and readied for public display appearances in 2018 and beyond. The new owners will also undertake restoration work on the interior of the cockpit section to try to return it to as close to its original status as possible.

LEFT Having previously been stored in a garage in Essex, the cockpit section of Buccaneer S.2B, XW550, was jointly acquired by the Buccaneer Aviation Group (TBAG) and Francis Wallace. It was photographed being extricated from the garage in May 2016 before it was loaded on to a lorry for its road journey to Bruntingthorpe. The cockpit section is currently being mounted on a trailer for public display and will be available at a number of forthcoming airshows and events.

(Francis Wallace)

A potentially flyable airframe in the UK?

With the future of the three South African Buccaneers being unclear, it could mean that no flyable Buccaneer exists anywhere in the world. However, it is refreshing to report that this may not be the case for long, as an airframe in the UK is currently maintained in a flyable condition, waiting for a sensible commercial offer to get it back into the air. If a commercial offer is forthcoming, the aircraft may then be available to appear on the airshow circuit. The former S.2B airframe, XX885, was registered as G-HHAA to Hawker Hunter Aviation Ltd on 6 December 2002 and since then has been the very first airframe to be accepted by the CAA on to the new Complex Aircraft Register.

XX885 joined the RAF on 30 April 1974, being issued to 16 Squadron at RAF Laarbruch. During the next few years it served with XV, 12 and 216 Squadrons, before being grounded along with all of the Buccaneer fleet. After undergoing a wing transplant with 19 MU at St Athan, XX885 was released back into service with 208 Squadron.

In September 1983, XX885 was one of six Buccaneer aircraft deployed to RAF Akrotiri for Operation Pulsator. In June 1988 XX885 was withdrawn from service and was allocated the maintenance serial number 9225M. However, it was returned to BAe at Woodford and underwent the Avionics Upgrade Programme (AUP) in 1989 and in March the following year was returned to service with 208 Squadron, having already been modified to carry the Sea Eagle missile in 1985/86.

In January 1991, XX885 was prepared for Operation Granby. Now in its new RTF temporary 'desert-pink' paint finish and coded 'L', it left for Muharraq on 7 February in the second batch of aircraft. Here it gained the artwork *Hello Sailor*, *Caroline* and *Famous Grouse* under the starboard-side cockpit along with seven mission symbols displayed on the starboard nose below the cockpit canopy. It returned from the Gulf on 17 March 1991 and rejoined 208 Squadron. Shortly afterwards it was transferred to 12 Squadron and had the desert-pink RTF removed, which revealed a medium sea grey and camouflage grey paint

scheme. The Gulf War artwork and code 'L' was, however, retained.

When 12 Squadron was stood down on 1 October 1993, XX885 was effectively withdrawn from service. However, the airframe – with only around 4,180 hours on it – was acquired by Hawker Hunter Aviation, a major contractor for the military and aerospace industry, and moved to its Scampton base.

Much-loved Buccaneer

Throughout its career, the Buccaneer has been an aircraft much loved by both its aircrew and groundcrew alike. The Buccaneer has a very active Air Crew Association along with a number of active social media sites for both air- and groundcrew.

The Buccaneer has also achieved a significant following from enthusiasts since the type was displayed on the airshow scene, but particularly since its withdrawal from RAF service back in March 1994; a very strong following that continues to this day. This following has in turn led to the formation of enthusiast groups whose aim is to preserve and, in some cases, continue to ground-run and fast-taxi Buccaneer aircraft for the public's (and their own) entertainment. As a consequence, the Buccaneer should remain in the public eye for many years to come.

At the time of writing, it is reported that Buccaneer S.2B, XV863, currently on display at Weston, may be for sale. Any offers anyone?

ABOVE It may just fly again! Following its participation in the Gulf War, Buccaneer S.2B, XX885, returned to 12 Squadron at RAF Lossiemouth and was repainted in this low-vis grey colour scheme, although it initially retained its Gulf War nose art. XX885 was retired from service on 1 October 1993 and later acquired by Hawker Hunter Aviation Ltd. On 9 December 2005, XX885 was the very first aircraft registered with the CAA on the new Complex Aircraft Register and allocated the civilian registration G-HHAA. Following an extensive rebuild at their Scampton base, G-HHAA now undergoes regular 'anti-det' maintenance and custodial ground runs and according to its owners, 'could be activated to flight status should a contractual tasking arise'.
(Francis Wallace)

Buccaneer production

UK air arms

XK486 to XK491 (6)
XK523 to XK536 (14)

Twenty prototype and pre-production Buccaneer S.1 shipboard strike aircraft were built by Blackburn Aircraft Limited at Brough. Initially the type was designated NA.39, derived from the Navy ASR NA.39; the Admiralty also issued the specification M.148T to cover the design.

XN922 to XN935 (14)
XN948 to XN973 (26)

Forty Buccaneer S.1 aircraft were ordered on 25 September 1959 under contract number KC/2F/05/CB.9(a). All were built by Blackburn Aircraft Limited at Brough and made their first flights at Holme-on-Spalding-Moor.

XN974 to XN983 (10)

Ten Buccaneer S.1 aircraft were ordered on 25 September 1959 under contract number KC/2F/O5/CB.9(a). The order was subsequently changed to Buccaneer S.2 aircraft in May 1961. All were built by Blackburn Aircraft Limited at Brough and made their first flights at Holme-on-Spalding-Moor.

BELOW A view of the production line in Brough's 'B' Shed on 5 December 1966, with S.2 aircraft for the Royal Navy in assembly. *(BAE SYSTEMS Image BAL21956-126)*

XT269 to XT288 (20)

The second production order for 20 Buccaneer S.2 aircraft for the Royal Navy was placed on 5 May 1964 under contract number KC/2F/048/CB.9(a). All were built at Hawker Siddeley Aviation, Brough, and made their first flights at Holme-on-Spalding-Moor.

XV152 to XV168 (17)

The third production order for 17 Buccaneer S.2 aircraft for the Royal Navy was placed on 25 October 1965 under contract number KC/2F/125/CB.58(b). All were built at Hawker Siddeley Aviation, Brough, and made their first flights at Holme-on-Spalding-Moor.

XV332 to XV361 (30)

The fourth production order for 30 Buccaneer S.2 aircraft for the Royal Navy was placed on 12 April 1966 under contract number KC/2F/153/CB.58(b). All were built at Hawker Siddeley Aviation, Brough. XV332 to XV351 made their first flights at Holme-on-Spalding-Moor, while XV352 to XV361 made their maiden flights at RAF Driffield.

XV863 to XV869 (7)

The fifth production order for 17 Buccaneer S.2 (Martel-capable) aircraft for the Royal Navy was placed on 27 June 1967 under contract number KC/2F/179/CB.58(b). Ten aircraft were subsequently cancelled (XV863 to XV877). The remaining seven aircraft were built at Hawker Siddeley Aviation, Brough, and made their first flights at Holme-on-Spalding-Moor.

XW525 to XW550 (26)

The first production order for Buccaneer S.2B strike aircraft for the RAF was placed under contract number KC/2F/258/CB.58(b). All were built at Hawker Siddeley Aviation, Brough, and made their first flights at Holme-on-Spalding-Moor.

LEFT 'Jackal Formation' flying around the north-east coast of Scotland on 3 December 1992. Leading the formation is 'Jackal 1', XW527, flown by Squadron Leaders Rick Phillips and Norman Browne; nearest the camera is 'Jackal 3', XV332, flown by Squadron Leaders Eric Wealleans and Dick Aitken; while furthest from the camera is 'Jackal 4', XZ431, flown by Squadron Leader Dave Bolsover and Wing Commander Nigel Maddox, the OC 12 Squadron.
(Keith Wilson)

XW986 to XW988 (3)

Four Buccaneer S.2B aircraft (XW986 to XW989) ordered for use by the Royal Aircraft establishment under contract number KA6a/316/CB.A6a. XW989 was subsequently cancelled, although XX901 was added to the next batch under the same contract. All three were built at Hawker Siddeley Aviation, Brough, and made their first flights at Holme-on-Spalding-Moor.

XX885 to XX901 (17)

Sixteen Buccaneer S.2B aircraft ordered for use by the RAF under contract number KA6a/316/CB.A6a. However, a further aircraft, allocated the serial number XX901, was added to the batch and delivered to the RAE. All aircraft were built at Hawker Siddeley Aviation, Brough, and made their first flights at Holme-on-Spalding-Moor.

XZ430 to XZ432 (3)

The final production order for three Buccaneer S.2B aircraft ordered for use by the RAF. All aircraft were built at Hawker Siddeley Aviation, Brough, and made their first flights at Holme-on-Spalding-Moor.

Export orders

411 to 427 (16)

Sixteen Buccaneer S.50 aircraft were ordered by the South African Government in January 1963 for use by the South African Air Force's (SAAF) No 24 Squadron. All were built at Hawker Siddeley Aviation, Brough, and made their first flights at Holme-on-Spalding-Moor. The first aircraft (411, G-2-1) made its first flight on 9 January 1965. One aircraft was lost on the delivery flight so only 15 aircraft were actually delivered. The South African Government also held an option on a further 20 aircraft but this was later cancelled after political pressure from the UK Government.

Summary of Buccaneer production

Prototypes and pre-production aircraft	20
S.1 aircraft converted to S.2	2
Royal Navy aircraft	124
Royal Air Force aircraft	46
Royal Aircraft Establishment	3
South African Air Force	16
TOTAL:	**211**

Full details of most Buccaneer airframe history and squadron allocations can be found on the excellent website www.blackburn-buccaneer.co.uk.

Buccaneers extant

Model	Serial	Code	Squadron markings	Location
United Kingdom				
Blackburn NA.39	XK488			Fleet Air Arm Museum Reserve Collection, Cobham Hall, Yeovilton, Somerset
Buccaneer S.2	XK526			RAF Regiment, Honington Airfield, Suffolk
Buccaneer S.2D	XK527			North Wales
Buccaneer S.1	XK532	'632'	736 NAS	Highland Aviation Museum, Inverness, Scotland
Buccaneer S.1	XK533			Dumfries and Galloway Aviation Museum, Dumfries, Scotland (held in deep storage)
Buccaneer S.1	XN923			Gatwick Aviation Museum, Charlwood, Surrey
Buccaneer S.1	XN928		736 NAS	Gravesend, Kent
Buccaneer S.1	XN957	'630'		Fleet Air Arm Museum, Yeovilton, Somerset
Buccaneer S.1	XN962	'XN972'		Royal Air Force Museum Cosford, Shropshire
Buccaneer S.1	XN964	'118'	801 Squadron	Newark Air Museum, Winthorpe, Nottinghamshire
Buccaneer S.1	XN967	'233'		City of Norwich Aviation Museum, Norfolk
Buccaneer S.2A	XN974			Yorkshire Air Museum, Elvington, North Yorkshire
Buccaneer S.2	XN979			South Yorkshire Air Museum, Doncaster, South Yorkshire
Buccaneer S.2B	XN981		12 Squadron	Errol, near Perth, Scotland (stored)
Buccaneer S.2B	XN983			Fenland and West Norfolk Aviation Museum, West Walton Highway, Norfolk
Buccaneer S.2B	XT277			Military Aircraft Cockpit Collection, Welshpool, Wales
Buccaneer S.2B	XT280			Dumfries and Galloway Aviation Museum, Dumfries, Scotland
Buccaneer S.2A	XT284	'H'		Felixstowe, Suffolk
Buccaneer S.2B	XT288		12 Squadron	Dumfries and Galloway Aviation Museum, Dumfries, Scotland
Buccaneer S.2B	XV165		12 Squadron	Ashford, Kent (unconfirmed)
Buccaneer S.2B	XV168	'AF'	208 Squadron	Yorkshire Air Museum, Elvington, North Yorkshire
Buccaneer S.2B	XV333	'234'	809 Squadron	Fleet Air Arm Museum, Yeovilton, Somerset
Buccaneer S.2C	XV344		RAE 'Raspberry Ripple'	Defence Science and Technology Laboratory (QinetiQ), Farnborough, Hampshire
Buccaneer S.2B	XV350			East Midlands Aeropark, Castle Donington, Derbyshire
Buccaneer S.2B	XV352			RAF Manston History Museum, Manston, Kent
Buccaneer S.2B	XV359	'035'	809 Squadron	Topsham, near Exeter, Devon

Condition	Remarks
Complete	Ex-Filton, BSE, DHE, Blackburn, RAE, DHE, Blackburn. Acquired 22 July 1967.
Complete	8648M, ex-RAE Bedford, RRE, A&AEE, RAE, A&AEE, RAE, A&AEE.
Cockpit section	
Complete	Ex-Inverness Airport, Lossiemouth 8867M, Manadon A2581, Arbroath, Lossiemouth, 736 Squadron. Arrived 23 December 2002.
Cockpit section	Ex-Arbroath, Lossiemouth, 809, 700Z, A&AEE, 700Z Squadron. Crashed 10 October 1963. Arrived 1972.
Complete – ground runs	Ex-Boscombe Down, West Freugh, A&AEE, RAE, A&AEE, RAE, A&AEE, 700Z Squadron. SoC 17 May 1954.
Cockpit section	Ex-Manston, Bruntingthorpe, Cardiff, St Athan 8179M, 736, 809, 801 Squadrons. Painted in 'desert-pink' with *Glenfiddich*, *Jaws* and *Lynn* on cockpit.
Complete	Ex-736, 809, 801 Squadrons. SoC 10 November 1973. Acquired 1974.
Cockpit section	Ex-Hendon, Cosford, St Athan 'XN972', Abingdon 8183M, Foulness, 736, 800, 839 Squadrons. Acquired July 1995.
Complete	Ex-Bruntingthorpe, East Midlands, Brough, Pershore, RRE, RAE, 803, 736, 801 Squadrons. Arrived 26 February 1988.
Cockpit section	Ex-Coltishall, Weybourne, Fleckney, Helston, Culdrose A2627, SAH-20, Lossiemouth, 736, 809 Squadrons. SoC 23 January 1970. Arrived 2006.
Taxiable	Ex-Warton, Holme-on-Spalding-Moor, RAE Bedford, Holme-on-Spalding-Moor, A&AEE, Driffield, RAE Bedford, A&AEE, Holme-on-Spalding-Moor. Flew on 19 August 1991.
Cockpit section	Ex-Stamford, Croydon, Popham, Stanbridge, Henlow, Cranfield, Fleetlands, 807, 700B Squadrons. Ditched 9 June 1966.
Dismantled – stored	Ex-Lossiemouth, 12, 208, 12, 809, 12, 900, 801, 700B Squadrons.
Cockpit section	Ex-Terrington St Clement, 12, 208, XV, 12, 809, A&AEE, Rolls-Royce. SoC 10 April 1994. Arrived 2002.
Cockpit section	Ex-Bruntingthorpe, Cosford 8853M, Shawbury, 237 OCU, 12, 800, 809, 801 Squadrons.
Cockpit section	Ex-Dundonald, Birtley, East Fortune, Lossiemouth, 208, 12, 208, 12, 16, 809, A&AEE, 809 Squadrons. SoC 10 April 1994. Arrived February 2003.
Cockpit section	Ex-Stock, St Athan, Abingdon 8855M, St Athan, 237 OCU, XV, 208, 809, 803, 736 Squadrons.
Complete	Ex-Lossiemouth 9134M, A&AEE, 208, 12, FAA 800 Squadrons. Arrived July 1994.
Cockpit section	Ex-Spanhoe, Bruntingthorpe, Farnborough, Staverton, Bentham, Staverton, Hucclecote, Heathrow, Stock, Shawbury, 12 Squadron.
Complete	Ex-Brough, Lossiemouth, 12, 208, 12, 801 Squadrons. SoC 15 October 1993. Arrived 18 August 2013.
Complete	Ex-208, 12, XV, 16, FAA, 237 OCU, 12 Squadron. Arrived 23 March 1994.
Complete – gate guardian	Ex-Boscombe Down, RAE, 809, 800, 809 Squadrons. Withdrawn September 1994. 'Nightbird'.
Complete	Ex-Shawbury, Warton, RAE. Arrived 11 December 1993.
Cockpit section	Ex-Gravesend, Manston, Stock, St Athan, Lossiemouth, 237 OCU, 208 Squadron.
Complete	Ex-Culdrose, A2693, Predannack, Lossiemouth, 208, 237 OCU, 12, 208, 12 Squadrons. Arrived 23 April 2005.

Model	Serial	Code	Squadron markings	Location
Buccaneer S.2B	XV361		208 Squadron	Ulster Aviation Collection, Long Kesh, Northern Ireland
Buccaneer S.2B	XV865		208 Squadron	IWM Duxford, Cambridgeshire
Buccaneer S.2B	XV867			Highland Aviation Museum, Inverness, Scotland
Buccaneer S.2B	XW530		12 Squadron	Buccaneer Service Station, Elgin, Scotland
Buccaneer S.2B	XW541			Lavendon, Bedfordshire
Buccaneer S.2B	XW544	'Y'	16 Squadron	The Buccaneer Aviation Group, Bruntingthorpe, Leicestershire
Buccaneer S.2B	XW547	'R'	Gulf War RTF	Royal Air Force Museum, Hendon, London
Buccaneer S.2B	XW550		16 Squadron	The Buccaneer Aviation Group and Francis Wallace, Bruntingthorpe, Leicestershire
Buccaneer S.2B	XX885	G-HHAA		Hawker Hunter Aviation, RAF Scampton, Lincolnshire
Buccaneer S.2B	XX888			Barnstaple, Devon
Buccaneer S.2B	XX889	'T'	Gulf War RTF	Gary Spoors, Bruntingthorpe, Leicestershire
Buccaneer S.2B	XX893			Blue Sky Experience, Perth, Scotland
Buccaneer S.2B	XX894	'020'	809 Squadron	The Buccaneer Aviation Group, Bruntingthorpe, Leicestershire
Buccaneer S.2B	XX895			Kidlington, Oxfordshire
Buccaneer S.2B	XX899		12 Squadron	Midland Air Museum, Coventry, Warwickshire
Buccaneer S.2B	XX900		208 Squadron	Cold War Jets Collection, Bruntingthorpe, Leicestershire
Buccaneer S.2B	XX901		Gulf War RTF	Yorkshire Air Museum, Elvington, North Yorkshire
Buccaneer S.2B	XZ431			Hinstock, Shropshire
Ireland				
Buccaneer S.2B	XV863		Gulf War RTF	Dublin Weston Airport, Kildare, Ireland
Buccaneer S.2B (mod)	XX897			Atlantic AirVenture, Shannon Aviation Museum, Shannon Airport, Clare, Ireland.
Italy				
Buccaneer S.2B	XW527			Albino Panigari
Netherlands				
Buccaneer S.2A	XV163			International Aircraft Solutions Park, Zeist
South Africa				
Buccaneer S.2B	XW986	ZS-NIP	RAE 'raspberry ripple'	Thunder City, Cape Town
Buccaneer S.2B	XW987	ZS-BCR		Thunder City, Cape Town
Buccaneer S.2B	XW988	ZS-AVI		Thunder City, Cape Town
Buccaneer S.50	412		24 Squadron	SAAF Waterkloof, Pretoria
Buccaneer S.50	414		24 Squadron	SAAF Museum, Swartkop, Pretoria
Buccaneer S.50	416		24 Squadron	SAAF Museum, Ysterplaat, Cape Town
Buccaneer S.50	421		24 Squadron	SAAF Museum, Swartkop, Pretoria
Buccaneer S.50	422		24 Squadron	National Museum of Military History, Saxonwold, Johannesburg

Condition	Remarks
Complete – stored	Ex-Langford Lodge, Lossiemouth, 208, XV, 208, 12, XV, 809, 800 Squadrons. Last flight 18 April 1994.
Complete	Ex-Coningsby 9226M, Lossiemouth, 208, 12, 237 OCU, 208, 12, 208, 237 OCU, FAA 809 and 736 Squadrons.
Cockpit section	Ex-Great Ayton, Leeming, 208, 12, 208, 237 OCU, FAA, 809, 736, 803 Squadrons. Crashed 10 September 1993. Arrived 2005.
Complete	Ex-Lossiemouth, 208, 12, 208, 216, 16, XV, 16 Squadrons.
Cockpit section	Ex-Welshpool, Ingatestone, Stock, Foulness, Honington 8858M, St Athan, 12, 16, XV Squadrons.
Taxiable	Ex-Shawbury, Cosford 8857M, Shawbury, 16, XV Squadrons. Arrived 3 October 2004.
Complete	Ex-Cosford 9169M, Shawbury 9095M, Gulf Det., 12, 237 OCU, 208, 12, 216, 12, 237 OCU, 12 Squadron. Acquired 20 January 1993. Desert-pink with *Guinness Girl*, *Pauline* and *The Macallan*.
Cockpit section	Ex-Stock, St Albans, 16, XV Squadrons. SoC 18 August 1980.
Restoration to flying condition	Ex-Lossiemouth 9225M, 12, 208, 12, 208, 216, 16 Squadrons.
Cockpit section	Ex-Dundonald, Ottershaw, Shawbury, St Athan, 16, XV Squadons. SoC 10 October 1991.
Complete	Ex-Kemble, Staverton, Bentham, Staverton, Enstone, St Athan, 12, 208, 12, 16 Squadrons. Arrived 8 May 2011.
Cockpit section	Ex-Forres, Lossiemouth, 208, 237 OCU, 16 Squadron.
Taxiable	Ex-Farnborough, Kemble, Bruntingthorpe, St Athan, 208, 16, 12, 208, 12 Squadrons. Arrived 28 September 2003.
Complete	Ex-Woking, St Athan, Lossiemouth, 208,12, 237 OCU, 12, 237 OCU, 16, XV, 12 Squadrons. SoC 13 January 1995.
Cockpit section	Ex-Kidlington, Stock, St Athan, Lossiemouth, 208, 12, Gulf Det., 237 OCU, 16, XV, 12, 208 Squadrons. SoC 10 October 1994. Arrived April 1996.
Taxiable	Ex-St Athan, 208, 12, 208, 216, 12, 208 Squadrons. Arrived 27 October 1994.
Complete	Ex-Kemble, St Athan, Lossiemouth, 208, 12, 237 OCU, 208 Squadron. SoC 10 January 1995. Arrived 26 May 1996. Desert-pink with *Kathryn*, *The Flying Mermaid*, *Glen Elgin*.
Cockpit section	
Complete – reportedly for sale	Ex-Lossiemouth 9145M, 9139M, 9115M, 16, 237 OCU, 208, 237 OCU, 208, 809 Squadrons. Desert-pink *Sea Witch*.
'Live' electrics and hydraulics	Ex-Bournemouth, DRA Bedford, RAE, RRE. Modified with Tornado nose. Arrived 26 August 2012.
Cockpit section	
Cockpit section	
Airworthy	Reportedly last flown in 2009.
Airworthy	Reportedly last flown in late 2016.
Airworthy	Reportedly last flown in 2009.
Gate guardian	
Complete	
Complete	
Complete	
Complete	

Technical specifications

	S.1		S.2		S.50	
Dimensions						
Wingspan	42ft 4in	12.90m	44ft 0in	13.41m	44ft 0in	13.41m
Width folded	19ft 11in	6.07m	19ft 11in	6.07m	19ft 11in	6.07m
Length	63ft 5in	19.33m	63ft 5in	19.33m	63ft 5in	19.33m
Length folded	51ft 10in	15.79m	51ft 10in	15.79m	51ft 10in	15.79m
Height	16ft 3in	4.95m	16ft 3in	4.95m	16ft 3in	4.95m
Height folded	16ft 8in	5.08m	16ft 8in	5.08m	16ft 8in	5.08m
Tailplane span	14ft 3in	4.34m	14ft 3in	4.34m	14ft 3in	4.34m
Wheel track	11ft 10.5in	3.59m	11ft 10.5in	3.59m	11ft 10.5in	3.59m
Wheelbase	20ft 8in	6.29m	20ft 8in	6.29m	20ft 8in	6.29m
Area						
Wings	508.5ft^2	47.24m^2	514.7ft^2	47.82m^2	514.7ft^2	47.82m^2
Ailerons	54.8ft^2	5.09m^2	54.8ft^2	5.09m^2	54.8ft^2	5.09m^2
Fin	68.6ft^2	6.37m^2	68.6ft^2	6.37m^2	68.6ft^2	6.37m^2
Rudder	10.74ft^2	1.00m^2	10.74ft^2	1.00m^2	10.74ft^2	1.00m^2
Tailplane	75.52ft^2	7.02m^2	75.52ft^2	7.02m^2	75.52ft^2	7.02m^2
Weight						
Take-off (typical)	42,000lb	19,051kg	46,000lb	20,865kg	46,000lb	20,865kg
Take-off (maximum)	45,000lb	20,416kg	62,000lb	28,123kg	62,000lb	28,123kg
Landing (typical)	31,000lb	14,000kg	35,000lb	15,876kg	35,000lb	15,876kg
Empty weight	29,980lb	13,602kg	31,000lb	14,065kg	31,000lb	14,067kg
Weapons load (internal)	4,000lb	1,815kg	4,000lb	1,815kg	4,000lb	1,815kg
Weapons load (external)	4,000lb	1,815kg	12,000lb	5,443kg	12,000lb	5,443kg
Weapons load (maximum)	8,000lb	3,630kg	16,000lb	7,258kg	16,000lb	7,258kg
Performance						
Maximum design speed (at 200ft/61m)	645mph (Mach 0.85)	1,038km/h	645mph (Mach 0.85)	1,038km/h	645mph (Mach 0.85)	1,038km/h
Range (typical)	1,730 miles	2,784km	2,300 miles	3,700km	2,300 miles	3,700km
Tactical radius	500 miles	805km	600 miles	966km	600 miles	966km
Endurance (including two in-flight refuellings)	9 hours		9 hours		9 hours	
Engines	2 × de Havilland Gyron Junior Mk.101 turbojets each developing 7,100lb st (31.6kN)		2 × Rolls-Royce RB.168-1A Spey Mk.101 turbofans each developing 11,100lb st (49.4 kN)		2 × Rolls-Royce RB.168-1A Spey Mk.101 turbofans each developing 11,100lb st (49.4 kN) and 2 × Rolls-Royce Bristol BS 605 rocket engines, developing a total of 8,000lb (3,630kg) for 30 seconds	

Appendix 4

The Buccaneer Aviation Group (aka 'the T-Baggers')

The Buccaneer Aviation Group is an organisation of volunteers who are dedicated to the preservation and maintenance of two ex-Royal Air Force Buccaneer aircraft in fast-taxi condition. They are the only group in the world who are dedicated entirely to this aircraft type.

Fondly known as the 'T-Baggers' they offer aviation enthusiasts the unique opportunity of becoming involved with the Buccaneer aircraft through their website, as well as experiencing them in person at their Bruntingthorpe Airfield base in Leicestershire.

The T-Baggers are a not-for-profit organisation, so any funds donated are spent directly on the ongoing maintenance and long-term preservation of the aircraft, as a testament to those who built and flew the Buccaneer, as well as for the enjoyment of present and future generations of Buccaneer enthusiasts.

Both Buccaneer S.2B aircraft – XW544 and XX894 – have been at Bruntingthorpe since early 2004, each with their own respective volunteer groups who worked independently on their aircraft's restoration, while gathering their own stock of spares. The two groups knew each other well and there was always a good spirit of cooperation.

In February 2011, Guy Hulme, the owner of XX894, decided that he no longer wanted to be involved with the project and offered the aircraft for sale. The volunteers involved with both Buccaneers saw this as an opportunity to acquire the aircraft to preserve and maintain it at Bruntingthorpe Airfield. With this objective in mind, both groups combined to form The Buccaneer Aviation Group (TBAG).

In March 2011, XX894 was sold by Guy Hulme to GJD AeroTech, who had originally sold the aircraft to him in 2003. The new owner, Gary Spoors, was happy to allow her be maintained and operated by The Buccaneer Aviation Group. Gary also offered to sell the aircraft and her spares to the newly formed group once funds became available.

On 23 May 2011 The Buccaneer Aviation Group held its first Annual General Meeting at Bruntingthorpe and on 29 May the group's

BELOW The two 'live' TBAG Buccaneers – XX894/020 (left) and XW544/O (right) – being prepared for an event at Bruntingthorpe in August 2012.
(Francis Wallace)

ABOVE A group of TBAG volunteers photographed with the Atlantic Air Venture Buccaneer S.2B (Mod) XX897 at Shannon during their visit in early April 2017. During this time, the group were able to bring both the electrical and hydraulic systems back to life, meaning future visitors to the Shannon Aviation Museum may occasionally be able to see the Buccaneer exercising them. Left to right: Mike Overs, Nathan Hayles, Andrew Webber, Kay 'Red' Bennett, Francis Wallace, Bob Lancaster and Andrew King. *(Mike Overs)*

BELOW TBAG members preparing their Buccaneer S.2B, XW544/O, for engine start at Bruntingthorpe on 29 May 2017, just ahead of a planned fast-taxi run during a Cold War Jets Day at the base. *(Keith Wilson)*

Buccaneer aircraft were displayed to the public alongside the Cold War Jets Collection Buccaneer S.2B XX900. This was the first time three Buccaneer aircraft had operated together since the type's retirement from RAF service in 1994.

In October 2011 XX894 was finally purchased on behalf of the new group, completing their initial objective. The group's mission is to preserve both these aircraft in a fast-taxi condition for the enjoyment of current and future generations of Buccaneer enthusiasts. The long-term goal is to get both

aircraft under cover, protecting them from the deteriorating effect of the elements.

In the short term the group have costs for fuel, insurance, tyres, repairs and servicing that need to be met. The group's first fund-raising event was held on 24 March 2012 and celebrated the completion of the restoration of XW544. The group is reliant on public donations to help meet the costs of both these short- and long-term objectives.

In 2016 The Buccaneer Aviation Group added the cockpit section of XW550, which had previously been in storage in a garage in Essex. This was jointly acquired with Francis Wallace, with the intention of creating a travelling exhibit to increase awareness of the group's activities away from Bruntingthorpe, and also to support the activities of the TBAG fund-raising shop.

Since 2012, The Buccaneer Aviation Group has participated in the twice-yearly events at Bruntingthorpe – the Cold War Jet Days – where at least one of the group's two jets has performed a fast-taxi run while the recently acquired cockpit section was open to interested enthusiasts.

The group's two Buccaneers participate in the regular photographic night shoots at Bruntingthorpe, which uses actors to recreate scenes from the Cold War era. These are well supported by aviation and photographic enthusiasts alike.

The Buccaneer Aviation Group would like to express their thanks and gratitude to David Walton for his support in providing a home allowing the T-Baggers to operate and store their aircraft; along with his assistance in their endeavours.

In order to achieve both their short- and long-term objectives, The Buccaneer Aviation Group requires significant funding, so all donations are gratefully received. If you wish to become part of the TBAG adventure, you are welcome to join as a friend of the organisation. You will then receive regular updates on the group's activities and developments.

More information on The Buccaneer Aviation Group can be found on their website at: www.thebuccaneeraviationgroup.com as well as on their Facebook page: The Buccaneer Aviation Group.

Bibliography and sources

Allward, Maurice, *Modern Combat Aircraft 7 – Buccaneer* (Ian Allan Ltd, 1981)

Andrews, C.F. and Morgan, E.B., *Vickers Aircraft since 1908*, 2nd edition (Putnam, 1988)

Boot, Roy, *From Spitfire to Eurofighter – 45 Years of Combat Aircraft Design* (Airlife Publishing Ltd, 1990)

British Aviation Research Group, *British Military Aircraft Serials and Markings*, 2nd edition, (BARG/Nostalgair/The Aviation Hobby Shop, 1983)

Brook, Mike, *Trials and Errors – Experimental Test Flying in the 1970s* (The History Press, 2015)

Caygill, Peter, *Flying the Buccaneer – Britain's Cold War Warrior* (Pen & Sword Aviation, 2008)

Chesneaur, Roger, *Buccaneer S Mks 1 & 2, Aeroguide 30* (Ad Hoc Publications, 2005)

Crosley, Commander R.M. 'Mike', DSC & Bar, RN, *Up in Harm's Way – Flying with the Fleet Air Arm* (Pen & Sword Aviation, 2005)

Doust, Michael J., *Buccaneer S.1, from the Cockpit* (Ad Hoc Publications, 2007)

Eeles, Group Captain Tom, BA, FRAes, *A Passion For Flying – 8,000 Hours of RAF Flying* (Pen & Sword Aviation, 2015)

Ellis, Ken, *Wrecks & Relics*, 24th edition (Crécy Publishing, 2014)

Jefford, Wing Commander C.G., MBE, RAF, *RAF Squadrons* (Airlife, 1988)

Lord, Brigadier-General Dick, *From Fledgling to Eagle – The South African Air Force during the Border War* (30° South Publishers (Pty) Ltd., 2008)

Pitchfork, Air Commodore Graham, MBE, BA, FRAes, *The Buccaneers – Operational Service with the Royal Navy and the Royal Air Force* (Patrick Stephens Limited, 2002)

Robertson, Bruce, *British Military Aircraft Serials 1878–1987* (Midland Counties Publications, 1987)

Skinner, Stephen, *Hawker Siddeley Aviation and Dynamics 1960–77* (The Crowood Press Ltd, 2014)

Thetford, Owen, *Aircraft of the Royal Air Force since 1918*, 8th edition (Putnam, 1988)

Trevenen James, A.G., *The Royal Air Force – the Past 30 Years* (McDonald and Jane's Publishers Limited, 1976)

Wynn, Humphrey, *The RAF Strategic Nuclear Deterrent Forces: Their Origins, Roles and Deployment 1946–1969: A Documentary History* (HMSO, 1994)

Various editions of *Air Clues* magazine, issued monthly for the Royal Air Force by the Director of Flying Training (MoD)

Various editions of the *Airplane* partwork (Orbis Publishing Limited, 1990)

Various editions of *Wings of Fame* (Aerospace Publishing Ltd)

Various editions of *Flight International* magazine, published weekly by IPC

Index